$10

A THEOLOGY
OF PERSONAL
MINISTRY

A THEOLOGY OF PERSONAL MINISTRY

SPIRITUAL GIFTEDNESS IN THE LOCAL CHURCH

LAWRENCE O. RICHARDS AND GIB MARTIN

ZONDERVAN PUBLISHING HOUSE
OF THE ZONDERVAN CORPORATION
GRAND RAPIDS, MICHIGAN 49506

A THEOLOGY OF PERSONAL MINISTRY
Copyright © 1981 by The Zondervan Corporation
Grand Rapids, Michigan

Library of Congress Cataloging in Publication Data

Richards, Lawrence O.
    A theology of personal ministry.

    Includes index.
    1.Pastorial theology. 2. People of God. 3. Priesthood, Universal. I. Martin, Gilbert R.
II. Title. III. Title: Spiritual giftedness in the local Church.
BV4011.R53   253   81 2193
ISBN 0-310-31970-6   AACR2

Edited by Leslie Keylock and Edward Viening
Designed by Paul M. Hillman

Printed in the United States of America

CONTENTS

PART 1: THEOLOGICAL CORE
THE IDENTITY OF THE BELIEVER

PART 2: PRACTICAL IMPLICATION

THEOLOGICAL CORE
THE IDENTITY
OF THE BELIEVER

PART 1

PART 1

THEOLOGICAL CORE
THE IDENTITY OF THE BELIEVER

A People of God
A New Covenant People
A Kingdom People
A Servant People
An Empowered People
A Gifted People

A PEOPLE OF GOD

Webster's simplest definition of *theology* is "a science which treats the facts and phenomena of religion and relations between God and man." For many, however, theology is perceived as a particular systematic formulation of beliefs about God and man stated in categories first devised in the seventeenth century.

We may have little or no quarrel with historic statements of the Christian faith. But we should never accept the notion that all that is significant about our faith was decided in the past. We should constantly challenge such thinking, for there is a living theology to be formulated in our day. In fact, each new generation is challenged by God and history to explore afresh the eternal Word and reflect on those truths that have a special relationship to the issues of the day.

It is in this sense that we are about to explore a "theology of personal ministry." While much has been said historically about the priesthood of all believers, a contemporary theology of the laity is sadly lacking. Of even more concern is the fact that today the people of God do not have a clear sense of their own identity as a ministering people, each one called, empowered, and gifted by God to continue the work of Jesus in our world.

CHAPTER **1**

But there is another vital issue to address. Theology should not be a treatment of abstract ideas. In exploring the relationship between God and man and examining the facts and phenomena of our faith, theology should and must deal with reality. It is not enough merely to say, "This is what the Bible says." The theologian is called on to move beyond such a statement and struggle with ways in which what the Scriptures reveal finds expression in the life of the individual and the Christian community. A theology of personal ministry must first describe our identity as the people of God. Then it must show how that identity is to be expressed in personal ministries, and how the community of faith ministry can encourage.

That, in brief, is the purpose of this work. Not to deny or attack past formulations of our faith; in fact, we build on them. But certainly to affirm that much more must be understood by the church today about the personal ministries of the people of God. Our purpose is also to explore how, in a local congregation, each believer can be encouraged and supported as he or she discovers that new identity as one of God's *laos* (people) and steps out in faith to live a life in harmony with who God says each of us is.

THEOLOGICAL CORE

VOICES FROM THE PAST

Who are the *laos,* the people of God? As we ask this question, it is fascinating to hear the voices of history speak out in such harmony. The Reformers agree with those theologians today who insist that the church is a company of believer-priests called by God to minister.

Listen to the voices of the three great Reformers: Calvin, Luther, and Zwingli.

> Now we must speak briefly concerning the purpose and use of Christ's priestly office: As a pure and stainless Mediator he is by his holiness to reconcile us to God. But God's righteous curse bars our access to him, and God in his capacity as judge is angry toward us. Hence, an expiation must intervene in order that Christ as priest may obtain God's favor for us and appease his wrath. Thus Christ to perform this office had to come forward with a sacrifice. For under the law, also, the priest was forbidden to enter the sanctuary without blood (Heb. 9:7), that believers might know, even though the priest as their advocate stood between them and God, that they could not propitiate God unless their sins were expiated (Lev. 16:2–3). The Apostle discusses this point at length in the Letter to the Hebrews, from the seventh almost to the end of the tenth chapter. To sum up his argument: The priestly office belongs to Christ alone because by the sacrifice of his death he blotted out our guilt and made satisfaction for our sins (Heb. 9:22). God's solemn oath, of which he "will not repent," warns us what a weighty matter this is: "You are a priest forever after the order of Melchizedek" (Ps. 110:4; Heb. 5:6, 7, 15). . . . now Christ plays the priestly role, not only to render the Father favorable and propitious toward us by an eternal law of reconciliation, *but also to receive us as his companions* in this great office (Rev. 1:6). For we who are defiled in ourselves, yet *are priests in him,* offer ourselves and our all to God, and freely enter the heavenly sanctuary that the sacrifice of prayers and praise that we bring may be acceptable and sweet-smelling before God. This is the meaning of Christ's statement: "For their sake I sanctify myself" (John 17:19).[1]
>
> From all this it follows that there is really no *difference* between laymen and priests, princes and bishops, "Spirituals" and "temporals," as they call them, except that of office and work, but not of "estate"; for they are all the same estate . . . this is the teaching of St. Paul in Romans 12, 1 Corinthians 12, and of St. Peter in 1 Peter 2, as I have said above, viz., that we are all *one body of Christ,* the Head, all members one of another. Christ has not two different bodies one "temporal," and the other "spiritual." He is one Head, and He has one body.[2]

---

[1]John Calvin, *Institutes of the Christian Religion,* 2 vols. (Philadelphia: The Westminster Press, 1960), pp. 501ff. Italics added. Calvin's writings on the priesthood of believers are rare and unsystematic. Yet according to editor John T. McNeill, "He gives to that doctrine substantially the content given to it by Luther."

[2]Martin Luther, "An Open Letter to the Christian Nobility," *The Works of Martin Luther* (Philadelphia: Muhlenberg Press, 1943), 11:69. Italics added.

For thus it is written in 1 Peter 2, "Ye are a chosen generation, *a royal priesthood,* and a priestly kingdom." Therefore we are all priests, *as many of us as are Christians* . . . the priesthood is nothing but a ministry, as we learn from 1 Corinthians 4, "Let a man so account of us as of the ministers of Christ, and the dispensers of the mysteries of God."[3]

And they quote 1 Peter 2: *regale sacerdotium;* a royal priesthood. And with the sword they now force Peter. What he meant was that the clergy can be temporal princes and wield secular authority. That is what the axe can do. But Peter's real meaning was that the Lord Jesus Christ has called all Christians to kingly honour and to the priesthood, so that they are all priests, offering spiritual gifts, that is, dedicating themselves wholly to God.[4]

In spite of such clear statements by the Reformers, most people continue to make a distinction between "clergy" and "laity." In fact, the failure of Christians to firmly grasp the truth that as God's people *each one* is called to ministry is recognized today as a major cause for the failure of the modern church to reach the world with the gospel or to serve effectively as God's salty preservative of society from injustice and immorality. John R. W. Stott asserts, "I do not hesitate to say that to interpret the Church in terms of a privileged clerical caste or hierarchical structure is to destroy the New Testament doctrine of the Church."[5]

We can go even further. In practical terms, to experience the church in terms of clerical caste or hierarchical structure will sap the strength, vitality, and fervor of the body of Christ. To live as a divided church will turn us aside from commitment to do the will of our living head, Jesus Christ.

Robert B. Munger of Fuller Theological Seminary observes that

Christianity in its beginnings was a lay movement . . . taking fishermen from their boats and nets, Jesus made them fishers of men. He dared to believe that ordinary people could become extraordinary servants of God. He would build his church upon believers like Peter. From among the common people he would call disciples who in turn he would send to disciple the nations. In our time it may well be that the greatest single bottleneck to the renewal and outreach of the church is the division of roles between clergy and laity that results in a hesitancy of the clergy to trust the laity with significant responsibility, and in turn to a reluctance on the part of the laity to trust themselves as authentic ministers of Christ, either in the church or outside the church.[6]

---

[3]Ibid., p. 279. Italics added.

[4]Ulrich Zwingli, *Valiant for the Truth,* ed. David Fuller (New York: McGraw-Hill, 1961), p. 151.

[5]John R. W. Stott, *One People: Laymen and Clergy in God's Church* (Downers Grove: Inter-Varsity).

[6]Robert B. Munger, *Training of the Laity for Ministry.*

In making such statements, these voices past and present are making a significant affirmation. They all insist that a believer's *identity* is not to be found in his role as clergy or in his position in any office within the institutional structure of the local church. Not only that, they insist that whatever role an individual may hold, his or her identity is *no different from that of other believers!* There is no essential difference in identity between a pastor and a new Christian, between a bishop and a blue-collar believer. There will be a difference of role, a difference in how each serves others. But each Christian is to find his identity in the fact that now, in Christ, he has become one of the people of God.

Each of the people of God is called to ministry. No clergy-laity distinction exists in the mind of God. Every believer is part of the *laos.* Everyone is to find personal significance in understanding what it means to be one of God's called-out people. Everyone is to shake off the shackles clamped on by past and present distortions. Everyone is to find freedom to *be who he is* through affirming that identity that is shared by all the people of God.

Laos

The biblical writers often take neutral or weak terms from the Greek language and give them new vitality. This happened with *agape,* a mild term for affection which, through association with the incarnation and crucifixion of Jesus became a bold statement of God's commitment to love His fallen creatures *anyway.* Such a transformation of a term by its association with a decisive act of God also took place in the case of the Greek word *laos.*

The Greek language knew a variety of words for "people." In harmony with the precision and richness of Hellenic thought, each term had its own shade of meaning. *Ethnos* portrayed a people who belonged together in virtue of a common heritage and customs. *Demos* pictured a people in political assembly, often in contrast to king or nobility. *Ochlos* referred to the people as a mass, a crowd. *Polis,* so significant in Greek experience and thought, viewed people drawn together in political unity, and then signified the "city-state" which was the primary Hellenic community.

By the time of the Septuagint, the Greek translation of the Old Testament completed at Alexandria *ca.* 284–247 B.C., the Greek word *laos* was rarely used in common speech and carried no distinctive connotation. It was this term that the translators fastened on and used more than two thousand times to make their special statement about the unique relationship that existed between Israel and Yahweh. By God's own amazing choice, Israel was declared to be "my people Israel" (Exod. 3:1). By God's amazing grace, Israel was invited to identify the Lord of creation as "the God of Israel" (cf. Ps. 69:6; 1 Sam. 2:30; etc.).

By choosing the term *laos* to refer only to Israel, God distinguishes it from all other words for "people." Thus in the Old Testament and the New the most common word, *ethnos*, came to be used in the sense of "foreigner." Those human beings who were held together merely by natural bonds of history and custom *were* different from Israel, for Israel found her identity not in natural history but in the supernatural work of God. Israel heard God speak to Father Abraham. She had been redeemed from slavery in Egypt, and had stood in wonder as God brought great plagues to punish His people's oppressors, split the seas to provide them escape, and provided the blood of the Passover lamb as a covering when the Death Angel struck. The identity of Israel was rooted in this special relationship with God. Israel's identity as a people could be understood only by reflecting on who God was to them, and who they were to God. Israel could not be understood by shared accidents of birth or customs held in common with others in the world of the Near East.

The identity of Israel is most clearly expressed, and the meaning of being God's people most clearly seen, in the Old Testament covenant. At the time of Abraham's call God gave him certain promises and confirmed them with an oath (*b'rith* "covenant"). Throughout the Old Testament this covenant was reaffirmed, and at times its provisions further unveiled.[7] This covenant was unlike most human contracts in that a *b'rith* contract between people was conditional on the performance of both parties. The biblical covenants, however, are covenants of *promise:* they are God's pronouncements of what He intends to do for His people. God's commitments under the covenant promises will be carried out, whether or not a particular generation of His people carries out its obligations.

Israel's history is a vivid commentary on God's continuing faithfulness to His Word. The people rebelled and turned back at the border of the Promised Land. Yet God remained faithful to His covenant promises. When the land had been possessed,

---

[7]An examination of the covenant system, and particularly the "new covenant," is included in chapter 2.

many generations during the time of the "judges" turned away from God to worship idols. Yet God continued to speak of His people and their land. Evil kings led Israel and Judah into an apostasy that God was forced to punish by exile. Yet at the time of their greatest despair, the Israelites saw God reaffirm His covenant promises . . . and bring His people back to the land, purged and cleansed. No matter how a particular generation might respond to the covenant, God remained unshaken in His determination to abide by His oath.

While the failure of a specific generation to seek its identity in the covenant did not shake God's purposes, it did have an impact on that generation. The promises point to the time of the end, when God will bring human history to a conclusion. But the benefits reserved for God's own at that time of final blessing were available to any generation of Israelites that would recognize the covenant relationship and live as God's people. When a generation failed to live for Him, it suffered the loss of blessings and a deterioration of life. But when it affirmed its identity as His people and lived in responsive obedience, God graciously permitted it to experience in space and time the blessings promised for eternity.

It was particularly important, then, for each generation of Old Testament believers to face the issues presented to it in the covenant. Would the people recognize God as their God? Would they accept and live out their identity as His people? Or would they turn aside to follow their passions and drift into idolatry, immorality, and injustice? The Old Testament record shows us several times when a generation was called to face this issue and to make a choice.

The people of God *('am Elohim)* gathered at Sinai were called on to make such a commitment (Exod. 24:7f.). Moses urged the next generation to "acknowledge and take to heart *this day*" its unique relationship with God (Deut. 4:39f.). Because the Israelites made that commitment, Moses said,

> . . . the Lord has declared *this day* that you are his people, his treasured possession as he promised, and that you are to keep all his commands. He has declared that he will set you in praise, fame and honor high above all the nations he has made and that you will be a people holy to the Lord your God, as he promised (Deut. 26:18, 19; italics are the authors').

Joshua then called yet another generation to commitment: "Choose for yourselves *this day* whom you will serve." And he set an example: "As for me and my household, we will serve the Lord" (Josh. 24:15f.).

And thus it happened in the days of the kings. When

16

Josiah called all the people together, he "renewed the covenant in the presence of the Lord" (see 2 Kings 23:1–3).

Each such renewal of the covenant relationship involved a commitment by the people to *obey the God of the covenant faithfully.* God Himself did not "renew" the covenant, for His promises stand no matter what His people might or might not do. Instead, the renewal of the covenant reminded each generation to consciously recognize who they were as the people of God, and to commit themselves personally to express that relationship in a life of obedience to Him. Even in times of greatest apostasy, God called out in invitation and promise. He urged His people to find their identity and live their life in Him. "Obey me, and I will be your God and you will be my people," He proclaims (Jer. 7:23; cf. 11:4). Realize who you are . . . and then live out your identity in beauty and holiness before the eyes of the world.

In the New Testament, the Hebrew '*am* becomes the Greek *laos,* in the special sense of a called-out covenant people. God has taken individuals who believe in Jesus, both Jew and Gentile, and has called them apart from the *ethnoi* (the nations) to make them a *laos* (people) for himself" (Acts 15:14). In Christ we are now both the temple and the people of God (2 Cor. 6:15f.). The God of holiness has taken up residence in our lives; because He now walks and lives among us as our God, we are in a unique way His own.

This unique relationship with God is the prized possession of all His children. All now being children of God through faith in Christ Jesus, there is among His people "neither Jew nor Greek, slave nor free, male nor female" (Gal. 3:28). Because we have been linked together in one body by the Spirit's action, the old distinctions by which men were weighed and their value assigned are irrelevant (1 Cor. 12:13). "Here," the Apostle affirms, "there is no Greek or Jew, circumcised or uncircumcised, barbarian, Scythian, slave or free, but Christ is all, and is in all" (Col. 3:11).

Equality in the church

The biblical concept of a people of God who find their identity in Him helps us guard against the particularly dangerous heresy of different classes of Christians. Christ, Paul affirms, "is all, *and is in all.*" In the same Colossian letter Paul speaks of Christ as the one "in whom are hidden all the treasures of wisdom and knowledge" (Col. 2:3). God has revealed that this same Jesus has entered into an amazing relationship with believers, "which is Christ in you, the hope of glory." Thus

Paul goes about his ministry "admonishing and teaching *everyone* with all wisdom, so that we may present *everyone* perfect in Christ" (Col. 1:28f.). This passage, with many others, makes it clear that every child of God has a full share of the common heritage. Hope, and glory, and the potential to grow toward maturity belong to us all.

This is important for us to grasp when we approach one of the basic issues raised in this book. When we deny a clergy-laity distinction, we are affirming the *equality* of all believers! To some this seems a threatening doctrine. It appears to drag the clergy down to the level of the laity. In fact, equality in the church must be understood as lifting every believer up to realize his full potential as one of the *laos* of God! The basic reality on which this commitment is based is simply that each believer *is* equal: no distinction can be made between "first-class" Christians (the clergy) and "second-class" Christians (the laity).

- Christ, who is all, is in *all*.
- With Christ in you, there is hope for *each* of glorious things to come.
- With Christ in you, *everyone* can be instructed and built up.
- With Christ in you, *everyone* can be perfected.

How tragic, then, when in our churches we hear people apologize, "I'm just a layman." How tragic when Christian schools take pride in graduates who are moving out into "full-time Christian service," as though their mission were somehow more significant than that of others who do not share their calling.

The biblical concept of the *laos* of God demands that we, like Moses and Joshua and Josiah, call the whole community of faith together to confront their true identity. Like them we are to show all believers the root of their identity in God's mighty acts and in His calling. Like them we are to invite all the people of God to a personal commitment to live out their identity as His own people by responsive obedience to a God whose voice calls each one to minister and serve.

To explore the issues raised in this text, we will seek to define the identity of the *laos* of God more fully. We will seek to discover and illuminate those truths that explain our relationship with God as His own special people. These truths must be taught to our generation, a generation that has lost itself. We will also suggest principles to guide individuals as they seek to express their identity in personal ministries. Finally, we will propose some guidelines to help those in the local congregation who want to enable it to minister in biblical ways. To explore such issues in the light of God's Voice in the Bible is to engage in the most significant form of theology possible. Together we will seek to analyze a contemporary problem that has great significance for the church of Christ and to discover the solutions the Word of God gives us.

PROBE

▶ case histories
▶ discussion questions
▶ thought provokers
▶ resources

1. Research in church history the origins of your own particular denomination or movement. What role did the "priesthood of all believers" play in the thought of the founders or systematizers? What role did the "laity" play in the growth of your group?

2. Elton Trueblood in *The Company of the Committed* speaks about the importance of the universal priesthood in witnessing. Read the following quote. Then see if you can determine one additional mission of the church in which the full involvement of all believers is vital. Write a paragraph (like Trueblood's) showing the importance of involvement by all believers in the denomination or mission you have selected.

   It is in the general setting of the necessity of giving witness and the consequent fellowship of witness that the famous doctrine of the universal priesthood of all believers begins to come alive. All Christians must be in the ministry, whatever their occupations, because the nonwitnessing follower of Christ is a contradiction in terms . . . we dare not let the witness be limited to a small group of the professionally religious. Therefore the ministry of Christ must be universal. It must be universal in three specific ways. It must involve all places; it must involve all times; it must involve all Christian persons. . . .

3. Do people in your congregation have a distorted view of their own identity? Is there a clergy-laity distinction? Try giving the quiz on the next page to about ten adults in the congregation:
   Before you distribute this questionnaire, write down the answers you think the respondents will give to each question. Also, write down *why* you think they will answer that way.
   When the questionnaire is returned, compare the actual responses you received with your predictions. How accurate were you? Why do you feel any unexpected answers were given? You

THEOLOGICAL CORE

FIGURE 1
QUESTIONNAIRE

Please answer the following questions briefly.

(1) Number of active ministers in my congregation: _____

(2) List three important things you believe anyone who is in the ministry should do.

-

-

-

(3) What does the word "clergy" mean to you?

-

(4) What does the word "layman" mean to you?

-

(5) Most Protestant denominations and groups hold a doctrine called "the priesthood of all believers." In a sentence or two, what does this phrase mean to you?

-

(6) What is the most important way in which you express your Christian faith?

---

may wish to interview those who respond to the questionnaire to get further insight into the reasons for unexpected answers.

You may also want to modify these questions or develop others.

4. The following is a case history concerning a seventy-year-old man from Phoenix, Arizona. Al has been in some eight churches since his conversion thirty years ago. He is currently a member of a house church that stresses the development of a family-community and encourages all members to reach out to each other and to non-Christians. Read the case history. Then, with others, carry out the case study procedure outlined on pages 22–24.

AL KASSAY

During the beginning of this year—the months of January, February, March, and April—I found myself in a state of spiritual depression. Having known Christ for thirty years, I was beginning to feel that I wanted to get away from Christianity altogether.

A People of God

Jim Evans made the difference. Jim and his wife showed me a Christian love that I have never experienced outside of my own family. They radiated love to me. They proved it. They showed it. I have eaten at their table time after time. Jim and I meet every Tuesday morning for breakfast at 7 A.M. Our meeting sometimes goes on for an hour or two.

Jim Evans had been in the same church I was in and was also withdrawing at the time. He loves the Lord and is unselfish, and he saw to it (or the Lord did) that my life was being redirected. Then he brought me here (to the house church fellowship), and I saw something I liked, something different. I said to Marlene a couple of times, "Marlene, is this for real?" It's a new world. It's a fellowship. They didn't have a preacher at the top of the pyramid. There was an atmosphere of love here that I hadn't felt before.

I come from a Hungarian community in Trenton, New Jersey. When people are in a community they are fantastically different from the world around them. They are in a foreign community or a bona fide Christian community such as we have here. Actually I had been prepared for this sort of thing.

I used to teach school, but I wasn't involved with people outside of my work. Today my whole life is dedicated to Christ—from morning to night.

For years I have felt that something should be done to bring people together. About three months ago we had a fire. I knew then that our street—the community in which I lived—was ready to do something. I went around and said, "I want to set up a directory with a map showing each house—eighteen houses—with their numbers." They said, "That's the greatest thing we've heard of." So I got the names of the people, their phone numbers, and emergency numbers in case of another fire.

I have dear friends across the street, and the husband had had major surgery. We became close because of it. I went to the neighbors and said, "Hey, these folks are going to be coming back. Let's do something for them. So I went from house to house and collected about $60, which I thought was good. One of the neighbors, Lorraine, sells crystal, so we got several boxes of crystal for them. Nothing great, but it was the neighbors showing an expression of love.

They call me "the mayor." That's how they express their appreciation. Now I can walk into any house and I am welcome. It is good to get your foot in the door. My daughter and I love the Lord and want to serve Him. And I think this is a wonderful way to serve Him. Show people that you love them. Show them that you are interested. Show them that you care.

The Lord is doing what He wants done on that street. I don't

21

know what's going to happen in the future but it has been a great experience. We are keeping our eye on Lorraine because she has gone through deep water. The people next door hardly ever spoke to us before the fire, but it is different now. I just keep my eyes on the people and what they want or need. There's one family who just moved in, and they are having trouble with their children. I hope the Lord will give us an opportunity to help them. The police cars have been there several times.

5. In many educational settings today, *case study seminars* are a basic tool of learning. A case study group may vary in size from three to twelve persons. The group follows a strict procedure—to focus on critical issues, to analyze, and to evaluate.

   In this book a number of the personal experiences of believers in Christ are shared. We suggest that whenever possible a group studying this text meet in a seminar setting to discuss together the cases included with each chapter.

HOW TO STUDY A CASE

Here are a number of things you might want to keep in mind when you examine a case history:

(1) *Persons.* How many are involved? What are their relationships? How do these people and relationships affect the case?

(2) *Time.* How much time is involved in the development of the event(s) described? Are there stages that can be determined? What kind of time intervals can be distinguished? Is there a clear sequence of events?

(3) *Cause-effect.* Are cause-effect relationships described? Is the person who shares his experience aware of cause and effect? Can you suggest possible cause-effect relationships in the case?

(4) *Role of church leaders.* Does a pastor or other church leader have an active or a passive role? Who most influences the individual? Does the experience relate to the programs of the church as an institution?

(5) *Revealing language.* Are there words or phrases people use that give clues to the feelings and attitudes of those involved? How do the feelings and attitudes they have revealed affect the experience?

(6) *Objectives.* What seem to be the objectives of each person in the case? Does the writer of the case have a clear idea of his own objectives and motives? Of those of others? Do you think his statements of objectives and motives are accurate?

(7) *Identification.* As you study the case do you identify positively or negatively with any of the participants? Why, or why not? What does this reveal about you? To what extent does the case

writer share and identify himself? Is he like or unlike you? How? Why?

(8) *Theories.* Does the case writer suggest theories to explain his own experiences and feelings? Are they justified? What theories would you present to explain what is reported? Do you or do you not have enough information to be confident that your hypotheses are justified? What additional information would you like?

(9) *Questions.* After studying the case, what questions should be asked? What questions would you like to ask the person who wrote the case? What questions should the case study group discuss?

(10) *Turning points.* Sometimes there is a single turning point in a case, sometimes more than one. Some cases may be written without a discernible turning point, although there is almost always a turning point at the heart of an individual's experience. Try to identify and clarify the turning point(s). In most situations, the ability to identify and understand turning points is a key to understanding problems and moving toward solutions.

(11) What concepts in this textbook are illustrated by or related to this case? What biblical principles are applied—or should have been applied—in it?

THE CASE STUDY STRUCTURE

Prior to the meeting, each participant in the case study seminar should spend a significant amount of time reading and thinking about the case. He should jot down observations related to the eleven general issues listed above. When the seminar meets, the following sequence must be followed strictly, with one member of the seminar group responsible for keeping to the schedule and keeping the members of the seminar from straying from the topic.

5 minutes: Clarification

The group members make statements about the facts of the case that seem significant. Much of the information in the case history may be interesting. Each member should be encouraged to make *significant* comments. Be careful to avoid interpretation, evaluation, or analysis.

25 minutes: Analysis of Dynamics

During this time the group should clarify its understanding of the dynamics of the event. It is not a time for evaluation, but for *analysis.* The group should concentrate on what seems significant in the case. Emphasize the eleven areas of exploration listed above. Such statements as "I think a turning point came when . . ." or "It seems to me the pastor had an impact here by . . ." are typical of analysis.

10 minutes: Evaluation

During this time focus on specific evaluations of the role church leadership, programs, structure, and activities played in the situation described. In what ways was the role positive? In what ways was it negative? *Why?* What concept of the church, leadership, and the layman is implied by the actions of the leaders or in the church structures described?

10 minutes: Application

What did you learn from this case? What practices would you want to avoid? What principles and practices would you want to adopt? What is the most significant thing here for your present experience? Future application?

PART 1

THEOLOGICAL CORE
THE IDENTITY OF THE BELIEVER

A People of God
A New Covenant People
A Kingdom People
A Servant People
An Empowered People
A Gifted People

A NEW COVENANT PEOPLE

The man, who had once been a prince in Egypt, was now in his fortieth year as a shepherd in Midian. Bent and near eighty, he was shocked to see a desert bush burning unconsumed. He was even more shocked by the words that God spoke to him from that bush, words that affirmed a unique relationship between the Creator and the people of Israel, whom the man had once dreamed of leading from slavery in Egypt to freedom in a Promised Land. The words that God spoke to the man, Moses, affirmed that distinctive relationship: I am your God; you are My people.

Listen to Him:

"I am the *God of your father*, the *God of Abraham*, the *God of Isaac* and the *God of Jacob*. . . . I have indeed seen the misery of *my people* in Egypt . . ." (Exod. 3:6, 7).

"Say to the Israelites, 'The LORD, the *God of your fathers*—the *God of Abraham*, the *God of Isaac* and the *God of Jacob*—has sent me to you.' *This is my name forever, the name by which I am to be remembered from generation to generation*" (Exod. 3:15).

"I have watched over you and have seen what has been done to you in Egypt. And I have *promised to bring you up* out of your misery in Egypt *into the land of the Canaanites.* Hittites, Amorites, Perizzites, Hivites and Jebusites—a land flowing with milk and honey" (Exod. 3:16, 17).

"Say to [the king of Egypt], 'The LORD, the *God of the Hebrews*, has met with us. Let us [go] . . . to *the LORD our God*'" (Exod. 3:18).

Note particularly the italicized phrases. God has chosen to identify Himself by His relationship with His people. Who is the Lord? By His own choice, He is to be known from generation to generation as

- the God of your fathers,
- the God of Abraham,
- the God of Isaac,
- the God of Jacob,
- the God of the Hebrews,
- the Lord *our* God!

What is more, God has chosen to act in harmony with that identity. He is committed to be faithful to His people and thus to keep the promise He made to Abraham. Because of the promise, He told Moses He would "bring you up out of your misery in Egypt into the land."

All such language—and the Old Testament is full of it—

brings us face to face with the concept of "covenant." God made a commitment (*b'rith*, "covenant") with Abraham and his seed. From the making of the first great biblical covenant,[1] the shape of the future was revealed, for God makes His purposes known through His promises.

THE COVENANT RELATIONSHIP

As Paul points out in Galatians 3:17, the covenant with Abraham was made prior to the giving of the Law. It is this covenant, and not the Mosaic covenant (the "Law"), that is our key to understand the relationship between God and His people. It is the Abrahamic covenant and the later covenants that amplify it that define who God is as "our God," and who we are as His *laos*. Therefore it's important to review these biblical covenants. They are rooted in the promise to Abraham and form the background for understanding the New Testament's teaching about the new covenant under which we as God's people live today.

Abrahamic covenant

Genesis 12 reports God's promise to Abraham. Abraham will become a great nation. He will be blessed, and his name will be great; he will be a source of blessing to all the peoples of the earth.

God attaches no condition to this commitment. He boldly affirms His intention to be Abraham's God.

Land covenant

Genesis 13 and 15 amplify the original covenant. Abraham is to become a great nation, and that nation is to be established in a particular land (Gen. 13:14–17). The land has geographical boundaries, and is to belong to Abraham's descendants (15:18–20).

Of particular note in the Genesis 15 account is the "covenant of blood" (the most binding of the recognized social compacts of that era), and its peculiar circumstances. The Scriptures report that Abraham fell into a deep sleep and that God alone, as a smoking fire pot with a blazing torch, passed between the halves of sacrificial animals laid out on the ground.

---

[1]Whereas Genesis 9:8f. tells of a covenant God made with Noah "and with every living creature," this covenant is not eschatological in nature. God promises "never again will all life be cut off by the waters of a flood." He does not, in the Noahic covenant, reveal the shape of the future He intends, as He does in the other biblical covenants, each of which builds on the promises given to Abraham.

This was the binding ceremony. Typically, both parties to a covenant would pass between the divided animals, signifying that each accepted the obligations laid on him and would perform them. That God alone acted out this significant ceremony is a clear statement within that culture of His intention to carry out His promises, no matter what Abraham or his descendants might do! Thus the normal covenant contract took on the character of a covenant oath. God made and testified to a decision that would not be changed by anything man might do or not do.

The nation promised to Abraham was to grow and become a kingdom in the Promised Land. Through it God intended to reveal His beauty to all the nations *(ethnoi)* of the world.

The Davidic covenant

We are given a further amplification of the Abrahamic promise in 2 Samuel 7:12–17. God appointed David and David's family to be hereditary rulers of the kingdom He intended to establish. From David's line the everlasting King was to be born.

The people God chose as His own now had a land in which to establish themselves and work out their unique identity. And they had a King from whose line the King of Kings was to come.

The new covenant promised

Finally, in the Book of Jeremiah, we see the promise of an additional covenant. The day would come, Jeremiah promised, when God would make a new covenant with the house of Israel. At that time, God would unfold a unique aspect of His eternal plan and institute a startling change in the way in which His people's relationship to Him would be expressed.

Note that each covenant is (1) rooted in the original promise to Abraham; (2) an unconditional statement of God's intention, a promise or oath defining His relationship with His people; (3) an anchor for God's people, giving them their identity in a distinctive relationship with Him.

THE LAW COVENANT

In our discussion of the biblical covenants we have not yet mentioned the Mosaic covenant (the "Law"). The reason is simple. The law covenant provided a constitution and defined how believers were to live in the Promised Land as God's people. But the law covenant was not a covenant of promise. It was not a covenant that focused on the future, nor was it

29

unconditional. The law covenant was distinctively *existential*, speaking to each generation about its personal relationship with God. All the benefits promised to Abraham could be experienced by a given generation *if* they would obey the Mosaic Law.

In addition, the Bible makes the law covenant stand in *contrast* to promise; it sees the law covenant as a covenant of performance (Gal. 3:10–14, 21–22). The law covenant is said also to be *temporary*, introduced after promise, and in force only until Christ should come (Gal. 3:23–25). The Old Testament says that a new covenant will replace the Mosaic covenant and be different from it. In the words of Jeremiah:

> "The time is coming" declares the LORD,
>   "when I will make a new covenant
> with the house of Israel
>   and with the house of Judah.
> It will not be like the covenant
>   I made with their forefathers
> when I took them by the hand
>   to lead them out of Egypt,
> because they broke my covenant,
>   though I was a husband to them,"
>   declares the LORD
>   (Jer. 31:31–32).

With this distinction drawn, we can understand something of great importance. *The identity of the believer in Old Testament times was rooted in the covenants of promise.* It was by God's free and sovereign choice that He identified Himself as "the God of Israel," and it was by His free and unconditional grace that He identified Israel as "the people of God." The law covenant showed *a people who were already God's own* how to live in a vital relationship with Him. God would "be" the God of each generation, and a succeeding generation could experience all the benefits of the relationship that existed between God and Israel when they responded to God with obedient love. The law covenant then guided God's people and showed them how to *live out their identity* as God's *laos*.

Jeremiah says the new covenant *will be made* [in the future] with God's people and "will not be like" the Mosaic covenant. We must be careful here to understand the differences and similarities between our own time and the Old Testament era. *Today, as then, our identity is rooted in the covenant promise.* Jesus has come, and through Him "those who have faith are blessed along with Abraham, the man of faith" (Gal. 3:8; cf. Rom. 4). Our relationship with God stands firmly established on His promise. He is our God and we are

His people because of *His* action, and not on the basis of any acts of our own.

But now we live under the new covenant, a replacement for the Mosaic covenant. The new covenant explains how we *live out* our promise-based identity. And this *is* different. In several significant ways the new covenant is "not like" the Mosaic covenant. What was once expressed externally in law as a guide to behavior is now implanted by God within the living personality, as a power for transformation. We who are God's *laos* today are called to and empowered for a life of ministry that Jeremiah hints at, but that is more fully explained in the New Testament in two key passages. Jeremiah says,

> "This is the covenant I will make with the house of Israel
>   after that time," declares the LORD.
> "I will put my law in their minds
>   and write it on their hearts.
> I will be their God,
>   and they will be my people
> No longer will a man teach his neighbor,
>   or a man his brother
>   saying 'Know the LORD,'
> because they will all know me,
>   from the least of them to the greatest,"
>   declares the LORD
>   (Jer. 31:33–34).

The *laos* of God from the least of us to the greatest has now been lifted up together. We are each one called to a life of ministry that is possible only because God has written *Himself* within us, on our minds and our hearts alike.

THE NEW COVENANT IN HEBREWS: ESTABLISHED

Jeremiah foretold a covenant that had not yet been made. When Jesus gathered with His disciples in the Upper Room the night before His crucifixion, He made it clear that His death was to institute the long-promised new covenant. When Jesus raised the symbolic cup of wine He announced, "This is my blood of the covenant, which is poured out for many for the forgiveness of sins" (Matt. 26:28). As the culminating covenant, it too would be a "covenant of blood." But now the blood would be drawn from the veins of the Savior Himself. His sac-. rifice would be God's ultimate, binding oath.

The Gospels do not explain the full significance of the new covenant. But two New Testament passages explore its meaning in detail. The most extensive exposition is Hebrews 4:14 through 10:18, with a digression in Hebrews 5:11–6:12. To understand this discussion of the new covenant we must

31

go back to the "old" Mosaic covenant with which it is contrasted.

Elements of the Mosaic covenant

The Mosaic code is often thought of as "the Ten Commandments," or the moral code of Israel. Law was, in fact, only one element of that covenant. With the introduction of the moral code sin also appeared as transgression of the Law (cf. Rom. 7:7–11; 1 John 3:3). Thus the history of events at Sinai tells us that immediately after stating the moral code, God gave His people (1) a tabernacle, in which His presence would rest; (2) a priesthood, which would make sacrifices for sins and thank offerings; and (3) sacrifices, by which the sins of His people could be covered, enabling them to approach Him.

The Mosaic covenant must always be understood as a total system, not simply as laws that once governed man's behavior toward God and others. Whenever any part of a human being's relationship with God has involved performance of any kind, there has been human failure. "All have sinned," the Scripture makes clear. Thus a legal system that sets standards must provide for forgiveness and restoration to fellowship. The very existence of "law" made a sacrifice, a priesthood, and a tabernacle (or temple) necessary.

This is the point of a statement made by the writer of Hebrews. "When there is a change of the priesthood, there must also be a change of the law" (Heb. 7:12). When the new covenant was made on Calvary, *the whole Mosaic system was replaced, in every element.* Life under the new covenant is a new kind of life for the *laos* of God.

As we analyze Hebrews we will see the writer dealt with every element of the Mosaic system to demonstrate how it has been transformed by Christ. And so "priesthood" must be reevaluated and understood in a fresh perspective provided by Christ.

Hebrews 1–4

The earliest chapters of Hebrews set about establishing the superiority of Jesus. He is the very Son of God, the "exact representation" (χαράκτηρ) of the Eternal (Heb. 1:3). As such He is greater than the angels (Heb. 1:4–14), who in the Jewish tradition were honored as mediators of the Mosaic covenant. Because of His higher position, those who honored the "message spoken by angels as binding" will surely honor His words.

Jesus entered the physical universe as a human being to

be a brother to all whom God intends to bring to glory as His sons (Heb. 2:5–18). His suffering in life and death was to free the *laos* of God and to make them a holy family. He became like us in every way, that He might "become a merciful and faithful high priest in service to God, and that he might make atonement for the sins of the people" (Heb. 2:17). In this, as apostle and high priest, Jesus is greater even than Moses, the lawgiver (Heb. 3:1–6). Because the higher honor belongs to Jesus, He must be heard and obeyed. Many in Moses' day refused to hear the words God spoke through him, and because of their unbelief they were condemned to wander the wilderness until they died. When God speaks today through Jesus, we must heed. A hardened heart will lead only to disobedience and disaster (Heb. 3:7–4:13).

Having established the importance of hearing the message that God communicates to us through Jesus, the writer of Hebrews immediately develops the theme of Jesus' high priesthood. He shows how Jesus' work on Calvary has initiated a new covenant and a new lifestyle for the *laos* of God.

Hebrews 4:14–5:10: Qualifications of a priest

Every high priest is (1) selected by God (2) from among men (3) to represent men in matters related to God and (4) to offer gifts and sacrifices for sin. God called Jesus to this office, and He is fully qualified for it. The writer stresses the full humanity of Jesus and assures us that, since He has experienced all the temptations humans are subject to, He is able to sympathize with us. Thus we can "approach the throne of grace with confidence."

Hebrews 6:13–7:28: Relationship of Jesus' priesthood to promise

The Mosaic (Levitical) priesthood was part of a temporary system that would pass away. The writer makes it clear that Jesus' priesthood is linked to promise. An oath confirmed the Abrahamic covenant (the "covenant of blood" reported in Genesis 15); an oath confirms the salvation offered by Jesus: "He has become a high priest forever, in the order of Melchizedek" (Heb. 6:20).

The writer reviews the Genesis history and recalls that Melchizedek, whose name meant "king of righteousness," functioned as a priest to Abraham and was given a tithe of Abraham's gain. The Old Testament gives no genealogy or subsequent history for this man. As a type he is "without beginning of days or end of days." In this he is similar to Jesus who, as God incarnate, has existed from eternity past and will continue into eternity future.

The writer's point is important. Old Testament prophecy spoke of a coming of One of whom God would declare "You are a priest forever, in the order of Melchizedek" (Ps. 110:4). If there is to be a new priesthood, then the Levitical priesthood and all the regulations associated with it must be set aside! Old Testament priests were ordained apart from an oath. But when Jesus became High Priest, He became a priest with an oath when God said to Him: "The LORD has sworn and will not change his mind: 'You are a priest forever'" (Ps. 110:4). The writer of Hebrews concludes that "because of this oath, Jesus has become the guarantee of a better covenant" (Heb. 7:22). All other priests died; Jesus lives forever. Because He has a permanent priesthood He is "able to save completely those who come to God through him, because he always lives to intercede for them" (Heb. 7:25). Unlike the former priests, who had to make sacrifices for the people, Jesus offered Himself, and in that once-for-all sacrifice accomplished fully what earlier sacrifices had merely pictured.

Hebrews 8:1–13: Priest of a new covenant

The sacrifice that Jesus made was infinitely better than those offered under the old system.

Thus His priesthood is conclusive evidence that a superior covenant has been introduced, one that makes the Mosaic system obsolete (Heb. 8:13). Specifically, under this new covenant, the writer of the Hebrews letter says,

> I will put my laws in their minds
> and write them on their hearts.
> I will be their God,
> and they will be my people.
> No longer will a man teach his neighbor,
> or a man his brother, saying, "Know the Lord,"
> because they will all know me,
> from the least of them to the greatest.
> For I will forgive their wickedness
> and will remember their sins no more
> (Heb. 8:10–12; cf. Jer. 31:33–34).

Hebrews 9:1–10:18: Impact of the new covenant

Just as the priesthood has been replaced, an earthly tabernacle is no longer the place of meeting with God. Christ has entered the true tabernacle, the very presence of the Father, and opened the way to immediate fellowship for all God's *laos*.

Also, the sacrificial blood under the old covenant was from

bulls and goats. These offerings covered (Heb. *kaphar*) the sin of God's people but were never able to perfect them. The need to bring sacrifices over and over again served only to remind God's people that their sin had not been dealt with! But the blood of Jesus *obtained,* not merely symbolized, eternal redemption (Heb. 9:12). Jesus' death set the believer free "from the sins committed under the first covenant" (Heb. 9:15). The language the writer uses is very specific. By Jesus' offering we have been made perfect and cleansed (cf. Heb. 10:2–3). We have been "made holy through the sacrifice of the body of Jesus once for all" (Heb. 10:10). Our sins have been taken away, and "by one sacrifice he has made perfect forever those who are being made holy" (Heb. 10:14). Because of Jesus, God no longer sees the sins of His *laos,* for "Their sins and lawless acts I will remember no more" (Heb. 10:17).

It is important to realize that this declarative act of God in pronouncing His people perfected is no license to sin. Instead it is part of God's new-covenant approach to righteousness. Under the Mosaic code, law was a statement of righteousness that stood *outside* the believer and spoke to him of obligation. Because people failed to live by the Law, God had to institute a system (priesthood, tabernacle, sacrifices), through which a believer might remain in fellowship with Him. *The moral law preceded and made necessary the priesthood and sacrifices.*

Under the new covenant this is reversed. Jesus came to serve us as ever-living High Priest. He offered His once-for-all sacrifice and dealt decisively and finally with sin. Because our sins have now been forgiven and are no longer an issue, we are freed to live transformed lives. Now law, which in the old system was a propositional expression of God's holiness, is no longer to be looked for *outside* us, but *within!* The Holy Spirit has taken it as His ministry to us to ". . . put my laws in their hearts, " and to ". . . write them on their minds." Under the new covenant the priesthood of Jesus and His sacrifice precede and make possible the moral transformation of God's people to His likeness.

It is now possible to sketch the contrast drawn by the writer to the Hebrews between the new and the Mosaic covenants that make the latter obsolete. We can also see something of the impact of these changes on the lifestyle of believers today. The contrasts are suggested in the chart on the following page.

The new covenant in 2 Corinthians: explained

In Hebrews the writer explains the basis for new covenant living. In 2 Corinthians the apostle Paul gives a striking exposi-

THEOLOGICAL CORE

FIGURE 2

MOSAIC CODE	NEW COVENANT	IMPACT
Levitical Priests	**Melchizedekian Priest**	
human imperfect sinners mortal not confirmed by oath	human perfect sinless immortal confirmed by God's oath	Jesus sympathizes with us in our weaknesses. Yet He ever lives to represent us to God, providing an eternal salvation. Knowing He is our high priest gives us confidence to approach God at any time, whether our need is for mercy (when we have failed) or for grace to help (that we might not fail).
Unrelated to Oath	**Confirmed by God's Oath**	
(e.g., not a promise covenant)	(thus an amplification of the Abrahamic "promise" covenant)	We can be greatly encouraged and secure in our hope, knowing that it is impossible for God to lie.
Earthly Sanctuary	**True Sanctuary**	
a copy and shadow of what is in heaven	Jesus entered heaven, appeared at the throne with the sacrifice of his own blood, and sat down at the right hand of God.	Jesus has dealt with the realities. Because of His finished work of sacrifice and continuing work as High Priest, we know that the "way into the holy place" is open to us.
Animal Sacrifices	**Jesus Himself the Sacrifice**	
repeated dealt with "outward cleansing" (9:13) reminded of sin could not perfect	once for all cleansed us within removed sin as an issue does perfect the worshiper	Jesus' blood fully meets all the righteous demands of God and provides full forgiveness. What is more, the sacrifice institutes a positive *cleansing* of the believer. We are declared perfect forever and at the same time in our daily life are "being made holy" (10:14).
Law	**"Law"**	
external written in stone an impossible standard a written expression of God's righteousness	internal written on mind and heart a practical lifestyle for *all* of God's people a living expression of God's righteousness	All God's people have a unique relationship with the spirit of God, who is now writing God's own character on the living personality of believers. Mind and heart are being transformed, so that life will increasingly reflect God's holiness and love. This action of the Spirit brings all believers to the highest possible relationship with God, "because they will all know me, from the least of them to the greatest" (8:11).
People	**People**	
select group	all	

tion of what the new covenant means to us, God's people. The argument, which we can once again only sketch, covers from 2 Corinthians 3:1 through 5:21. Paul's main point is summed up in 2 Corinthians 4:10 and 11. Because of God's work in our lives under the new covenant, we who are His *laos* in fact *incarnate the living Jesus in today's world.* "We always carry around in our body the death of Jesus," Paul says, "so that the life of Jesus may also be revealed in our body. For we who are alive are always being given over to death for Jesus' sake, so that his life may be revealed in our mortal body." This central new-covenant reality orients and guides us in tracing Paul's argument.

Second Corinthians 3:1-18

Paul points out that the impact of his ministry is visible to all, being "written not with ink but with the Spirit of the living God, not on tablets of stone but on tablets of human hearts" (2 Cor. 3:3). This is a clear reference to Jeremiah's new covenant promise. In fact, Paul speaks of Christ making him [and others] "competent as ministers of a new covenant" (2 Cor. 3:6).

Paul then contrasts the glory of the old (Mosaic) and the new covenant. The old covenant reveals holiness but condemns, for "I would not have known what sin was except through the law" (Rom. 7:7). The new covenant is more glorious, for it "brings righteousness" (2 Cor. 3:9). Here Paul contrasts an experience Moses had with the experience of believers who live under the new covenant. When Moses came down from Mount Sinai with the tablets of the Law, his face was radiant. But that radiant glow began to fade when Moses left Sinai and the presence of God. So Moses "put a veil over his face to keep the Israelites from gazing at it while the radiance was fading away" (2 Cor. 3:13). In contrast, believers living under the new covenant are able to remove their veils boldly and live openly with each other. We are free to do this, Paul says, because under the new covenant we are continually in the very presence of God ["Where the spirit of the Lord is, there is freedom" (2 Cor. 3:17)]. Our lives reflect that presence, and demonstrate God's new-covenant promise to write His law on heart and mind. Thus our unveiled faces "all reflect the Lord's glory," for we "are being transformed into his likeness with ever-increasing glory, which comes from the Lord, who is the Spirit" (2 Cor. 3:18).

Second Corinthians 4:1-16

Paul's startling affirmation in chapter 3 is that Christ Himself is being formed and revealed in each believer. Paul continues to point out that Christ "who is the image of God" (2 Cor. 4:4), shines in and through us. We continue to be human, subject to all the weaknesses and failures of mankind. Yet through us "his life" is "revealed in our mortal body" (2 Cor. 4:11). The confidence we have in His work of inward renewal outweighs any daily frustrations we may know, for "we fix our eyes not on what is seen, but on what is unseen." We know "what is unseen is eternal" (2 Cor. 4:18), and we have in Christ God's covenant promise of eternal salvation.

Second Corinthians 5:1–21

In this great chapter Paul applies what he has been teaching. In light of new-covenant realities, ministry can focus, not on externals, but on the work God does within the heart (cf. 2 Cor. 5:12; Jer. 31:33). In a new-covenant ministry we rely on "Christ's love [which] compels us," . . . not on manipulation of authoritarian demand (2 Cor. 5:14). Christ's death for all was purposive and effective. He died that we might live for Him (2 Cor. 5:15), and He accomplished His purpose. Now each believer is a new creation (2 Cor. 5:17). Thus ministry within the body of Christ is a ministry of reconciliation, that is, ministry is focused on bringing the experience of the believer into harmony with his or her new-covenant identity "in Christ" (2 Cor. 5:18–20).

THE NEW-COVENANT IDENTITY OF THE LAOS OF GOD

The Reformers of the sixteenth century reacted against a number of errors institutionalized in the Roman Catholic Church of their day. They stressed salvation by faith alone in contrast to a salvation by works and indulgences. They stressed a "priesthood of all believers" to affirm the significance of each Christian, against a system that viewed the clergy as the church. In their teaching of this doctrine the Reformers moved toward a fresh understanding of the idea of the people of God. Through the Reformers, many believers caught a glimpse of the glory that was theirs.

However, it is doubtful that the Reformers' concept of the "priesthood of all believers" gave full expression to the biblical content. "Priesthood" still carried then, as it does today, a sacerdotal meaning. Biblically, the concept of priesthood is rooted in a much earlier time than the age of law, and its basic meanings are not expressed in vestments and sacraments.

We've seen in our survey of Hebrews and 2 Corinthians the impact of the new covenant, of which Christ is High Priest. By that covenant and through His sacrifice Jesus has brought each believer into the immediate presence of God and planted the life of Christ within him. Thus Peter can say we are "not just mortals now but sons of God; the live, permanent Word of the living God has given [us] his own indestructible heredity" (1 Peter 1:23 PHILLIPS). We live today in intimate fellowship with God.

It is in examining fellowship—life in the presence of the Lord—that we best understand the root meanings of priesthood. In the original creation Adam and Eve lived in close fellowship with God. But sin entered, and the original pair was led out of the Garden. Then God Himself acted as the first priest. He slew animals and brought Adam and Eve their skins for a covering. This picture of redemption (sin covered by blood through the personal action of God) was transmitted to the children of men. People were to bring sacrifices to the altar when they approached God. Cain's condemnation came when he refused this act of confession of sin and instead brought the bloodless sacrifice of his garden produce. Throughout history, sacrifice has been seen as essential when people met God.

In families like those of Job (who predates the Law) and Abraham (who was possibly Job's close contemporary), the leader of the clan took on the duty of priest. He guarded the integrity of the family and stood before God representing them at the time of sacrifice. The priest was, in his person and his ministry, a channel or doorway. He approached God with worship or confession on behalf of others. And God worked through him to teach the ways of holiness.

The introduction of the Law at the time of the Exodus led to the institutionalization of the priesthood. Specific laws meant specific sins were being or would be committed. A people made guilty before God (cf. Rom. 3:19) needed a remedy. Thus the system of tabernacle, sacrifice, and priesthood was essential. And God set aside a single family to perform priestly functions that mirrored the work Christ would do—and continued the essential ministries that had existed from Eden. These lasting ministries were to represent man to God, as the Book of Hebrews says. And in turn, they were to instruct the people in the ways of God (cf. John 17:5; 18:5f.; Deut. 27:9f.; 31:4f.). The priests, to whom all Israelites came when sin interrupted their fellowship with God, were the doorway to fellowship and represented both mercy and help.

And then Jesus came to fulfill in Himself all the functions of priesthood. Through the one perfect sacrifice of Himself He laid the foundation for full forgiveness. Through Him all believers gain direct and immediate access to God. Because Christians are "in Christ" they are in direct and immediate contact with God Himself. Thus they need no priest to represent them other than Jesus Himself. *But the rest of mankind still requires a priesthood* and God Himself calls us to perform these priestly duties. Thus it is that the New Testament sees the whole people of God as a royal priesthood, called to proclaim the knowledge of God (1 Peter 2:9). Thus, too, Paul speaks of His ministry of sharing the Gospel as a priestly duty (Rom. 15:16).

This priesthood no longer offers sacrifices. But the priesthood in which every believer today is a full participant continues to be the "point of contact" people have with God. We live in His presence, and He lives in us. Thus our lives and our words have a priestly function. We represent God to men and men to God, pointing always to the finished sacrifice of Jesus, whose work brought this change to priesthood by making it the ministry of the whole people of God.

A grasp of our priesthood and our identity under the new covenant is a necessary foundation for understanding the nature of the personal ministries of believers today.

- Under the new covenant, every believer lives in the very presence of God, with full and immediate access to Him.
- Under the new covenant, God is at work within every believer, making him holy and writing his Maker's law on his transformed mind and heart.
- Under the new covenant, Jesus Himself is "revealed in our mortal bodies." In essence, the Bible teaches a *continuing incarnation and presence of Jesus in today's world in every believer.*
- Under the new covenant, each believer is now enabled to fulfill the changeless functions of priesthood. While the sacrificial function has been fulfilled by the High Priest, all the other "contact" functions of that ministry are ours.

The implications of these truths are staggering. Because each believer has personal and immediate access to and authority with God, there is no need for hierarchical structures as under the old covenant. Instead, each Christian needs to be taught how to live responsive to His Lord, to listen for His voice, and to follow obediently. Structures in a local church designed to give a pastor or a board *control* of others violate the freedom and responsibility of Christians to live in the immediate presence of God.

Because God is at work in believers to transform them, teaching and motivation within the church are not to focus on behavior [the issue dealt with by the Law] but on the heart. Ministry in the church should seek to build a commitment to Christ that will be expressed by responsive obedience to His voice.

Because Jesus incarnates Himself in each believer, there can be no lifting up of some as more significant than others. There can be no higher calling than that of bearing Jesus about in our mortal bodies to express His continuing presence in the world. Distinctions between "clergy" and "laity" become totally meaningless when every Christian realizes he is stamped with the presence of his Lord. Compared to Jesus' presence in us, the roles or positions or gifts that are sometimes emphasized are seen to be completely irrelevant in defining our identity.

A ministry by each believer and the building of a congregation to become a ministering people are possible today because we live under the new covenant. Because each genuine believer is in touch with God, experiences personal transformation, and is infused with the very life of Jesus, it is a realizable goal to expect each local congregation freed and taught to become the ministering people of God in our tangled world.

PROBE

▶ *case histories*
▶ *discussion questions*
▶ *thought provokers*
▶ *resources*

1. For additional study, select one of the following projects and write out your findings in a paper at least five pages long.
   A. Study *diathēkē,* the Greek word for "covenant."
   B. Select the most significant paragraph from Hebrews 3–10 and write about its teaching, explaining why you selected it as the most significant.
   C. Select the most significant paragraph from 2 Corinthians 3–5 and write about its teaching, explaining why you selected it as the most significant.
   D. Explore the "transformation" process by which the believer becomes "like Jesus." Key words to check include "example," "like," and "image."

2. Review carefully the content of this chapter. Then make a list of at least twenty practical implications of the believer's identity as one

41

of a new-covenant *laos*. Implications can range from personal ("I should learn how to receive guidance directly from God") to cultural ("We should abandon the terms 'clergy' and 'laity' because they cloud the Christian's understanding of his identity") to institutional ("There should be a way to structure a local church so that leaders do not 'control' others"). (Later in this text many of these implications will be spelled out in detail. For now it is adequate to begin seeking some of the implications on your own.)

3. Here is a list developed in 1976 from questionnaires by Gilbert R. Martin and Chet Bartholomew of the Trinity Church in Seattle. They describe relationships between the congregation and individual believer-priests. Which of these areas seems most significant to you? Why?

WHAT DOES THE BELIEVER-PRIEST BRING TO THE CHURCH?

I. Reproductive Function—To build disciples.
  A. To bring new people to the Lord:
    1. To greet new people
    2. Show hospitality
    3. Meet the needs of individuals
    4. Share the Lord
  B. To help Christians grow:
    1. Encouragement*
    2. Exhortation*
    3. Be example*
    4. Teaching*
    5. Fellowship*
    6. Joy in what God is doing
    7. Meeting individual needs—physical, spiritual*
    8. Love
    9. Prayer*

II. Responsibilities to the Whole Body—To keep it a growing, healthy organism.
  A. Exercise of spiritual gifts*
  B. Prayer*
  C. Protection of the body from falseness
  D. Keeping relationships right between brothers—discipline and exhortation
  E. Service*
  F. Obedience
  G. Support of elders
  H. Stewardship of resources
  I. Sound teaching*

  (Note: Those with an * were mentioned several times)

WHAT DOES THE CHURCH DO FOR THE BELIEVER-PRIEST?
(Responses from the body; group interaction)

I. Teaching:
  A. The nature of God

B. The nature of man
C. The leading of God
D. Spiritual gifts
E. Prayer

II. Development of Spiritual Gifts:
   A. Recognition of individual gifts
   B. Provision of opportunity to use gifts through service
   C. Ordination

III. Protection:
   A. From world system
   B. From false teaching and Satan
   C. From the rough world; greenhouse for growing little Christians

IV. Opportunity for Growth:
   A. Bringing people to maturity
   B. Showing us weak areas, so we aren't allowed just to "hang in there"
   C. Rubbing off some of the "rough corners" so the refining process is carried on
   D. Providing a sounding board to exercise what the believer has learned
   E. Challenging the growth
   F. Giving to believers the example of other believers
   G. Exhorting

V. Affirmation of Each Other:
   A. Giving a structure to minister in and be ministered to
   B. Supporting various ministries of believer-priests
   C. Supporting each person as an individual
   D. Providing an opportunity to serve God and other believer-priests
   E. Providing strength to overcome temptation
   F. Supporting in times of trouble—a group of people to depend on when you can't handle something yourself
   G. Giving a family

VI. Unity as a Body:
   A. A center of operation
   B. Strength in corporate worship
   C. An opportunity to meet others—a place to meet
   D. Fellowship, sharing, and recreation
   E. Availability of different viewpoints from other believers
   F. "Oneness of mind"
   G. A structure for believers to meet others of same mind
   H. Love relationships with people you would never otherwise associate with in the world. This demonstrates God's grace and offers acceptance

4. *Case History.* This case history comes from Gilbert R. ("Gib") Martin, who shares the story of his conversion. What is of special note is the role of Charlie—and the relationship of Charlie to the churches of his community.

   Follow the procedure outlined on pages 22–24 and examine this experience in a case seminar.

THEOLOGICAL CORE

GIB MARTIN

I was converted at the age of twenty-seven, more than twenty-one years ago. At that time a man who had the gift of mercy was God's instrument in leading me to Jesus Christ. This man, who had been an alcoholic for many years, was a carpenter in the community I had moved to. He had been led to the Lord many years earlier by my great-grandmother, and God put such a burden on his heart for souls that he would spend literally every day in the local bar after work, drinking coffee and talking and sharing his life with the people who came in.

I was one of those who came into the bar. I was a school teacher, and after teaching I would stop and get a beer. Drinking wasn't my thing, but a drink was and I would sit there and sort of bemoan life to myself. I always tried to separate myself from everyone else. I wanted to be alone at that point; working with twenty-seven kids all day long, I didn't want to be with anyone.

I had been an atheist for three years. I tried to be an atheist. At least I confessed to being an atheist. I had come out of a religious system but had not met the Lord in a personal way. I was going through a period of desperation.

Charlie, with his gift of mercy would sit at the end of the bar, and I would see him there every night. He would look at me and smile. Pretty soon he knew my name. Then one night I was so miserable he could probably read it all over my face. He just waited for the Lord to tell him the night. Well, he came over and brought his cup of coffee and sat down beside me at the bar and we had an exchange of words. They weren't very nice because I really didn't want his company. But he had a way of not being offended. In a marvelous way God gave him gentleness.

He couldn't actually share Christ with me then. He perceived that he wasn't on the right side of the track, because I was arrogant, was haughty, thought too highly of myself. He discerned all of those things in me (as he told me later). That was humbling, but it was good for me, because he had a gentle way of doing that, too.

But Charlie knew a man who had a doctor's degree who was going to be speaking in the community. That impressed me. So he suggested I go hear him. I said I would do it on condition that we discussed what the man had to say. I didn't know that he was a preacher, just a doctor who was going to give a talk. So Charlie trapped me all the way!

I went to hear this doctor give a talk and I heard the gospel for the first time. It was so traumatic that I came home and vomited all night long. I laid in the bathroom, and my mother thought I was

44

dying—and I was sure I was. I was so convicted of my sin. I went back to school the next day, and you know how (if you're a school teacher) to feed the kids a lot of work to keep them quiet. I did that, and at noon I went down on my knees and asked Jesus Christ into my life.

The surprising thing about my experience with Jesus was that it was real. I was afraid it wouldn't be real. I had known about Jesus Christ for so long, but I was always afraid He could never mean much to me. But He did! An encounter with Him had occurred. Christ came into my life.

That first night I couldn't wait to get back to talk to Charlie. As we met I was anxious to share with him what had happened. But we just hugged.

Then I said, "How did you know?"

He said, "Because God told me at 7 o'clock this morning to get up off my knees!"

He said that his friends, the ones he had led to Christ, had joined him and all night long they had been on their knees praying.

That was how it happened. Because one man was exercising his spiritual gift.

And he did it with the rebuke of the local churches. They didn't like what he was doing. Because he went to a bar, many churches would not allow him to associate with them. Even the church to which he directed me would not allow him to become a member. Charlie had such a heart that this rejection didn't bother him at all. I would sometimes say, "How about coming to church with me this Sunday, Charlie." And he would reply, "Well, it wouldn't be good for you if I did."

So that's the way Charlie was. He died a couple of years ago. I'll never forget him."

5. *Case History.* One of the difficulties the contemporary church faces in affirming the priesthood of all believers and working out that reality in the congregation's lifestyle is the role people expect ministers to play. Jack Wood, whose ministry in Spokane, Washington, as one of the pastors of a fellowship of some nine hundred people committed to new covenant realities, shares in the following paragraphs his experience of some of these pressures and their personal impact.

Explore his experience in a *case study seminar,* especially if you are planning to serve as a pastor or other church staff member.

JACK WOOD

It costs a pastor to realize that he is limiting the grace of God within his flock by being a dominant leader or by assuming the traditional role of "superstar shepherd."

THEOLOGICAL CORE

I learned early in the ministry that the typical congregation expects a lot of its shepherd. It fit right into my personality to try to live up to those expectations. I have, in fact, been living up to people's expectations all my life, from my boyhood. Growing up without a father and kicked around from pillar to post, I found myself working doubly hard to win people's approval. I fell right into doing the same thing in the ministry.

I wanted to live up to everyone's expectations. And they were more than glad in most cases to put me in the position of the superstar shepherd. I suppose subconsciously they didn't want the responsibility of being ministers themselves. So very early I learned that that was the way you did things.

Deep down inside I wasn't happy, but I just didn't know any other way. So for the first ten years of my ministry the church hired me to do its thing. That was the understanding we had. And it began to chip away at something inside me. I felt dehumanized by performing all the time, by feeling responsible for everybody's spiritual welfare. I thought that's what a shepherd was. I didn't realize I was limiting God's grace and other people's growth and maturity by doing everything for them.

Then God began to work away at this superstar image. He sent people into my life. He took me out of the denominational box I was in. And he opened me up to other perspectives on shepherding. When I first heard that every Christian is to be a minister, that every believer is to be a priest, I thought, "Oh, no, not another school of thought!" I thought of it as similar to the school of thought I had adopted, and I didn't want to leave that box and crawl into another.

And I thought of it as just a way of saying, "I don't want to be responsible." Nor did I want to give up being the superstar shepherd, either. It met my ego needs, which were enormous at times. I suppose because of my childhood background and normal human egocentricity, I enjoyed the adulation that came from "riding the pulpit." I hid my real self behind my clerical robes. No one was supposed to touch or question or pull down or confront the superstar.

When God began to talk to me about being vulnerable and open and honest, all that changed. Others began to confront me, and I was devastated. It cost me. I was depressed and confused about the two schools of thought. The church was split, too, because the Lord was leading us into a priesthood of all believers and involving people in groups so they could minister to one another.

At first two-thirds of the congregation did not *want* to be responsible for their own spiritual welfare. These members were

46

looking to me as their leader, and they too found it extremely difficult to be responsible for their own spiritual welfare, for ministering to one another, confessing their faults one to another, praying for one another, and growing as ministers in the Christian community. After four years we still haven't made the transition from the church dependent on the superstar shepherd to the "Christ is sufficient" church of believers who have learned to be ministers in their own right. It's been quite a process. Many people have dropped out and gone elsewhere, because when I stopped performing and being the superstar shepherd, they were disappointed.

And I was still holding onto the role of superstar shepherd. People tried to pump my yellow balloon up again, and I heard conversations like, "Jack, we're behind you. Don't worry about a thing." They thought I was in a power struggle with the church council or board. Yes, there were struggles. But most of them were inside me, over my willingness to let my ego die, my ego that thought it needed all the adulation. God was producing that death in me. He humbled me, and I was completely crushed. Though God always surrounded me with loving people, I couldn't feel their love because of the devastation of discovering that the call of God is a call to humility, not a call to be a superstar shepherd.

The big ego and congregational expectations of me went hand in hand. I was working all the time. And had no time for my family and no time for my own personal spiritual welfare. I was trying my best to meet all the needs of my congregation. And so when my ego died, my pastoral role had to change. I am still in the lifelong process of being broken. I still have a great deal of pride and ego need in me.

Then I found that preaching to other congregations met my ego needs. But I knew that God was calling me to surrender to Him and that if speaking to other groups interfered, I would have to give it up.

I had to stop listening to people, too. Their assurance of their prayers for me kept pushing me to assume the role I was trying to shed. They had a hard time understanding that the death I was dying was a good thing and that the depression I was in wasn't altogether bad. The "performer" in me had to die.

I had learned to be a showman at a very early age. All those things I had grown so skillful at in ten years of ministry had to die—the ability to influence people, raise money, promote programs, build buildings, and build the kingdom of my denomination.

It left me dangling with nothing. I had to start all over again until I realized my work had to be *all* of Jesus and none of me. As

I look back on the process now I am grateful to God for the people He sent into my life at the right time and for the books, especially those of Larry Richards, that influenced me so strongly. Particularly helpful were *The Priesthood of All Believers, Everyone a Minister,* and *Bodylife*.

God has now given our church peace. Those who were so disappointed that I was not performing to their expectations began to change. They either got into a group, grew up and embraced the priesthood of all believers, or they left. I wept over those who left. But in many cases there was nothing I could do. They demanded a pastor who did everything for them and they couldn't get out of the groove they were in. And the Lord has given my church a spiritually biblical unity it had never had before, one that lets me be a shepherd in the biblical sense. Praise the Lord!

THEOLOGICAL CORE
THE IDENTITY OF THE BELIEVER

A People of God
A New Covenant People
A Kingdom People
A Servant People
An Empowered People
A Gifted People

A KINGDOM PEOPLE

In a great statement about what it means for believers to know Christ, Paul speaks of giving thanks to the Father "who has qualified you to share in the inheritance of the saints in the kingdom of light." "For he has rescued us," Paul continues, "from the dominion of darkness and brought us into the kingdom of the Son he loves" (Col. 1:12–13). The *laos*, the people of God, live in the kingdom of the Son.

It's difficult to apply this affirmation to contemporary church life. The biblical concept of "kingdom," for example, is rich and complex. More than one writer has written a whole book on the subject. Some have argued over possible distinctions between the "kingdom of heaven" and the "kingdom of God." The Bible clearly speaks of a kingdom that is both universal and local, both future and present. George Eldon Ladd reached the following conclusions about the kingdom:

> The Kingdom of God is basically the rule of God. It is God's reign, the divine sovereignty in action. God's reign, however, is manifested in several realms, and the Gospels speak of entering into the Kingdom of God today and tomorrow. God's reign manifests itself both in the future and in the present and thereby creates both a future realm and a present realm in which man may experience the blessings of his reign.[1]

What we must be concerned with in this study is God's present reign, and specifically what it means to the *laos* of God to live "in the kingdom of the Son he loves." We are a kingdom people. We need to understand what it means to be citizens of God's kingdom. Our identity and our ministry are rooted in this reality as well as in that of the new covenant.

"KINGDOM"

The Greek word for "king" in our New Testament is the same word the translators of the Septuagint chose to render the Hebrew word *melek*. In various forms both words refer to a ruler or king. A related word refers to kingly rule or to a kingdom. In the Old Testament the words are first used of earthly kings and secular governments. But increasingly the concept is applied to God and His reign. Psalm 47 reflects something of the Old Testament picture of God as universal ruler:

> For God is the King of all the earth;
> sing to him a psalm of praise.
> God reigns over the nations;
> God is seated on his holy throne.

---

[1]George E. Ladd, *The Gospel of the Kingdom* (Grand Rapids: William B. Eerdmans Publishing Co., 1959), p. iii.

> The nobles of the nations assemble
>> as the people of the God of Abraham,
> for the kings of the earth belong to God;
>> he is greatly exalted (Ps. 47:7–9).

Even though God did not have the covenant relationship with the *ethnoi* (people) He had with Abraham, His authority nevertheless extended to all creation, and everyone who peopled it.

But the Old Testament does more than speak of God's general rule. As its revelation unfolded over the centuries, more and more emphasis was given to picture a future time when a literal kingdom would be established on earth, with God Himself present to rule in the person of the Messiah. Thus Isaiah says,

> For to us a child is born,
>> to us a son is given,
>> and the government will be on his shoulders.
> And he will be called
>> Wonderful Counselor, Mighty God,
>> Everlasting Father, Prince of Peace.
> Of the increase of his government and peace
>> there will be no end.
> He will reign on David's throne
>> and over his kingdom,
>> establishing and upholding it
>> with justice and righteousness
>> from that time on and forever (Isa. 9:6–7).

Later Isaiah goes on to describe the impact of the Messiah's rule.

> He will not judge by what he sees with his eyes,
>> or decide by what he hears with his ears;
> but with righteousness he will judge the needy,
>> with justice he will give decisions
>>> for the poor of the earth.
> He will strike the heart with the rod of his mouth;
>> with the breath of his lips he will slay the
>>> wicked.
> Righteousness will be his belt
>> and faithfulness the sash around his waist.
>
> The wolf will live with the lamb,
>> the leopard will lie down with the goat,
> the calf and the lion and the yearling together;
>> and a little child will lead them.
> The cow will feed with the bear,
>> their young will lie down together,
>> and the lion will eat straw like the ox.
> They will neither harm nor destroy
>> in all my holy mountain,
> for the earth will be full of the knowledge of the LORD
>> as the waters cover the sea (Isa. 11:3–9).

These quotes from Isaiah and the one from the Psalms show the tension between the various uses of "kingdom." They also reveal a unifying principle. In the Psalms God is said to reign over the nations whether or not they know and acknowledge Him. Here the Bible affirms an *indirect control* [as far as human perceptions are concerned]. Isaiah speaks of a time when God's *direct control* [as far as human perception is concerned] will be experienced. In the coming kingdom the "mighty God," who is born to sit on David's throne in accord with the Davidic covenant, will "establish and uphold" His kingdom "with justice and righteousness." He will act immediately to judge the wicked, will exercise justice on behalf of the poor of the earth, and will even change ecological systems so that wolf and lamb as well as mankind can live in peace with no fear that anyone might harm or destroy.

In the Old Testament, then, God's kingdom is pictured primarily as the indirect control He exercises over everything in the universe. But God's kingdom as a future time when full and direct control will be exercised also appears. In both portraits the kingdom extends to the whole universe. In both portraits, "kingdom" is a word of power rather than of locality. To speak of the "kingdom" of God is to speak of God's exercise of His power.

To be "in the kingdom of the Son he loves" is to live in the presence of the King and thus in that realm where His power is directly exercised.

"Kingdom" in the Gospels

The major occurrence of kingdom language in the New Testament is in the Gospels. There are some fifty-five references in Matthew, twenty in Mark, forty-six in Luke, and five in John.

Matthew's Gospel is particularly instructive. Matthew begins by telling of Jesus' birth, and in the first two chapters he frequently refers to Old Testament prophecies that show Jesus as the promised messianic King.[2] When John the Baptist is introduced, we are told the theme of his preaching: "Repent, for the kingdom of heaven is near" (Matt. 3:2). Immediately after Jesus' baptism and temptation, the Scriptures tell us that He "went throughout Galilee, teaching in their

---

[2]Note in Matthew 1–2 not only the titles "king of the Jews" and "Messiah," but also quotes from or references to Isaiah 7:14; Micah 5:2; Hosea 11:1; Jeremiah 31:15; and Isaiah 40:3. In context these Old Testament references emphasize the Messiah's role as a world ruler.

synagogues, preaching the good news of the kingdom, and healing every disease and sickness among the people" (Matt. 4:23). This association of the kingdom message with the relief of suffering is particularly significant, as we shall see later.

Matthew 5–7 is a statement by the King concerning the constitution of His kingdom. We know the passage better as the Sermon on the Mount. The words of Isaiah, "He will not judge by what he sees with his eyes" (Isa. 11:3), indicate the nature of this passage. Jesus shifts our attention from righteous behavior in harmony with law (the old covenant) to righteous inner attitudes of heart and mind (the new covenant).[3]

After the King's declaration of the principles on which His kingdom will function, Matthew in 8–11 reports a series of miracles. The miracles authenticate Jesus as God's spokesman. But they also demonstrate to everyone the ruling power of the King over every aspect of life on earth that keeps human beings in bondage. One who claims authority as the messianic King must demonstrate God's kingly power, and this Jesus did fully.

Even more, the kind of miracle Jesus chose to perform is in full harmony with those concerns which are the focus of Old Testament messianic prophecy. Jesus' miracles were not the spectacular but impersonal display we often associate with the word "miracle." He moved no mountains. He leaped off no temple parapet. He stopped no sun in its course. But when John's disciples came and asked Jesus if He was the Promised One, our Lord replied, "Go back and report to John what you hear and see: The blind receive sight, the lame walk, those who have leprosy are cured, the deaf hear, the dead are raised, and the good news is preached to the poor" (Matt. 11:5).

Matthew 12 reveals the reaction of the Pharisees to Jesus' ministry. They rejected Him as their King and tried to pass off His compassionate concern for others as demonic. They dared Jesus to heal on the Sabbath—and when He did, they complained that Satan, not God, was at work through Him. At that point Jesus confronted them with a striking statement about the kingdom: "If I drive out demons by the Spirit of God, *then the kingdom of God has come upon you*" (Matt. 12:28)!

---

[3]This is why righteousness in the kingdom of Jesus (Matt. 5:20) must surpass the righteousness of the Pharisees and teachers of law. It is also why Jesus shifts attention from murder to the anger that precedes it (Matt. 5:21–22) and from adulterous acts to lust (Matt. 5:27–30). In the kingdom over which Jesus rules God will act *within* believers and exercise authority over the inner person.

We are no longer speaking of the kingdom as coming.
We are no longer speaking of the kingdom as near.
We are speaking of the kingdom as *already come!*

A parallel passage is found in Luke 17. The Pharisees asked Jesus when the kingdom of God would come. He answered, "The kingdom of God does not come visibly, nor will people say 'Here it is,' or 'There it is,' because the kingdom of God *is in the midst of you*" (Luke 17:20–21).[4]

Matthew 12–16 portrays growing opposition to the King and His kingdom. The religious leaders of Israel fought against Him, while the people hesitated. They honored Him as a prophet (Matt. 16:13–14) but would not commit themselves to Him as their King. In the light of this rejection and His disciples' subsequent profession of faith in Jesus as the Christ (i.e. "Messiah" or "King") and Son of God, Jesus announced that He would give the keys to the kingdom of heaven to Peter and the other disciples. And He foretold His own coming crucifixion (Matt. 16:15–21; cf. 18:18).

From the perspective of the new covenant we can understand this enigmatic promise. The kingdom exists where Jesus is and where He exercises His power. In Jesus' resurrection His presence was placed within His *laos*. Believers bear the keys of the kingdom, for in them the King continues His presence in our world.

Klappert points out that the kingdom must always be linked with the person of the King:

> The kingdom of God is utterly transcendent and supernatural: it comes from above, from God alone. When God's kingdom comes, the hungry will be filled and the sad will be comforted (cf. the Beatitudes, Matt. 5:3–10; Lk. 6:20ff.). It demands that men should love their enemies (Matt. 5:38–42; Lk. 6:27f., 32–36), and they will be as free from care as the birds of the air and the lilies of the field (Matt. 6:25–33; Lk. 12:22–31). Here again it is Jesus himself, in whom alone the future kingdom of God is present, in whose words and deeds that kingdom has already appeared. It has come already, in that Jesus seeks out the company of tax-collectors and sinners, offering them fellowship at table and so promising them forgiveness of their sins. As the king invites to his feast the beggars and homeless (Matt. 22:1–10), as the father's love receives back again the prodigal son (Lk. 15:11–32), as the shepherd goes out after the lost sheep (Lk. 15:4–7), as the woman searches for the

---

[4]The Greek phrase ἐντὸς ὑμῶν ἐστιν is traditionally translated "is within you." Either rendering, "among" or "within" is possible. However, in context it is unlikely Jesus would say the kingdom is within the *Pharisees*. Also, the parallel passage in Matthew clearly means that the kingdom "has come" in the person of the King. Since the same argument is made by Luke, it seems we should take these words to mean "among you." I have therefore changed the wording of the NIV text at this point.

lost coin (Lk. 15:8–10), as the master out of the goodness of his heart pays the labourers hired at the last hour the full day's pay (Matt. 20:1–15), so Jesus goes to the poor to give them the promise of forgiveness, "for theirs is the kingdom of heaven" (Matt. 5:3). Only sinners, who know what it is like to have a great burden of → guilt (Lk. 7:41–43), can appreciate the remission of sins through the goodness of God. For "those who are well have no need of a physician, but those who are sick" (Mk. 2:17; cf. Matt. 9:12; Lk. 5:31).

The distinctive feature of Jesus' proclamation of the kingdom of God is not therefore that he brought a new doctrine of the kingdom, or that he revolutionized people's apocalyptic and eschatological expectations, but that he made the kingdom of God inseparable from his own person. The new thing about Jesus' preaching of the kingdom is "He himself, simply his person" (J. Schniewind).[5]

We can summarize by saying that the kingdom concept implies God's universal rule—*and* all the ways that rule is exercised. In the broadest sense, "kingdom" means God's sovereignty over all beings and events in His universe: a sovereignty exercised indirectly in that it is not evident to men.

The Bible, however, speaks of at least three additional ways through which God's rule is exercised. Each of the three relates specifically to the presence of the King. The Old and New Testaments both refer to a *coming kingdom* in which Christ will take His rightful place on the throne of David to completely transform the order, ecology, and economic structure of society. The Gospels sometimes refer back to a *historical kingdom*, God's kingdom in Israel some two thousand years ago. In Jesus the kingdom was a *present kingdom* "in the midst of" people, one that had "come upon" them. The evidence of the kingdom's presence was not then found in the transformation of society, as it will be in its eschatological form. The King's actions were a prelude as He touched and healed the suffering and brought good news to the poor (Matt. 11:5). The miracles this care produced demonstrated the King's power. But it was the focus of the King's attention that gives us the link between history and the future. In both cases the King's power is utilized in the cause of justice and righteousness. The power of Jesus is expended to do good.

The third special way in which the rule of God is exercised is in the establishment of His *present kingdom*. As does the power of God's eschatological and historical kingdoms, its power depends on the personal presence of the King. Today, in

---

[5]B. Klappert, "King, Kingdom," in Colin Brown, ed., *Dictionary of New Testament Theology* (3 vols; Grand Rapids: Zondervan Publishing House, 1976–1978), 2:386.

the believer who reveals "his life . . . in [his] mortal body" (2 Cor. 4:11), Jesus' presence and power still operate! The kingdom is now expressed in the way the King continues His rule of good in and through His *laos*.

THE KINGDOM PRESENT

The words of Paul with which we began this chapter remind us that we must treat the kingdom as a present reality for God's *laos*. God has rescued us, Paul affirms. God has "brought us into the kingdom of the Son he loves" (Col. 1:13). We are in that kingdom now . . . and so must find our identity and our mission as a kingdom people.

Here we can do no more than sketch concepts that are significant enough to have received volumes of attention from others. And we must select aspects of kingdom life that are directly related to our subject. It goes without saying that we are to live the holy life commanded by the King (Matt. 5-7) and be obedient to Him as Lord. It is perhaps not as obvious, but nevertheless basic to our grasp of personal ministries, to realize that we who are the *laos* of God are channels for the power of the King and are to participate in His mission.

It is fascinating to explore the power of Jesus active in believers' lives now. Paul speaks of "his incomparably great power for us who believe." "That power," he adds, "is like the working of his mighty strength, which he exerted in Christ when he raised him from the dead and seated him at his right hand in the heavenly realms" (Eph. 1:19-20).

But there is more to the exercise of the King's power than its working in our inner lives.

Power on our behalf

Jesus taught that in His kingdom God orders the physical universe even when men are not able to observe any supernatural acts. Because God's power is exercised in the natural course of events, each member of His *laos* is free to concentrate on those things that please Him. We can live a life of commitment without fear.

> Then Jesus said to his disciples: "Therefore I tell you, do not worry about your life, what you will eat; or about your body, what you will wear. Life is more than food, and the body more than clothes. Consider the ravens: They do not sow or reap, they have no storeroom or barn; yet God feeds them. And how much more valuable you are than birds! Who of you by worrying can add a single hour to his life? Since you cannot do this very little thing, why do you worry about the rest?
>
> "Consider how the lilies grow. They do not labor or spin. Yet I tell you, not even Solomon in all his splendor was dressed like one of these.

> If that is how God clothes the grass of the field, which is here today, and tomorrow is thrown into the fire, how much more will he clothe you, O you of little faith! And do not set your heart on what you will eat or drink; do not worry about it. For the pagan world runs after all such things, and your Father knows that you need them. But seek his kingdom, and these things will be given to you as well.
>
> "Do not be afraid, little flock, for your Father has been pleased to give you the kingdom" (Luke 12:22–32).

Assurance that God's kingdom rule involves ordering the details of our lives frees us for obedience. His power is not simply "spiritual." He is actively involved in shaping the physical universe so that the needs of His *laos* might be met.

The impact of this truth is illustrated in Hebrews 4. The writer has dealt at length with the importance of responding to God's voice in our "today" (Heb. 3:7–15). He has pointed out that Israel's disobedience, when God first called the people to enter Canaan, was prompted by unbelief. They did not trust God to care for them if they obeyed His Word and crossed into the Promised Land. The disobedience caused them to wander in the wilderness for forty years until their bodies fell in the desert (Heb. 3:16–18).

Then in Hebrews 4 the writer moves on to urge believers today to be attentive to God's voice. When we hear Him in our "today" we must not harden our hearts. We must trust God and respond in the full obedience of faith. The writer adds this promise: "There remains, then, a Sabbath-rest for the people of God; for anyone who enters God's rest also rests from his own work, just as God did from his. Let us, therefore, make every effort to enter that rest, so that no one will fall by following their example of disobedience" (Heb. 4:9–11).

The argument here is striking. The Genesis story tells of six days in which God labored over His creation. Each day is marked off in the Genesis account with a morning and an evening. Then comes the seventh day during which God rested. What is striking is that in Genesis there is a seventh-day morning . . . but *no evening!* The work of creation is finished! God is still at rest.

This does not indicate that God is *inactive.* It does tell us His *labor is complete.* No problem can arise for which God has not already developed the solution. No need can develop for which He has not already provided. To enter into God's rest simply means to listen to His voice and follow His leading . . . along the pathway He has planned for us. We will be active— but at rest. We will have needs—but they will be met. With this assurance we can freely seek His kingdom and righteousness, knowing "all these things will be given to you as well."

Power through our lives

God's kingdom power is exercised in space and time on our behalf. But God is also committed to exercise His kingdom power *through* us.

John 14 contains a brief paragraph that is a rich and complex expression of this great kingdom truth.

> Philip said, "Lord, show us the Father and that will be enough for us."
>
> Jesus answered: "Don't you know me, Philip, even after I have been among you such a long time? Anyone who has seen me has seen the Father. How can you say, 'Show us the Father'? Don't you believe that I am in the Father, and that the Father is in me? The words I say to you are not just my own. Rather, it is the Father, living in me, who is doing his work. Believe me when I say that I am in the Father and the Father is in me; or at least believe on the evidence of the miracles themselves. I tell you the truth, anyone who has faith in me will do what I have been doing. He will do even greater things than these, because I am going to the Father. And I will do whatever you ask in my name, so that the Son may bring glory to the Father. You may ask me for anything in my name, and I will do it" (John 14:8–14).

In response to Philip's request to "see the Father" Jesus explains, "Anyone who has seen me has seen the Father." This is because Jesus is in the Father and the Father is in Him. The incarnation of Jesus is not only the coming of the Second Person of the Trinity in human flesh. It also involves the presence of the First Person in the living, incarnate Son. "It is the Father, living in me," Jesus explained, "who is doing his work."

Once we understand this reality we can grasp the meaning of Jesus' next amazing affirmation: "I tell you the truth, anyone who has faith in me will do what I have been doing" (John 14:12). How is this possible? It is possible because Jesus is returning to the Father. From His location outside space and time Jesus is present within His people. This is why He assures us, "You may ask me for anything in my name, and I will do it" (John 14:14). The works that the believer performs are in actuality the works of Jesus Himself, who under the new covenant now incarnates Himself in us, just as the Father expressed Himself in Jesus!

The Acts of the Apostles begins with Luke's mention of his "former book" [the Gospel of Luke] in which he wrote about "all that Jesus *began* to do and to teach" (Acts 1:1). The Book of Acts is the chronicle of what Jesus *continued* to do and teach through the persons of His disciples! The history of the true church is the history of Jesus' continuing incarnation. And that history is still being written by citizens of the kingdom of the living Christ, for we embody the continuing presence of Jesus in our world.

The kingdom, as we have seen, exists wherever the King is present in power. Today the *laos* of God are the kingdom. In us Jesus is vitally, powerfully present, eager and able to continue His mission.

Power through prayer

John 14 links the working of Jesus the King through us to prayer. "I will do whatever you ask in my name," Jesus promises, "so that the Son may bring glory to the Father. You may ask me for anything in my name, and I will do it" (John 14:13–14).

The supernatural power that flows through believers to touch those around them is not their own power. It is not founded on their wisdom, intelligence, zeal, commitment, sincerity, efforts, intentions, or works. It is Jesus who acts through them, and it is the power of the King that accomplishes His purposes. Our part in the present expression of the kingdom is first to be available to the King, listening and responsive to His voice. Second, it is to act in total dependence on the King, committing to Him in prayer all those things He calls us to be involved in.

There are many illustrations in the Scriptures of the role of prayer in present expressions of the kingdom. One of the most beautiful is found in Acts 4. Peter and John had been dragged before the Sanhedrin for their bold proclamation of Jesus and the healings they had performed. They were questioned and threatened . . . but released because the Jewish court feared the people, who were praising God for the miraculous healing that had occasioned the two disciples' arrest. On their release, the two immediately rejoined the people of God, reported what had been said, and with them raised voices in this prayer:

> "Sovereign Lord," they said, "you made the heaven and the earth and the sea, and everything in them. You spoke by the Holy Spirit through the mouth of your servant, our father David:
>
>> 'Why do the nations rage
>> and the peoples plot in vain?
>> The kings of the earth take their stand
>> and the rulers gather together
>> against the Lord
>> and against his Anointed One.'
>
> Indeed Herod and Pontius Pilate met together with the Gentiles and the people of Israel in this city to conspire against your holy servant Jesus, whom you anointed. They did what your power and will had decided beforehand should happen. Now, Lord, consider their threats

and enable your servants to speak your word with great boldness. Stretch out your hand to heal and perform miraculous signs and wonders through the name of your holy servant Jesus."

After they prayed, the place where they were meeting was shaken. And they were all filled with the Holy Spirit and spoke the word of God boldly (Acts 4:24–31).

God's people recognized the reality of His sovereign power over their present experience. Their prayer was answered and they were infused with power to continue the works of Jesus the King.

To live "in the kingdom of the Son he loves" means that we are privileged, as God's *laos,* to experience the supernatural power and rule of Jesus today.

- As we commit ourselves to obey our King we can be sure that God will work in and through our circumstances. Jesus' words are uniquely for us: "Do not be afraid, little flock, for your Father has been pleased to give you the kingdom" (Luke 12:32).
- Because of the presence of Jesus in us we can be channels through which Christ exercises His present reign. We can do what Jesus did on earth, for it is Jesus in us who acts.
- Prayer is a resource for the kingdom lifestyle. "Ask in my name," Jesus promised, "and I will do it." Our reliance is not on ourselves but on Jesus working through us.

THE PRESENT MISSION OF THE KING

The Old Testament is full of images of the kingdom and its righteousness. Here are just a few from the prophet Isaiah that describe the impact of the presence of the King:

In that day the deaf will hear the words of the scroll,
    and out of gloom and darkness
    the eyes of the blind will see.
Once more the humble will rejoice in the LORD;
    the needy will rejoice in the Holy One of Israel.
The ruthless will vanish,
    the mockers will disappear,
    and all who have an eye for evil will be cut down—
those who with a word make a man out to be guilty,
    who ensnare the defender in court
    and with false testimony deprive the innocent
        of justice (Isa. 29:18–21).

Then will the eyes of the blind be opened
    and the ears of the deaf unstopped.
Then will the lame leap like a deer,
    and the tongue of the dumb shout for joy.
Water will gush forth in the wilderness
    and streams in the desert (Isa. 35:5–6).

And these words, which Christ related to His own mission and ministry . . .

> The Spirit of the Sovereign LORD is on me,
>> because the LORD has anointed me
>> to preach the good news to the poor.
> He has sent me to bind up the brokenhearted,
>> to proclaim freedom for the captives
>> and release the prisoners,
> to proclaim the year of the LORD's favor
>> and the day of vengeance of our God,
> to comfort all who mourn,
>> and provide for those who grieve in Zion
>> (Isa. 61:1–3 [cf. Luke 4:18f.]).

Jesus did not institute the eschatological kingdom when He came the first time. But still He was the King, present in the world of men. As King He acted in harmony with His nature and His commitment to righteousness. Thus we have in the Gospels a whole series of compassionate actions that *are part of the kingdom.* Here are several from Matthew's Gospel:

> These twelve Jesus sent out with the following instructions: "Do not go among the Gentiles or enter any town of the Samaritans. Go rather to the lost sheep of Israel. As you go, preach this message: 'The kingdom of heaven is near.' Heal the sick, raise the dead, cleanse those who have leprosy, drive out demons. Freely you have received, freely give" (Matt. 10:5–8).

In response to John's inquiry as to whether Jesus truly was the promised King, the Lord offered this evidence:

> Go back and report to John what you hear and see: The blind receive sight, the lame walk, those who have leprosy are cured, the deaf hear, the dead are raised, and the good news is preached to the poor (Matt. 11:4–5).

A little later Jesus' actions are interpreted as follows:

> Many followed him [Jesus], and he healed all their sick, warning them not to tell who he was. This was to fulfill what was spoken through the prophet Isaiah:
>> "Here is my servant whom I have chosen,
>>> the one I love, in whom I delight;
>> I will put my Spirit on him,
>>> and he will proclaim justice to the nations.
>> He will not quarrel or cry out;
>>> no one will hear his voice in the streets.
>> A bruised reed he will not break,
>>> and a smoldering wick he will not snuff out,
>> till he leads justice to victory.
>>> In his name the nations will put their hope"
>>> (Matt. 12:15–21).

There can be no question that the nature of Jesus' acts of compassion and righteousness were an essential part of His presentation of Himself to Israel as their King. This explains in part the reaction of many crowds, as in the following incident:

> Jesus . . . went up into the hills and sat down. Great crowds came to him, bringing the lame, the blind, the crippled, the dumb and many others, and laid them at his feet; and he healed them. The people were amazed when they saw the dumb speaking, the crippled made well, the lame walking and the blind seeing. And they praised the God of Israel (Matt. 15:29–31).

The extent to which this account parallels the prophecies of Isaiah concerning what will happen when the King comes is too clear to be misunderstood by a people brought up to be familiar with the Book of God.

The religious leaders also understood the claim implicit in Jesus' actions. They had understood, in fact, since the beginning of John's ministry. Yet Jesus had to condemn them for a lack of the compassion that marked His ministry. The Pharisees were even willing to use a human being to trap Jesus . . . and He chided them with Scripture: "If you had known what these words mean, 'I desire mercy, not sacrifice,' you would not have condemned the innocent" (Matt. 12:7). Later He condemned them even more bluntly: "Woe to you, teachers of the law and Pharisees, you hypocrites! You give a tenth of your spices—mint, dill and cummin. But you have neglected the more important matters of the law—justice, mercy and faithfulness" (Matt. 23:23).

No wonder Jesus would soon pronounce judgment on those who had seen the King and had experienced the shape of the kingdom in His acts of mercy and yet rejected Him. "I tell you that the kingdom of God will be taken away from you and given to a people who will produce its fruit" (Matt. 21:43).

This is, of course, the point we are trying to make concerning the kingdom's present aspect. The kingdom of God always produces fruit! The *people of the kingdom are to produce that fruit.*

Where God's kingdom exists on earth there is compassion for the needy. There is justice for the poor. There is healing for the sick. There is His loving, transforming touch for society's outcasts: the addict, the prostitute, the homosexual. Kingdom people do not ignore the widow and the orphan. They do not desert the fatherless child. They do not leave the hopeless without encouragement. They do not isolate the rejected. They do not write off the retarded. Wherever the kingdom of God exists in the world an island of love and compassion and deep concern can be found. For the King is present in His people. And the mission of the King is "to preach good news to the poor. . . . bind up the brokenhearted, to proclaim freedom for the captives and release for the prisoners . . . and . . . to comfort all who mourn" (Isa. 61:1–2).

Kingdom terminology is found primarily in the Gospels. But the call of the believer to a life of love and compassion is not limited to them. In what may have been the first epistle to be written after the synoptic Gospels, James says, "Religion that God our Father accepts as pure and faultless is this: to look after orphans and widows in their distress and to keep oneself from being polluted by the world" (James 1:27). These words are an echo of the kingdom ethic.

Paul tells Titus to remind the believers in Crete to "be ready to do whatever is good," for "those who have trusted in God" are to "devote themselves to doing what is good" (Titus 3:1, 8, 14). Here, too, is an echo of the kingdom ethic.

Writing to Timothy, Paul describes the widow who may be enlisted for special ministry as "well-known for her good deeds, such as bringing up children, showing hospitality, washing the feet of saints, helping those in trouble and devoting herself to all kinds of good deeds" (1 Tim. 5:9–10). Once again we have an echo of the kingdom ethic.

We have not been saved *by* our good works, Paul tells the Ephesians. But we have been "created in Christ Jesus to do good works, which God prepared in advance for us to do" (Eph. 2:10). And so the ethic of the kingdom echoes and resonates again.

The King is present *now* in our world, in His people. He gives His people the task of continuing His mission of compassion and righteousness. The apostle John makes the point clearly and simply: "Whoever claims to live in him must walk as Jesus did" (1 John 2:6).

PROBE

▶ *case histories*
▶ *discussion questions*
▶ *thought provokers*
▶ *resources*

1. Study Jesus' "high-priestly prayer" in John 17. What elements of new covenant and kingdom can you distinguish? What key truths from this prayer would you want to be sure God's *laos* grasp today?

2. Debate the following proposition, or write a five-page paper arguing for or against it.

    Resolved: The fruit of the kingdom is not simply acts of compassion and justice, but also *miraculous* acts.

3. Read A. T. Pierson's biography of George Muller, *George Muller of Bristol* (Old Tappan, N.J.: Revell, 1971). In what ways did he experience the active involvement of the King *in* his life? *Through* his life? What was the role of prayer in Muller's ministry? In what ways was his ministry a "fruit of the kingdom"? What is the most important thing God is saying to you through Muller's life?

4. The following case history shares something of the ministry of the first director of the "Grapevine Shelter" at Trinity Church in Seattle, Mark Million, now on its staff and an elder. Use the case study method explained on pages 22–24 to explore this case history with others.

MARK MILLION

I graduated from college in 1971 and that summer came to Trinity. My main fellowship had been with the Navigators on campus, so I was used to an action group. I came to Trinity with the expectation that I could probably find a place to function and make a contribution in that way. The Grapevine Shelter needed help, but at first I wasn't committed to its vision or people of Trinity Church particularly. But once I started the work became so absorbing that it quickly became the focus of my life.

The experience changed my Christian life. During my four years of college I had thought in terms of my very simple spiritual needs. Through the Navigator "Wheel," I knew Christ through fellowship, witnessing, practical obedience, and study. But campus life is different from work. Then I could fill in the hours however I wanted. At the Grapevine you couldn't do that. As a result my spiritual life began to wobble.

There were thirteen of us in the group. Five were staff, but I couldn't identify with them any more readily than with the residents. They didn't quote Bible verses the way I did. I still quoted Bible verses in my conversation because they were new to me. The group was more deeply spiritual and less inclined to follow certain disciplines that I assumed were part of what it meant to be a Christian.

Most of the residents at that time were court referrals and some had already served some time in prison. They seemed to be rugged and tough. They made it clear to me that we were the guards and they were the inmates. I wanted to have a "family" orientation, but any time you have to be somewhere because of court restraints, there is a different environment.

We had an understanding that the staff would be resource people to the residents, available both when they were having problems and when everything was fine. We thought that by living among them and trying to grow ourselves and to confess when we failed we would help them most. So our treatment was pretty simple—try to meet their spiritual, emotional, mental, educational, and physical needs by making them part of a larger body. We tried to make opportunities for relationships to develop. We had a small enough staff so that we didn't have to be very organized.

It was hard to say how many staff workers we had at a given moment because we had at least twenty-six people, each working between five and thirty hours a week. Most of the staff were unpaid, but they had a direct, continuing involvement with the residents.

Every Wednesday night we had a dinner, a sharing time, and prayer for the whole church family at the Grapevine. At first about one hundred people came. That broke down a lot of barriers and destroyed a lot of stereotypes. That was much more important than getting the residents to go to church, though church attendance was one of the requirements. We tried to form friendships in the group so the residents would relate to us as friends as well as staff members.

During my four and a half years, the average time a young person would stay with us was about six months. We could handle five or six at a time, sixteen to eighteen a year. So I worked with about seventy people during that time.

In 1973 and 1974 we added more psychiatric aftercare, more hospital contacts. The drug scene diversified. Kids got more into the polydrug scene, not exclusively heroin. So we were dealing with a different group. For the first year and a half they were much more passive than earlier groups, so we had to learn a different style of life. The heroin addict we had earlier tended to be a little more pushy and sly.

But our goal was the same. The staff learned to rely on the sufficiency of Christ for every situation. We could serve without knowing all the answers by being available and by loving the people we were responsible for. Our goal was for the residents to find an alternate lifestyle based on Christ. Even if they didn't choose Jesus as their Lord at least there were some people they could count on as friends, and they could see the church as a caring community, not just an institution. We were trying to show them who the people of God were and what Christianity was all about.

We knew that Christ had freed us from sin and cared for us as individuals. We knew that most of our residents needed to go back to school and pick up skills.

One criticism secular groups made of us at the Shelter was that we assumed we had the only real solution. But in fact we were influenced by the philosophy of the Sky Club that had worked in the area earlier. Our counseling ministry showed a lot of concern. The Grapevine was the treatment arm. It gave long-term support. But many people extended mercy to the kids in many ways.

5. To get a feeling of the impact of a kingdom-like "mercy" ministry, here is the story of a resident.

IVAN

My first contact with Christ's body here at Trinity was in 1972. I had been arrested for armed robbery. I was sent to live with my aunt and she introduced me to Gib Martin. My initial contact with the body was Grapevine Shelter, a Christian living and learning center for people who had drug-related problems. Because Gib was involved with Grapevine, he knit me into the work they were doing.

I went there with my aunt and talked with the staff about a process that might help me get out of the trouble I was in with the law.

After a few weeks I went to stay at the Grapevine, about forty-five days before I had to appear in court. The only reason I wanted to be there was because I thought, "These people can help me get out of the trouble I'm in." That was as far as my commitment went! I didn't want to be involved with God because I didn't believe there was a God. In fact, I remember one time sitting in Gib's office and telling him, "Hey, I don't want any of this Christian _____!" That was my attitude. But he wasn't too concerned; in fact he seemed to appreciate my honesty.

On my first contact with the guys on the staff I thought they were kind of weird if they wanted to help me out. But as a resident at the Grapevine I watched the way they lived their lives, and I was impressed. They loved and cared about me even though I was a creep. When I was living there I was going out, getting and taking drugs and coming back, and nobody said anything. I thought they didn't know. But they did. They were pretty sensitive to what was going on in my life, and sometimes they had to say, "No, you can't do that anymore if you are going to live here." So it was the way they lived day after day after day in many situations that really made me think, "What is it that they have that I don't have?"

On Wednesday nights they had a group come and prepare dinner. Older people, younger people—the age span was from one to seventy-five. That impressed me. I was really offended by older people. They grossed me out. I just didn't like them. The little old ladies were there every Wednesday night for Bible study. They *never* missed. Somehow their lives made an impact on me, too, because they were faithful and they loved me. And, of course, I had contact with the body on Sunday mornings, because Sunday morning worship was something that we had to be a part of.

In the beginning I would watch them. When they were praying, I thought they were praying to the walls because there was no God. I was fighting church all the way. I would go back and spend time with my friends, and I would make fun of the Christians. Jesus freaks I called them.

I spent forty-five days living at the Grapevine. Whatever it took to be a nice guy and get out of the trouble I was in with the law I was willing to do. But when I went to court, the judge didn't see it that way. Because I had a well-to-do family and my parents had gotten me out of trouble every time in the past, the judge said, "I'm not going to let that happen again. This time you're going to pay the price." So they sent me to jail for ninety days, which was really grace because for armed robbery they had just made a ten-year sentence mandatory. And I had to sit in that jail for ninety days and think about who I was.

It was during that time that I accepted Christ as my Savior. I made the decision because of those contacts with Christian people who had loved and cared about me. There wasn't anybody in the room with me or anybody telling me that I needed to ask Jesus into my heart. It was simply that I liked the way those Christians lived. There was something dynamic about it. I wanted that. I realized that I was lost, and in King County Jail, Cell C-3, all by myself, I let Christ take control of my life.

I was in the middle of writing Gib a letter telling him what a creep I was and how I had lied and been dishonest in relationships at the Grapevine when I began to cry. I realized at that moment that Jesus was there and that He wanted to be a part of my life, so I asked Him to take over.

I was changed at that moment. I knew that there was something different about me. My grandmother had been a Christian. She had walked with Jesus for sixty-nine years and prayed for me constantly. God showed me in a dream that it was through her prayers I came into the kingdom. That dream was an affirmation that I had become a different person.

After that I got out of jail. I went back to the Grapevine because I knew that that was where I needed to be. I needed help;

my life was so undisciplined. I had never been a disciplined person, from brushing my teeth to cleaning my body, even though I had well-to-do parents. They hadn't taught me any discipline at all. So part of the process at the Grapevine was to make me aware of some of these deficiencies in my life.

That was the *start* of the process, and it's been going on for seven years now.

Even though Jesus was in my heart, I was still deceptive and deceitful. This fact came up and was exposed. I remember one time when the whole house thought that I was still doing drugs and stuff, and Gib approached me in a very stern way and told me, "Satan will not run this house." Man, that changed my life, because I realized I wanted Jesus to run my life. I didn't want Satan running it. That was a major turning point in my life. There were lots of them, but that one somehow really changed me. I realized that I wanted Jesus to be the Lord of my life. I wanted others to know He was the Lord of my life. I wanted my life to be a demonstration of Jesus' influence.

THEOLOGICAL CORE
THE IDENTITY OF THE BELIEVER

A People of God
A New Covenant People
A Kingdom People
A Servant People
An Empowered People
A Gifted People

A SERVANT PEOPLE

To the Greeks becoming a servant or a slave was repulsive. Freedom was their most prized right, and one of their goals of life was to be independent of others and to live as one chose. To be a servant involved surrender of such freedom. Slavery meant subjection to another's will. To a Hellenist, who was convinced that a man was morally obligated to develop his own potential, to give himself to the service of others was more than alien. It was contemptible.

Paul's teaching in the Epistles directly confronts this aspect of Greek thought. He shows those who are proud of their "freedom" that they are in fact slaves to sin. The obsessive desire of the Greek to live only in reference to his own desires and only by his own resources is shown up as foolishness in view of sin's grip on mankind. Paul unmasks such illusions and shows the need of Jew and Greek alike for redemption from man's hidden master, sin.

But, according to Paul, redemption (the Greek word means "purchase out from the marketplace") does not mean release to the kind of freedom the Greeks idealized. Redemption involves a price paid that man might no longer be a slave to sin but instead become a slave to righteousness. Paul explains the concept carefully in Romans 6:

CHAPTER 4

What then? Shall we sin because we are not under law but under grace? By no means! Don't you know that when you offer yourselves to someone to obey him as slaves, you are slaves to the one whom you obey—whether you are slaves to sin, which leads to death, or to obedience, which leads to righteousness? But thanks be to God that, though you used to be slaves to sin, you wholeheartedly obeyed the form of teaching to which you were entrusted. You have been set free from sin and have become slaves to righteousness.

I put this in human terms because you are weak in your natural selves. Just as you used to offer the parts of your body in slavery to impurity and to ever-increasing wickedness, so now offer them in slavery to righteousness leading to holiness. When you were slaves to sin, you were free from the control of righteousness. What benefit did you reap at that time from the things you are now ashamed of? Those things result in death! But now that you have been set free from sin and have become slaves to God, the benefit you reap leads to holiness, and the result is eternal life. For the wages of sin is death, but the gift of God is eternal life in Christ Jesus our Lord (Rom. 6:15–23).

Theologically, it is always true that slavery to God is the one true freedom open to mankind. Only by submitting ourselves to God can all the good He desires for us be experienced.

Therefore when we turn to Scripture we find a very different picture of servanthood than the one that dominated the ancient world. From the earliest Old Testament roots of the

73

idea of service to its expression in Isaiah's picture of the Servant of the Lord, the understanding is positive. And in the Incarnation we are shown the splendor of the servant's role, as Jesus empties Himself of His prerogatives as God to take on Himself "the very nature of a servant" (Phil. 2:7; cf. vv. 5–8). In Jesus' example and teachings about servanthood we discover the essence of our identity as the *laos* of God.

SERVANT IN THE OLD TESTAMENT

The Hebrew root word translated "slave" or "servant" *('bd)* means "laboring, or doing work," and thus "serving another by labor." It was used not only of physical toil but of subjection in general. It is often used of the service we owe to God. Since the Old Testament understands the relationship of Israel to God in terms of a covenant, the servant idea also has a covenantal dimension. Many scholars suggest that "servants of God" and "people of God" are parallel Old Testament expressions. God brought Israel out of Egypt with a mighty hand and an outstretched arm (Deut. 5:15). No relationship of love or commitment existed between the Egyptians and Israel. Servitude in Egypt was slavery of the most negative sort. But to be a servant of God is completely different, for "the Lord will judge his people and have compassion on his servants" (Deut. 32:36). Thus the Hebrews realized that to identify themselves as servants of God was to affirm the same high distinctive calling involved in being His special people (cf. Neh. 1:6; Ps. 105:25; 135:14; Isa. 63:17).

To accept the title "servant of the Lord" was to identify oneself as a worshiper of the Lord (Ps. 34:22; 89:50; 90:13, 16; 102:28). It was also to affirm complete dependence on Him: "As the eyes of slaves look to the hand of their master, as the eyes of a maid look to the hand of her mistress, so our eyes look to the LORD our God, till he shows us his mercy" (Ps. 123:2). God in His amazing loving-kindness had chosen to make Israel His special people and possession. The wonder of this great act of Jahweh and all the subsequent evidence of His commitment to Israel fill the Old Testament with a humbling sense of wonder.

> Ask now about the former days, long before your time, from the day God created man on the earth; ask from one end of the heavens to the other. Has anything so great as this ever happened, or has anything like it ever been heard of? Has any other people heard the voice of God speaking out of fire, as you have, and lived? Has any god ever tried to take for himself one nation out of another nation, by testings, by miraculous signs and wonders, by war, by a mighty hand and an outstretched arm, or by great and awesome deeds, like all the things the

LORD your God did for you in Egypt before your very eyes?

You were shown these things so that you might know that the LORD is God; beside him there is no other. From heaven he made you hear his voice to discipline you. On earth he showed you his great fire, and you heard his words from out of the fire. Because he loved your forefathers and chose their descendants after them, he brought you out of Egypt by his Presence and his great strength (Deut. 4:32–39).

The Greek would cringe from such an identification as a servant or slave. But the people of the Old Testament see it as their claim to greatness.

Servant terminology does more, however, than suggest Israel's covenant relationship to God. It suggests that Israel will find fulfillment in actively serving Him. From the time of Moses onward part of the service Israel rendered to God was obedience to the Law of Moses. This service was not meant to be an end in itself. The unique lifestyle of love and justice that the Law prescribed for Israel was intended to testify of God's presence and power to all the nations. In this same passage from Deuteronomy Moses explains something of the service Israel would do for God and others by obeying the Law:

Observe them carefully, for this will show your wisdom and understanding to the nations, who will hear about these decrees and say, "Surely this great nation is a wise and understanding people." What other nation is so great as to have their gods near them the way the LORD our God is near us whenever we pray to him? And what other nation is so great as to have such righteous decrees and laws as this body of laws I am setting before you today? (Deut. 4:6–8).

By obedience Israel would serve God's purpose of providing a witness to Himself among the nations.

But the prophets are increasingly aware that Israel has repeatedly failed to be an obedient servant. Isaiah pictures the people of Israel as a vineyard planted and cared for by God. In spite of ideal conditions, the fruit brought forth is sour and shriveled.

Now you dwellers in Jerusalem and men of Judah,
    judge between me and my vineyard.
What more could have been done for my vineyard
    than I have done for it?
When I looked for good grapes,
    why did it yield only bad?

                     * * *

The vineyard of the LORD Almighty
    is the house of Israel,
and the men of Judah
    are the garden of his delight.
And he looked for justice, but saw bloodshed;
    for righteousness, but heard cries of distress (Isa. 5:3–4, 7).

The prophets deal with this failure of the servant people to be responsive to their Lord in two ways. On the one hand they beautifully affirm God's covenant commitment. God continues to call Israel His servant and, though the people have failed to live obediently, He promises His ultimate redemption.

> But now listen, O Jacob, my servant,
> Israel, whom I have chosen.
> This is what the LORD says—
>   he who made you, who formed you in the womb,
> and who will help you . . . (Isa. 44:1–2).

In this and many other passages, God confirms His commitment to Israel even in its failure to be a servant (cf. Isa. 44:21; 45:4; 48:20; 49:3; Jer. 30:10; 46:27–28).

There is a second way the prophets deal with the failure of Israel. "Who is blind but my servant," God asks, "and deaf like the messenger I send? Who is blind like the one committed to me, blind like the servant of the LORD?" (Isa. 42:19). Since God's servant Israel has failed to carry out His purposes, the prophets tell of *another Servant who will not fail!* In Isaiah there are four passages that describe "the Servant of the Lord." These passages are often called the "Servant Songs" and are recognized as messianic. They portray the Messiah, the promised King of Israel, in the amazing role of a servant!

First song: Isaiah 42:1–4

In this passage God promises to put His Spirit on the Servant, "and he will bring justice to the nations." His coming will be marked by no fanfare or shouting attendants. He will not even break a bruised reed or snuff out a smoldering wick (42:3). This beautiful reference reveals the Servant's attitude toward the outcasts of society. The reference to a bruised reed alludes to the tender branch a shepherd cuts to make a flute. If the bark is bruised as he works on it, it is worthless and fit only to be discarded. The wick is a bit of flax dropped in a bowl of olive oil and ignited to serve as a lamp. When carbon forms on the wick it sputters and smokes and is worthless, fit only to be taken out of the lamp and thrown away. The Servant of the Lord, however, will hold the worthless, the bruised, those burned out by life's fires, to be of value. "In faithfulness he will bring forth justice; he will not falter or be discouraged till he establishes justice on earth" (Isa. 42:3b–4).

Second song: Isaiah 49:1–6

In this passage the Servant is pictured as a weapon in the hand of God (49:2). His labors seem to be a failure (49:4), but through his work Israel will be regathered to the Lord (49:5). In fact, God will also make Him a light for the Gentiles, that He may bring God's salvation to the ends of the earth (49:6).

Third song: Isaiah 50:4–9

This Servant Song speaks beautifully of the sensitivity of the Servant to the voice of God. Because God guides and instructs Him, the Servant will "know the word that sustains the weary."

Yet the obedience of the Servant brings Him unjust accusations, beatings, mocking, and spitting. Through it all the Servant continues to set His face like flint and live in full obedience to God. He says, "He who vindicates me is near. Who then will bring charges against me?" (Isa. 50:8; cf. vv. 5–8).

It is significant that in this section the primary name given God is "Sovereign LORD." In spite of all the suffering the Servant experiences because of His obedience, He remains confident that God is the sovereign ruler of the universe. He is sure that the God who guides will be faithful to Him.

Fourth song: Isaiah 52:13–53:12

This most familiar of the Servant Songs describes the death of the Servant "for our transgressions" (53:5). By His self-sacrifice the Servant "will see his offspring and prolong his days" (53:10). Thus, the prophet says, "After the suffering of his soul, he will see the light of life and be satisfied" (53:11).

Many themes are found in this description. The Servant does not win recognition from men (53:1–2). In His obedience to God He is despised and rejected by those who fail to grasp who He is or understand the significance of a Servant lifestyle (53:3). The things that attract people to their leaders ("beauty" and "majesty") He does not have (53:2). The suffering of the Servant is caused by the transgressions of others, rather than his own (53:4–5). He bore the suffering quietly (53:7), living honestly and without deceit (53:9). Yet His servanthood and suffering for the benefit of others bore fruit. Through His work men were freed from the power of sun and justified (53:11). In the end, God will exalt the Servant and "give him a portion among the great" (53:12).

The *Zondervan Pictorial Encyclopedia of the Bible* describes the character of the Servant of the Lord shown in these Isaiah passages as follows:

> The Servant was chosen by the Lord (42:1; 49:1) and endued with the Spirit (42:1); He was taught by the Lord (50:4), and found His

strength in Him (49:2, 5). It was the Lord's will that He should suffer (53:10); He was weak, unimpressive, and scorned by men (52:14; 53:1-3, 7-9), meek (42:2), gentle (42:3), and uncomplaining (50:6; 53:7). Despite His innocence (53:9), He was subjected to constant suffering (50:6; 53:3, 8-10), so as to be reduced to near despair (49:4). But His trust was in the Lord (49:4; 50:7-9); He obeyed Him (50:4-5) until He was victorious (42:4; 50:8, 9).[1]

Though Israel has failed in the servant's task, the Coming One will not fail. Through a strange and splendid humility, the promised Messiah will Himself accomplish all that God wants to do for the lost and suffering of our world.

INCARNATION OF THE SERVANT

Old Testament teaching about servanthood stresses the covenant relationship that exists between God and His *laos*. Even when Israel failed in her servant calling, God remained faithful to His chosen people. But His purposes will not be allowed to fail, despite Israel's failure. There will come another Servant, an individual who will undertake God's intended work with the human race. In the Old Testament portrait of the Servant of the Lord we learn much of the character and mission of a servant. In humility and in spite of suffering the Servant of the Lord reaches out to the rejected and hurting. He speaks a word to sustain the weary, and He brings the lost into a personal relationship with God.

The New Testament reveals dimensions of a servant ministry. We see clearly what was only intimated in the Old Testament: the Servant is God Himself, and servanthood involves a distinctive self-emptying. The key New Testament passage is Philippians 2:5-8, which speaks of Jesus

> who, being in very nature God,
>> did not consider equality with God something
>>> to be grasped,
>> but made himself nothing,
>>> taking the very nature of a servant,
>>> being made in human likeness.
> And being found in appearance as a man,
>> he humbled himself
>> and became obedient to death—
>>> even death on a cross!
> Therefore God exalted him to the highest place
>> and gave him the name that is above every name,
> that at the name of Jesus every knee should bow,
>> in heaven and on earth and under the earth,

---

[1]"Servant of the Lord," Merrill C. Tenney, ed., *Zondervan Pictorial Encyclopedia of the Bible*, 5 vols. (Grand Rapids: Zondervan Publishing House, 1975), 5:361.

and every tongue confess that Jesus Christ is Lord,
to the glory of God the Father.

The stress in this passage is not on what Christ surrendered to take on the "very nature of a servant," but on the *attitude* demonstrated in His action. Thus Paul urges the church at Philippi to exchange self-interest and selfishness for a humility demonstrated by putting others first. "Do nothing out of selfish ambition or vain conceit," Paul writes, "but in humility consider others better than yourselves. Each of you should look not only to your own interests, but also to the interests of others. Your attitude should be the same as that of Christ Jesus" (Phil. 2:3–5).

Wherever Jesus is shown in His servant character, there are exhortations to us to follow His example. "Whoever wants to become great among you must be your servant," Jesus taught, "and whoever wants to be first must be your slave— just as the Son of Man did not come to be served, but to serve, and give his life as a ransom for many" (Matt. 20:26–28).

This servant attitude was reflected in everything Jesus did, and especially in the way He reached out in compassion to those in need. It was reflected in His ultimate self-giving, foreshadowed by the portrait of the cross in Isaiah 53.

The disciples were never too comfortable with Jesus' servant approach to life. They knew who He was, the Son of God, so when He chose to take a Servant posture among them they were embarrassed. This embarrassment was brought into focus by an act of Jesus at the Last Supper. What Jesus did was both symbolic and didactic. His actions graphically symbolized His whole approach to ministry. At the same time they taught His disciples that they were to adopt His attitude in their relationship with each other. The Bible tells us

Jesus knew that the Father had put all things under his power, and that he had come from God and was returning to God; so he got up from the meal, took off his outer clothing, and wrapped a towel around his waist. After that, he poured water into a basin and began to wash his disciples' feet, drying them with the towel that was wrapped around him.

He came to Simon Peter, who said to him, "Lord, are you going to wash my feet?"

Jesus replied, "You do not realize now what I am doing, but later you will understand."

"No," said Peter, "you shall never wash my feet."

Jesus answered, "Unless I wash you, you have no part with me."

"Then, Lord," Simon Peter replied, "not just my feet but my hands and my head as well!"

Jesus answered, "A person who has had a bath needs only to wash his feet; his whole body is clean. And you are clean, though not every one of you." For he knew who was going to betray him, and that was why he said not every one was clean.

When he had finished washing their feet, he put on his clothes and returned to his place. "Do you understand what I have done for you?" he asked them. "You call me 'Teacher' and 'Lord,' and rightly so, for that is what I am. Now that I, your Lord and Teacher, have washed your feet, you also should wash one another's feet. I have set you an example that you should do as I have done for you. I tell you the truth, no servant is greater than his master nor is a messenger greater than the one who sent him. Now that you know these things, you will be blessed if you do them" (John 13:3–17).

Notice the process:

- Jesus was fully aware of His own identity as God.
- Yet Jesus purposely took a role reserved for the most humble of household servants (unless the householder purposely wanted to honor a visitor greater than he by washing his guest's feet himself).
- Peter in particular was disturbed by this role reversal in which the greater washed the feet of the lesser.
- Jesus explained His action as an example. He *is* superior: Teacher and Lord. If He is willing to take the servant's role, surely they should accept that same role in their relationship with one another.

The Incarnation, then, is more than the entry of God into history in human form. It is His becoming man *to serve.* Incarnation involves self-emptying (Philippians puts it "to make himself nothing") in that Jesus' own interests and rights are set aside for the benefit of others.

Today as the body of Christ we are expected to participate in the servanthood of Jesus. We are to maintain his humble attitude (Phil. 2:3–4). We are to give ourselves to serve others (Matt. 20:28). We are to follow His example in all things, do as He has done for us (John 13:15).

This is a message for the whole people of God. But the New Testament applies it especially to leaders, perhaps because those who are leaders in the body are so often exalted by others (cf. 1 Cor. 1–4). It is difficult for members of the church to remember that "men ought to regard [leaders] as servants of Christ" (1 Cor. 4:1) and never "take pride in one man over against another" (1 Cor. 4:6). It is also difficult for those who have a secular concept of leadership to grasp how a pastor or elder can function as the servant-leader of the body of Christ.[2] Yet Christ's teaching on this point is extremely clear:

---

[2]This theme is developed in another book by the author, *A Theology of Church Leadership* (Grand Rapids: Zondervan Publishing House, 1980).

> You know that the rulers of the Gentiles lord it over them, and their high officials exercise authority over them. *Not so with you.* Instead, whoever wants to become great among you must be your servant, and whoever wants to be first must be your slave—just as the Son of Man did not come to be served, but to serve, and to give his life as a ransom for many (Matt. 20:25–28 [italics added]).

Thus a servant approach to ministry is to dominate in every expression of the church. The servant church is composed of members each of whom is to continue Jesus' servant life. The body is to be composed of members who are to serve one another. Leadership in the body is composed of those who are committed not to control the members of the body but to give themselves for them. The body is to be composed of members each of whom is to care for those outside the church as Jesus cared for the outcasts of His society.

SERVANT IN THE NEW TESTAMENT

There are two word groups for "servant" and "serving" in the New Testament. One of them, *diakonon,* is concerned primarily with serving others in the church or the world. This service may involve waiting on tables (Acts 6), communicating the gospel (Eph. 3:7; Col. 1:23), nurturing believers who have come to faith (2 Cor. 11:23), or collecting money to meet human needs (2 Cor. 8:4; 9:1, 12f.). This practical service links proclamation of the Good News with a variety of helps. Help and proclamation complement one another and express God's concern for every man.

The other Greek word is *doulos* or "slave." It stresses the subjection of the believer to the Lord.

The two aspects of servanthood are linked in the Old Testament term 'bd and in the Old Testament portrait of the Servant of the Lord.

Like the Old Testament, the New Testament contains no hint of contempt for servants, as though they belonged to some "lower class" that made them subhuman. In Jesus' parables, servants are pictured as those with positions of responsibility (Matt. 24:45). At the same time it is clear that a servant owes his master complete obedience, for "no man can serve two masters" (Matt. 8:9). The work a servant performs earns him no mandatory profit or thanks (Luke 17:7–10). Our relationship with God always rests on grace, never on works, even works done in obedience to Him after salvation. To give service is only right, for we belong to Him, and a master has unlimited power over his slaves (Matt. 18:27, 34; 25:30). In our deliverance from slavery to sin we have been brought into a relationship with a new Master. Our new Master commands us to live a life of righteousness and commits Himself to us even when we fall short. His righteousness is no abstract holiness that isolates spirituality and service to God from service to one's neighbor. Instead, God's righteousness is a call to such involvement.

> This is how we know what love is: Jesus Christ laid down his life for us. And we ought to lay down our lives for our brothers. If anyone has material possessions and sees his brother in need but has no pity on him, how can the love of God be in him? Dear children, let us not love with words or tongue but with actions and in truth (1 John 3:16–18).

The implications are striking and clear. The Servant of the Lord, who in Matthew's Gospel gives His life a ransom for many and calls on us to serve as He served (Matt. 20), taught us what love is and calls on us to love others as He loved us. We, too, are to love not with words or tongue but through action and in truth. Servanthood is nothing more, and nothing less, than living out Jesus' own self-sacrificial love, a love that responds to the needs of others, whatever that need may be, as God responds to our needs through Jesus Christ. This is the servanthood God calls us to as His people, His own contemporary incarnation in our world.

PROBE

▶ *case histories*
▶ *discussion questions*
▶ *thought provokers*
▶ *resources*

1. Look over the following list of key concepts related to the biblical doctrine of servanthood. Which of them do you personally feel is most important? Which is least understood by members of your congregation? Which have you seen expressed in others? How? Which have you sought to express in your own life? How?
   A. Servanthood speaks of a covenant relationship with God in which He accepts us as His special and loved possession.
   B. Servanthood speaks of the fulfillment to be found in actively serving God.
   C. Servanthood does not speak of a conditional relationship with God. He remains committed to us even when we fail.
   D. Servanthood has always been focused on providing a witness concerning the person of God to the whole world.
   E. Servanthood as revealed in the Old Testament Servant of the Lord involves caring for the outcasts of society and bringing others to the Lord.

F. Servanthood as revealed in the Old Testament Servant of the Lord requires obedience to God, even though God's will may involve us in misunderstanding, hostility, and suffering.

G. Servanthood as revealed in the Old Testament Servant of the Lord is acting for the benefit of others even when it involves self-sacrifice.

H. Servanthood as revealed in the incarnation of Jesus involves a surrender of personal rights and interests in consideration of the concerns of others.

I. Servanthood as revealed in the Incarnation demonstrates the values of God, who sees greatness not as the power to control others but as the willingness to serve them.

J. Servanthood as revealed in the Incarnation is a model for personal relationships that all of Jesus' followers are to adopt.

K. Servanthood as revealed in the Incarnation is the primary qualification for and responsibility of spiritual leaders.

L. Servanthood as revealed in the New Testament includes all the services that Christians might render to those within or outside the body of Christ.

M. Servanthood as revealed in the New Testament and in the example of Jesus is nothing more nor less than love given practical and self-sacrificial expression.

2. Undertake one of the following Bible studies, and write a five-page paper on what it teaches you about your own life.
   A. Study the Servant Songs in Isaiah 42:1–4; 49:1–6; 50:4–9; 52:13–53:2.
   B. Study occurrences of the word "deacon" or "servant" in the New Testament Epistles. (Check *diakonos* in a concordance such as *Strongs'* or *Youngs'* that lists Greek originals.)
   C. Study occurrences of the word "slave" in the New Testament Epistles. (Look in the Greek section of a concordance for *doulos*.)
   D. Examine in detail one of the following three New Testament passages reflecting on Christ's servanthood: Philippians 2:1–11; Matthew 20:20–28; John 13:3–17.

3. One aspect of servanthood stressed in Scripture is that of obedience. In the following case history you meet a young woman of thirty with terminal cancer of the liver. Many members of her church in Spokane, Washington, identified her to me as a woman with the gift of intercessory prayer. She does not seem to have as strong an awareness of her gift as do her brothers and sisters in the body. However, her story illustrates a gift in action and shows something of the relationship of obedience to our life as the servant people of God. Explore it using the case study method (p. 22–24).

THEOLOGICAL CORE

SANDY

My becoming aware of my ministry was not an overnight affair. God didn't wake me up in the middle of the night and say, "from this point on you are going to do this." I became aware that I was a little different from most people when I was quite small.

In my first grade at school I was very aware that classmates who were underprivileged or from broken homes had certain problems. If a child was deeply disturbed, *I* became deeply disturbed. I felt a great empathy for him or her, and I did not understand it.

My family made a great deal of fun of me. "Sandy's a little light in the head. Don't worry about her." About my feelings they said, "Sandy's just moody—don't pay any attention to her." Yet I would become quite deeply disturbed, and I prayed for people even then.

Then I became aware of what Jesus was all about when I was eight years old and accepted Him as my Savior.

Through high school I was a Christian but I was more Southern Baptist. The highest calling for a Southern Baptist is to be a medical missionary, and my parents wanted me to do this. While they didn't say so explicitly, Mom and Dad bought me a lot of books about missionaries. One was *Through Gates of Splendor,* the story of five missionaries in Ecuador who were killed. But I think that my Mom's and Dad's greatest ambition was for me to go to Africa. So I went forward at a revival and accepted the "call."

My life was very planned out then. I went into college with medical missions in mind. In school, however, I forgot about this great "calling" and went in my own direction for quite a while. But the Lord still had His hands on my life. When I came back to the Lord I again decided that I was going to have a ministry. Of course, again it was my own thinking. It was something that *I* decided I would do for the Lord. So I decided that counseling was my calling. I was going to get people straightened out. I was going to solve their problems and point them in the right direction.

Then I found I had cancer. The doctors thought they had gotten it all, but on December 5 they told me that it had spread to the liver and was inoperable. When you suddenly find out that you are going to die, your whole life changes. It was when I was in the hospital that I found myself very burdened for another person in the church who was going through some things similar to what I had gone through earlier in my life. This person was very deeply depressed, very heavily burdened. And the Lord just shifted the burden from this person to me and allowed me to carry his burden. That was my first experience in intercessory prayer. Here again we come to the labeling and even at that time I didn't think of labeling it as that. I just knew I had been burdened. As I said, I had felt for people all along. But this was the first time I was conscious of having a burden that was not going to leave me until I prayed about it and the Lord released me from it.

I knew it was not just something *I* wanted to pray about. It was much more than that, because I felt the agony that this person felt. I had heard from people in the Christian Life Center who talked about intercessory prayer, but I still didn't realize that was what I was doing.

Well, one night my husband and I had been out for a drive and stopped in a 7-11 store to get something to drink. We got out just in time to see one person shoot another person. The victim was a young man, only about eighteen years old. We went over and gave him first aid and prayed for him. Then the ambulance came and took him to the hospital.

Dan and I went home and washed all the blood off and went to bed. But the Lord wouldn't let me go to sleep. He told me to get back up and get dressed and go to the hospital and pray for the young man. Now, getting dressed for me was a little more complicated than for a normal person. When I went through chemotherapy I lost all my hair, so I wear a wig. I had to get my wig back on. It doesn't sound like a big deal but it isn't like natural hair, it gets all messed up. I told the Lord, "Oh, Lord, can't I just pray here?" I kept arguing back and forth with Him and He finally just said, "You go and you pray."

That was when I learned that obedience plays a huge part in intercessory prayer. I had to get up and get dressed, and I went to the hospital and I prayed for the young man. He was in surgery, so I went into the waiting room. His grandmother was there alone, with no one to wait with her. So the Lord used me to witness to this lady. I don't mean that I said any great things of wisdom; I just comforted her and prayed for her.

Later the Lord showed me that, if I had not obeyed, the young man would not have lived. Now I don't begin to understand that. Part of me says that is really silly, that I didn't understand what the Lord said. But then part of me knows that the Lord *did* say that, if I hadn't obeyed, the young man would not have lived. Because I obeyed, *I* received as much as or more than anyone else from this experience. I think obedience is a tremendous part of anything you do for the Lord.

So this was the way I came to know my gift. I found out that my abilities are not worth anything to the Lord, that when it comes to serving Him my abilities are not important but obedience is.

AN EMPOWERED PEOPLE

"I will put my Spirit on him and he will bring justice to the nations." These words from Isaiah 42 introduce us to another dimension of our life as the *laos* of God. We are a new covenant people charged as servant-citizens to bring forth kingdom fruit. We have also been given the resources needed to live as God's people. We have been given the Holy Spirit!

The Spirit was the person Jesus relied on in His ministry on earth. We've already seen His claim to drive out demons "by the Spirit of God" (Matt. 12:28). The amazing fact we confront in this chapter is that when Jesus emptied Himself to take on the form of a servant, He purposefully limited Himself. He chose to rely not on Himself but on the Spirit, even as every believer must do.

In this exploration of theological core truths on which the personal ministry of the *laos* of God is based, we will look first at the role of the Spirit in Jesus' life and ministry. Then we'll look at the role of the Holy Spirit in the church since Christ's ascension. Through it all we will discover more of what it means to be a people in whom the Spirit dwells.

**THE ROLE OF THE SPIRIT
IN JESUS' MINISTRY**

The prophets looked forward to the coming of the Messiah as a time when the Spirit would be poured out. Isaiah 32 describes the kingdom reign of righteousness and justice and longs for an ending to the empty years. For then

> the Spirit is poured upon us from on high,
> and the desert becomes a fertile field,
> and the fertile field seems like a forest.
> Justice will dwell in the desert
> and righteousness live in the fertile field.
> The fruit of righteousness will be peace;
> the effect of righteousness will be quietness and
> confidence forever (Isa. 32:15).

While the Old Testament does not speak of the Holy Spirit as a separate person of the Trinity, there is a deep awareness of the vital role the Spirit of God plays in His renewing work.

The creation account tells of the Spirit of God hovering over the waters of a formless and empty earth. As God spoke, the Spirit acted—forming, shaping, vitalizing, renewing, beautifying. "When you send your Spirit," Psalm 104 praises, "they are created: and you renew the face of the earth" (v. 30). "Sing joyfully to the LORD," Psalm 33 exhorts, and recounts that "By the word of the LORD were the heavens made, their starry host by the breath [*ruah*, "Spirit"] of his mouth" (vv. 1,

6). The Spirit brings order to desolation and beauty to the whole of God's creation.

The Spirit is viewed in the Old Testament as having the same creative relationship to mankind. The Spirit is the source of man's reason (Job. 32:8) and wisdom (1 Kings 3:28). Inspiration for the prophet's insight comes from the Spirit (Num. 11:17, 25f.; 2 Sam. 23:2; Dan. 4:8–9). Righteousness, too, comes from Him, as David was particularly aware after his sin with Bathsheba. Thus he cries out in Psalm 51, "Do not cast me from your presence or take your Holy Spirit from me. Restore to me the joy of your salvation and grant me a willing spirit, to sustain me" (vv. 11–12). Cunning in war (Deut. 34:9), special gifts (Gen. 41:38; Exod. 28:3), and even craftsmen's skills (Exod. 31:6) are traced to the Spirit's action in men.

God's Old Testament people were well aware that the Spirit of God operated on human beings. A number of phrases expressed that divine endowment. The Spirit was known to come on God's people in power (Judg. 14:6; Judg. 6:34), enter into them (Ezek. 2:2), rest on them (Isa. 11:2), and stir them (Judg. 13:25). The Spirit was thus the source of the mighty deeds accomplished by the people through whom God chose to act (cf. Num. 27:18; Judg. 3:10; 6:34; 11:29; 1 Sam. 11:6; 16:13).

Against this background it is not surprising that the prophets looked forward to the messianic age. At that time the Spirit of God was to be poured out on all flesh (Joel 2:28–29). Israel stood in desperate need of such a renewal. Like the earth of Genesis 1, God's people were crushed and formless. Like prophets and mighty men without the Spirit, God's people were helpless and had no hope of accomplishing their mission as His servant.

But the Spirit would rest on the Messiah. He would accomplish all God's will and give the Spirit to all.

It is no wonder, then, that the New Testament carefully documents the relationship of Jesus Christ to the Holy Spirit, who in the Gospels and Epistles is shown to be a Person co-equal with the Father and the Son. Jesus' conception is by the supernatural activity of the Holy Spirit, so He who is born can be called holy (Matt. 1:18, 20; Luke 1:35). When Jesus was about to enter into His public ministry, the Spirit descended on Him to consecrate Him for His task (Matt. 3:16; Luke 3:22). This consecration is later described in Acts in these words: "God anointed Jesus of Nazareth with the Holy Spirit and power, and . . . he went around doing good and healing all who were under the power of the devil, because God was with him" (Acts 10:38). John says Jesus was given the Holy Spirit without limit, for He was sent to speak the very words of God (John 3:34). Jesus Himself ascribes His healing powers to the Spirit (Matt. 12:28). So both kingdom proclamation and kingdom righteousness are rooted in Jesus' relationship to the Spirit of God.

The New Testament portrait of Christ as dependent on the Spirit in His ministry on earth raises questions. Why didn't the Second Person of the Trinity act in His own power? Why rely instead on the power of the indwelling Spirit?

We see the answer in the report of Jesus' temptation. Scripture tells us that Jesus was "led by the Spirit into the desert" to be tested by Satan. The tests took place after a forty-day fast, when He was physically weak. The first test, recounted by both Matthew and Luke, involved that weakness and hunger.

> The tempter came to him and said, "If [i.e. since] you are the Son of God, tell these stones to become bread."
>
> Jesus answered, "It is written: 'Man does not live on bread alone, but on every word that comes from the mouth of God'" (Matt. 4:3–4).

What is significant to us is the nature of the challenge and Jesus' response. There are several different kinds of "if" in the Greek language. The "if" here is like an English "since": the condition is assumed to have been fulfilled. Thus Satan's temptation focused on Jesus' very nature as God the Son. The test was to move Jesus to *act in His own essential deity* to meet His needs.

Jesus met the temptation with a quotation from Deuteronomy that stresses the dependence of all humanity on the word and will of God. God is free to act in harmony with His essential nature. Human beings are by nature limited—limited within the physical universe, limited by their bodies, limited by their characters, limited by their mortality. Jesus chose to respond as a human being. Jesus' response shows how complete the Incarnation was. He was not *like* a human being; He *was* a human being. In becoming one of us in every essential respect (cf. Heb. 2:10–18), Jesus set aside His prerogatives as God. He limited Himself to live on earth as we who are His brothers and sisters must live. Jesus lived in dependence on the Holy Spirit, and His works and teaching were accomplished in the power of the Holy Spirit, so that you and I might realize that *in the Spirit we have the same source of power that operated in Christ.* What He did in His incarnation is not "impossible" for us, but is completely possible because the same Spirit resides in our lives.

91

Paul Jewett comments on this as follows:

> The question might well be asked, Why, if Jesus is Himself God the Son, was the power of the Spirit so necessary to carry out His mission? A part of the answer must lie in the real humanity that Jesus assumed when He became incarnate. Jesus was no less a man because He was divine, as though He were divine omnipotence masquerading as human frailty. Since God had made man by His Spirit, and since man always lived in dependence upon God's Spirit, therefore Jesus, if He was one with mankind, must also have depended upon the indwelling Spirit of God. That is why, in the economy of salvation, He assumed the role of the Messiah, the One who was anointed by the Spirit of God. Yet He was also conscious of His own divine, absolute authority. Unlike the prophets in their dependence upon the Spirit, He did not say, "Thus says the LORD," but "truly, I say unto you."[1]

One of the themes of Jesus' teaching to His disciples dealt with their future relationship to the Spirit. The Twelve were familiar with the prophecies. The Spirit would rest on the Messiah. But through His work the Spirit would be "poured out" on everyone. Thus Joel had promised

> And afterward,
>   I will pour out my Spirit on all people.
> Your sons and daughters will prophesy,
>   your old men will dream dreams,
>   your young men will see visions.
> Even on my servants, both men and women,
>   I will pour out my Spirit in those days (Joel 2:28–29).

The age of the Spirit was approaching. The Messiah had come; could the Spirit be far behind?

Certainly Jesus spoke of the Spirit's outpouring as imminent. "Whoever believes in me, as the Scripture has said, streams of living water will flow from within him." John interprets, "By this he meant the Spirit, whom those who believed in him were later to receive. Up to that time the Spirit had not been given, since Jesus had not yet been glorified" (John 7:38–39). Although the coming of the Spirit had to await the ascension of Jesus, the Gospels speak much of that coming. John the Baptist's preaching promised that soon One would come who baptized with the Holy Spirit (Matt. 3:11; John 1:33). With the Spirit would come guidance from God as to how the disciples ought to respond and speak (Mark 13:11). As late as the time of the Last Supper Jesus spoke of the Spirit's coming upon His *laos* as future: "I will send him to you" (John 16:7). After the Resurrection, walking to the As-

---

[1]Paul Jewett, "The Holy Spirit," Merrill C. Tenney, ed., *The Zondervan Pictorial Encyclopedia of the Bible.* 5 vols. (Grand Rapids: Zondervan Publishing House, 1975), 3:185f.

cension hill, Jesus gave these final instructions: "Wait for the gift my Father promised, which you have heard me speak about. For John baptized with water, but in a few days you will be baptized with the Holy Spirit" (Acts 1:4–5). With the work of Jesus on the cross complete and His return to glory accomplished, the Spirit was about to be given to all in accordance with the age-old vision of the prophets. The day of the Holy Spirit was about to dawn.

The work of the Spirit in Jesus' ministry was, then, foreshadowed by the work of the Spirit in creation and in God's Old Testament people. The Spirit was intimately connected with every significant aspect of Jesus' life. He was born through the agency of the Spirit, was endowed at His baptism by the Spirit for His ministry, accomplished His teachings and His works in the power of the Spirit, and lived in dependence on the Spirit. Thus He modeled for us the possibility of a supernatural lifestyle that we too are to live in the Spirit's power. During His time on earth Jesus also promised that, in accordance with Old Testament prophecies, the Spirit would soon be poured out on all of God's *laos*. At the time of Jesus' return to the Father, the promise was to be kept: "in a few days."

There is one last theme we need to explore briefly before we examine the role of the Spirit in the life of the church. In what is often called the Upper Room Discourse (John 13–16), Jesus taught His disciples much about the Spirit. We need to look at this teaching of Jesus to learn about our present relationship to the Spirit.

There are four sections that teach about the relationship of believers and the Spirit. The first speaks of the Spirit as the link between the believer and the Lord (John 14:9–20). The second presents the Spirit as our Teacher (John 14:21–26). The third speaks of the Spirit's relationship to the believer as he lives his life in a hostile world (John 15:8–16:11). The fourth speaks of the Spirit's ministry as God's contemporary voice and interpreter of His Word (John 16:12–15).

The living link: John 14:9–20

In response to Philip's request to be shown the Father, Jesus responds that "anyone who has seen me has seen the Father" (John 14:9). This is true because Jesus is in the Father, and the Father is in Him (John 14:10). Christ points out that the Father living in Him is expressed in all Jesus' words and works, for they are in fact the words and works of the Father Himself.

At this point Jesus promises that anyone who has faith in

Him will do what He has been doing, and even "greater things" (John 14:12). This is possible, He explains, because on His return to the Father He will answer prayer by Himself, doing those things asked in His name (John 14:13).

Jesus adds a further explanation: "Because I live, you also will live. On that day you will realize that I am in my Father, and you are in me, and I am in you" (John 14:19–20). The same indwelling relationship that Jesus experienced with the Father is to be possible for the believer and the persons of the Trinity (cf. John 17:21–23). All this will become reality, Jesus tells the disciples, when He returns to the Father and sends the Spirit of Truth, who "will be in you" (John 14:16–17).

The thrust of this teaching is that the Spirit, who will be given to "anyone who has faith" in Jesus, is the living link between the believer and the Godhead. In the Spirit, the Father and the Son also take up residence in the believer, making it possible for him to do the works of Christ because the King is Himself present in the citizens of His kingdom.

Counselor and guide: John 14:21–27

In our look at the Servant of the Lord in the previous chapter, we saw that willing submission to the will of God is a key to servant ministry. Now Jesus stresses the importance of obedience for the personal experience of the indwelling Lord. "Whoever has my commands and obeys them, he is the one who loves me. He who loves me will be loved by my Father, and I too will love him and show myself to him" (John 14:21). Love-motivated obedience is essential if we are to experience the reality of this indwelling relationship.

The obedience God seeks is not an obedience to external laws governing our behavior, as under the old covenant. Obedience instead is to the inner prompting of the Spirit. The Spirit-led life must be in full harmony with God's objective revelation in the Bible, but differs from it in that both behavior and motivation are reshaped by God. "The Counselor, the Holy Spirit, whom the Father will send in my name," Jesus says, "will teach you all things and will remind you of everything I have said to you" (John 14:26). The remembered and written words of Jesus will be given specific application by the Spirit as He calls them to mind to guide in every situation in our lives.

Companion in the world: John 15:18–16:11

In this section Jesus reminds His followers that the world has hated Him. Because we, like Jesus, do not belong to this world system but live in the kingdom of the Son, "they will persecute you also" (John 15:20). When Jesus sends the Spirit from the Father to live within believers, He will testify to the world about Jesus. But, Jesus adds, "you also must testify" (John 15:27).

At this point Jesus tells His disciples that it is to their benefit that He return to the Father. "Unless I go away, the Counselor will not come to you; but if I go, I will send him to you" (John 16:7). The believer's effectiveness in communicating the love of God depends on the work of the Spirit, for "When he comes, he will convict the world of guilt in regard to sin and righteousness and judgment" (John 16:8).

The believer is called on to live as Jesus lived in a hostile world. He is enabled to reveal by the quality of his life and the teaching of his lips the great realities of the gospel. The Holy Spirit is our constant Companion and lifelong Counselor in this world. It is through His power in us that our witness can be effective in overcoming the power of the evil one over the minds of the lost (cf. John 16:8–11).

Contemporary voice: John 16:12–15

In a few brief phrases Jesus now restates something of the present teaching ministry of the Spirit. "I have much more to say to you, more than you can now bear" (John 16:12). Thus it is essential for the Spirit to come to guide "into all truth." The Spirit will function as the voice of God to the believer, constantly bringing us insight into Jesus' will, so that we might live in intimate fellowship with our Lord as His servants.

When we look at the relationship of Jesus to the Spirit, we find that He Himself depended on the Spirit for power to carry out His ministry. Jesus' dependence is in total harmony with what the Bible tells us in the Old Testament about how the Spirit works. In Jesus' teachings about the Spirit, we see the same relationship that He enjoyed with the Spirit in His life on earth promised to "anyone who has faith in me." *Thus each believer today is fully equipped for personal ministries. Jesus Himself has provided that equipping by the gift to all believers of the Holy Spirit of God!*

THE ROLE OF THE HOLY SPIRIT IN THE CHURCH

Acts 2 describes the fulfillment of Jesus' promise to send the Spirit "in a few days" (Acts 1:5). The rest of the Book of Acts shows the impact of the Spirit's presence on believers. Several passages in the Epistles instruct us on the meaning of that presence.

THEOLOGICAL CORE

Directing the church

One of the most significant teachings of Scripture is that Jesus is head of the church. This is not simply a "theological concept." It is a practical reality to be experienced by all Christians. In Acts we see the church of Christ functioning under His headship, with the Spirit of God as the promised voice and guide. For those of us who have assumed that the church of Christ can function only in a highly organized form, with pastors acting as the "chief operating officers" and boards and committees functioning to make decisions and set up and staff programs, the Acts' picture of the church living in simple response to the voice of the Spirit is a foreign and amazing thing. Yet the church *did* function this way, as individuals and smaller groups. And the body as a whole listened to God's voice and was conscious of the Spirit's leading.

Here is how Acts portrays this ministry of the Holy Spirit. It begins with the promise of the gift of the Spirit, to be given "in a few days" (Acts 1:5). When the Spirit has come, His presence will provide power "and you will be my witnesses in Jerusalem, and in all Judea and Samaria, and to the ends of the earth" (Acts 1:8). The next chapters of Acts outline the working of that power, as many receive the witness and turn to the Lord, forming a unique community of faith. As the core community in Jerusalem and Judah was formed, it was soon time to reach out to the rest of mankind. We see many evidences of the Spirit's function as the voice of Jesus, the head of the body. It is the Spirit who guides Philip when he meets the Ethiopian eunuch to "go to that chariot and stay near it" (Acts 8:29), leading to the conversion of this important official in the court of his queen.

When it was time for the Gentiles to be admitted to the community of faith, the Spirit instructed Peter (Acts 11:12, 19). Later leaders of the gentile church at Antioch were directed by the Spirit while fasting and praying to set apart for Him Barnabas and Saul for the work to which He had called them (Acts 13:2). At the time of the first great controversy in the church (about the relationship between Jewish customs and gentile believers), the decision was arrived at by a consensus superintended by the Spirit. Thus the leaders wrote, "It seemed good to the Holy Spirit and to us . . ." (Acts 15:28). Paul's journeys were directed by the Spirit. In one instance he was "kept by the Holy Spirit from preaching the word in the province of Asia" (Acts 16:6). Later, he warned the elders of the church at Ephesus to guard themselves "and all the flock of which the Holy Spirit has made you overseers" (Acts 20:28).

The picture we have in Acts is of active and personal direction of the affairs of the church of Christ by the Holy Spirit. Local congregations or leaders were not charged with "making decisions" but with seeking the will of God by listening for the voice of the Spirit. This supernatural operation of the community of believers is, as Jesus' instructions to the disciples made clear, not only possible for the church; it is to be the norm. We are to be a people who, individually and together, are responsive and open to the leading of the Spirit of God.

The voice of God

Emphasis on the Spirit as teacher and revealer often causes concern. Some fear a subjectivism that might lead to heresies and chaos. Why, if each Christian were taught to listen for the voice of God to him, wouldn't the result be a chaotic individualism? They are also concerned that such a doctrine might lead to the rejection of leaders. Humanly speaking, it is much more comfortable to insist that an authoritative pastor or a church structure designed to control through organization be given the role of controlling and directing lives. This seems much more "safe" than the surrender of control that the doctrine of Christ's headship "over all things for the church, which is His body" and the doctrine of direction by the Spirit demand. However, as the experience of the early church illustrates, the Spirit is wiser than men in guiding the life of God's people. Our obedience as servants of God is owed directly to Him.

In point of fact, the Spirit's guidance is *not* in the nature of that subjectivism feared by those who require control to feel comfortable. Scripture is clear in teaching that the Holy Spirit was the active agent in the giving of the written Word. According to Acts 28:25 it was the "Holy Spirit [who] spoke the truth to your forefathers." In Hebrews the words of Deuteronomy are identified as what "the Holy Spirit says" (Heb. 3:7). The whole system of Law is an illustration of realities revealed by the Spirit (Heb. 9:8). The prophets who spoke God's words in the Old Testament era later studied those words in an attempt to grasp "the time and circumstances to which the Spirit of Christ in them was pointing" (1 Peter 1:11). Peter sums up the doctrine clearly when he says "prophecy never had its origin in the will of man, but men spoke from God as they were carried along by the Holy Spirit" (2 Peter 1:21).

Against this background, then, it's clear why Paul, writing of our life in the Spirit, would speak of "the righteous requirements of the law" being "fully met" in "those who live in accordance with the Spirit" (Rom. 8:4–5). Of course the "mind controlled by the Spirit is life and peace" (Rom. 8:6). Certainly no one living in vital association with the Spirit of God and under His control would wander into a subjectivism that turns him away from the written Word. The existential voice by which the Spirit speaks to a contemporary follower of the Lord will always be in harmony with the written Word, the enscripturated voice of the Spirit. That written Word will always serve as a check against subjectivism.

But it is also important to realize that each believer is *responsible to listen to the voice of God speaking to him in a personal, directing, or instructing way.* The objective Word without the living voice has often led to a dead orthodoxy, just as the concept of a living voice apart from Scripture has led to a subjective mysticism. In the church of Christ, Scripture and voice are both essential in the experience of the *laos* of God.

In this context, 1 Corinthians provides vital teaching. In chapters 1–4 Paul contrasts the wisdom of the world with the wisdom of God. In chapter 2 he explains that the wisdom of God is ours through the ministry of the Spirit. In the fifth century B.C. Empedocles wrote:

> Weak and narrow are the powers emplanted in the limbs of man; many the woes that fall on them and blunt the edges of thought; short is the measure of the life and death through which they toil. Then are they borne away; like smoke they vanish into air; and what they dream they know is but the little that each hath stumbled upon in wandering about the world. Yet boast they all that they have learned the whole. Vain fools! For what that is, no eye hath seen, nor ear hath heard, nor can it be conceived by the mind of man.

Now Paul refers to this quote, when he says, "No eye has seen, no ear has heard, no mind has conceived" and adds "what God has prepared for those who love him" (1 Cor. 2:9). Yet "God has revealed it to us by his Spirit" (1 Cor. 2:10).

Without the Spirit a man cannot grasp spiritual truths or penetrate the meaning of spiritual words (1 Cor. 2:13). Thus it is clear that even *the meaning of the written revelation must be interpreted to humans by the Holy Spirit.* The living voice of God, illuminating the Word and interpreting its impact on the life of community and individual, is an essential element of Christian experience. Because spiritual discernment is involved (1 Cor. 2:14), the one with the Spirit "makes judgments about all things, but he himself is not subject to any man's judgment" (1 Cor. 2:15). Through the Spirit, each believer has the amazing capacity of coming to know and understand

God's will for his own life, for in the Spirit "we have the mind of Christ" (1 Cor. 2:16).

If it were true that only *some* believers possessed the Spirit, it might be reasonable to argue that God has given them the task of being interpreters of Scripture for the others, or has charged them to structure organizations through which the work of Jesus in the world could be accomplished. But the emphasis in Scripture is on the coming of the Spirit "on all flesh." It was Jesus who promised that *"anyone* who has faith in me will do what I have been doing" (John 14:12), and who based this promise on the gift of the Spirit, who "will be in you" (John 14:17). In speaking of the life we live in the Spirit, Paul testifies that any person without the Spirit does not belong to Christ (Rom. 8:9).

Knowing, then, the presence of the Spirit in each believer and honoring the right of Christ as Lord to direct those who are His servants, Paul insists that we pass no judgment on one another nor look down on others who differ from us. "Who are you to judge someone else's servant?" he asks. "To his own master he stands or falls. And he will stand, for the Lord is able to make him stand" (Rom. 14:4). Paul makes this very clear in what follows:

> For this very reason, Christ died and returned to life so that he might be the Lord of both the dead and the living. You, then, why do you judge your brother? Or why do you look down on your brother? For we will all stand before God's judgment seat . . . So then, each of us will give an account of himself to God (Rom. 14:9–12).

The immediate lordship of Jesus over each of His laos is clearly taught in Scripture

No man and no institution can claim the right to guide, nor can they provide the empowering that Jesus spoke about in the Upper Room. Teacher, guide, and empowerer are all included in the role of the Spirit.

Scripture is thus clear that each believer must learn to live in responsive obedience to the voice of the Spirit and look confidently to Jesus Christ to exercise personal lordship in his or her life.

As the Spirit directed and taught the early church, so we today must expect the Spirit to direct and guide us and all our brothers and sisters.

Transforming the believer

This is a third dimension of the Spirit's present work that is emphasized in the New Testament. We have already pointed out that Jesus continues His incarnation in believers today. Paul says to the Galatians, ". . . Christ lives in me. The life I live in the body, I live by faith in the Son of God, who loved me and gave himself for me" (Gal. 2:20). To "walk as Jesus did" (1 John 2:6) involves far more than simply going about doing good; it involves being godly. When the new covenant speaks of the law being written on our hearts and minds, it is speaking of an inner transformation toward Christlikeness. In that context Paul says we are "being transformed into his [Jesus'] likeness with ever-increasing glory, which comes from the Lord, who is the Spirit" (2 Cor. 3:18).

Everywhere this new quality of life is associated with the presence and work of the Holy Spirit in believers. We are urged to "live by the Spirit" (Gal. 5:16), because the fruit that the Holy Spirit produces is "love, joy, peace, patience, kindness, goodness, faithfulness, gentleness and self-control" (Gal. 5:22–23). We consciously reject the pull of the sinful nature and consciously choose to follow the promptings of the Spirit. This leading relies on our responsiveness to the voice of the Spirit and not to written codes, as though the code itself were God (Gal. 5:8; cf. Rom. 7:4–6). As we learn to walk and live in the Spirit (Gal. 5:16, 18, 25), He works in us as well as through us to shape the character of Jesus in our personalities.

In dealing with this aspect of the Spirit's work, it is important to note that the Bible implies a transformation. Maturity is not something that magically appears at the time of conversion. Everywhere we find the language of process. Hebrews speaks of the mature as those "who by constant use have trained themselves to distinguish good from evil" (Heb. 5:14). We *are being* transformed (2 Cor. 3:18). We are to "*Become* mature, attaining to the whole measure of the fullness of Christ," at which time "we will no longer be infants" (Eph. 4:13–14). The new self that we become in Christ "*is being* renewed in knowledge in the image of its Creator" (Col. 3:10; cf. 1–11). As Peter puts it, "you are not just mortals now but sons of God; the live, permanent Word of the living God has given you his own indestructible heredity" (1 Peter 1:23 PHILLIPS). Thus we have the potential to be like Jesus. In His work the Holy Spirit guides and guards that transformation, so that the intent of the Father for us may be achieved (cf. Rom. 8:29).

This is particularly important in the exercise of any ministry. Jesus acted out of compassion and love in meeting human needs. He not only told of a God who is love; His whole life demonstrated the reality of that love. Of our witness Jesus said, "Love one another. . . . All men will know that you are my disciples if you love one another" (John 13:34–35). Paul writes pointedly that actions, no matter how right or noble, that are undertaken without the harmony of godlike motives are of no value. "If I speak in the tongues of men and of angels, but have not love," he says in 1 Corinthians 13:1–3,

> I am only a resounding gong or a clanging cymbal. If I have the gift of prophecy and can fathom all mysteries and all knowledge, and if I have a faith that can move mountains, but have not love, I am nothing. If I give all I possess to the poor and surrender my body to the flames, but have not love, I gain nothing.

To incarnate Jesus in this world, the Christian must experience an inner transformation in which he not only behaves as Jesus behaved, but also shares His love, His valuing of persons, His compassion, and His zeal for justice and righteousness. This character, stamped indelibly on his heart and mind, will be read by all men (2 Cor. 3:2).

Summary

This brief exploration of the role of the Spirit among the *laos* of God has touched on a number of significant themes. Consistently throughout the Old Testament the Spirit is portrayed as the active agent in the renewal of God's creation and in the empowering of human beings for God's service. The Old Testament looks toward the coming of the Messiah and sees it as ushering in an age of the Spirit. Then the Spirit's work will be seen in the whole people of God.

Jesus' whole ministry was marked by a dependence on the Spirit. He taught His disciples that they too would soon have a special relationship with the Spirit of God. Everyone who believed in Jesus was to be indwelt by the Spirit, the living link between the individual and the Godhead. The Spirit is to be the believer's Counselor and Guide, teaching him how to obey the Lord. As a constant Companion, the Spirit will be present in our conflict in a hostile world, and will testify to and convict the men of the world.

After Jesus' ascension, that promise was kept. The Spirit came at Pentecost to initiate the new relationship. From this point on, Acts not only speaks of filling and empowering, but also describes the Spirit's specific direction to individuals and to the community of faith. The Epistles pick up and amplify the concept of the Spirit as the living voice of God. He interprets Scripture, directs and guides the people of God by an existential revelation of His voice. Through the Spirit the lordship of Jesus over every individual and over His body as a community is exercised. Because of the Spirit's working "we have the mind of Christ." Finally, the Spirit works within a believer's personality as the active agent in writing God's law on his mind and heart. Transformation toward the likeness of Jesus, so essential if we are to represent Him adequately in the world, takes place through the Spirit. This is a progressive transformation, a growth toward maturity. But we are dependent for it on learning to live in and walk by the Spirit of God.

How vital, then, is the teaching of Scripture that we who are the *laos* of God are the possessors of the Spirit! How essential that each Christian comes to understand himself and his potential as a ministering person by recognizing the meaning of the Spirit's presence and acknowledging the power that this makes available in and through him.

PROBE

▶ *case histories*
▶ *discussion questions*
▶ *thought provokers*
▶ *resources*

1. In the *New International Dictionary of New Testament Theology,* edited by Colin Brown, J. D. G. Dunn writes about life in the Spirit. Many aspects of our Christian experience are related to the ministry of the Spirit in us. Locate as many aspects as you can in the following quotation:

> *For Paul, the believer has a responsibility to live his life in the power of the Spirit. In general terms that means to let his character be moulded by God according to the pattern of Jesus Christ—not as something which the believer achieves for himself . . . but as something which by attentive openness to God he allows the Spirit to produce through him . . . (2 Cor. 3:18; Gal 5:18–23; cf. Rom. 8:28; 9:1; 14:17; 15:13, 30; 2 Cor. 6:6; Gal. 6:1; Col. 1:8). In particular, it means that Paul was able to talk of his daily conduct as a "walking by the Spirit," a being "led by the Spirit," as an "ordering one's life by the Spirit" (Rom. 8:4–6, 14; Gal. 5:16, 18, 25; cf. Rom. 8:13; Gal. 6:8). It is noticeable that he contrasts this experience of daily guidance with the sort of dependence on the rule book of the law which had characterized his previous religious practice (Rom. 7:6; 2 Cor. 3:6; Gal. 5:1, 16). That is to say, he experienced the Spirit precisely as the fulfilment of the prophetic hope that the law would be written on the heart not just on*

> tablets of stone, that men would know God for themselves and be able to discern God's will immediately without having to refer to the Scriptures and the case-law of tradition each time (Rom. 12:2; 2 Cor. 3:3, alluding to Jer. 31:31–34). Similarly worship and prayer were not a matter of liturgical rote or outward form, but worship was characterized precisely as worship in or by the Spirit of God (Rom. 2:28f.; Phil. 3:3; cf. Eph. 2:18, 22), and prayer precisely as prayer in the Spirit (Eph. 6:18; see also Rom. 8:15f., 26f.; 1 Cor. 14:4–7; Gal. 4:6) (NIDNTT, 3:702).

2. The Scriptures stress the fact that *all believers* are possessors of the Spirit and are thus to live their lives "in the Spirit." This has been clouded in many ways across the centuries. One of the most obvious was mentioned earlier, the clergy-laity distinction that was institutionalized in Catholicism and continues in Protestantism. Yet today another cloud exists, with its own long, historic tradition, the distinction between men and women in the church.

   Here are two quotations, one from Lord Chesterfield, and one from Joel as quoted by Peter in Acts. Read each quotation carefully.

Lord Chesterfield (Eighteenth Century)

● Women are only children of larger growth; they have an entertaining rattle and sometimes wit; but not solid reasoning or good sense. . . .

● A man of sense only trifles with them, plays with them, humors and flatters them, as he does a slightly forward child. . . .

● Women are much more like each other than men; they have in truth but two passions, vanity and love; these are their universal characteristics.

Joel/Peter (Joel 2:28–32; Acts 2:17–18)

And afterward,
I will pour out my Spirit on all people.
Your sons and daughters will prophesy,
    your old men will dream dreams,
    your young men will see visions.
Even on my servants, both men and women,
    I will pour out my Spirit in those days.

Now for each quotation develop a list of ten descriptive statements. The statements in each list are to describe a local congregation that essentially accepts the point of view of each quotation.

For instance, a congregation living out the view expressed by

Chesterfield might be described as: "Strongly holds to 'chain of command' ideas of authority." Or "Seldom gives women any significant place of leadership," etc.

3. Review your two lists (from 2 above). *Which statements from each list seem to portray your own congregation?* What conclusions do you draw from comparing your congregation with the descriptive statements you have developed?

4. The key concept developed in this chapter is simply this: we, the *laos* of God, are an empowered people. When we realize His presence and power and live in confidence that He will work through us, our lives change.

   In several references we've learned about the counseling ministry carried out by believers at Trinity. The following case history, for your exploration in a *Case Study Conference,* is in the form of an interview Larry Richards held with Nettie, one of the believer-priests at Trinity whose ministry is counseling . . . and whose confidence is in the indwelling Holy Spirit.

Nettie: I'm the wife of an airline pilot, and we've been married twenty-one years. The Lord brought us to Seattle in a special way and took us through a number of experiences that brought us to Trinity. We became connected with this church after an experience of restlessness in the church where we were. No deep problems, but we felt that our own giftedness was not. . . .

Larry: Were you aware then of what your giftedness was?

Nettie: Not exactly. I had somewhat of a ministry working with women, mostly my own age or younger. There was uncertainty, but I knew that the Lord had something for me. At the time my husband and I had no idea of where we could minister and where we couldn't.

Larry: How have your ministries developed here?

Nettie: I attended a counseling seminar that Gib Martin was giving a number of years ago. It focused on the gift of encouragement and the belief that if the Holy Spirit is in you, He has a word for any person you might encounter. Hopefully, the Spirit might minister through you to that individual.

   Even though I had a degree in psychology and graduate work in counseling and guidance, I realized that it wasn't the degree that gave me any authority. It was the power of the Holy Spirit working through me that would allow me to encourage or exhort.

   I have a handicapped child whose schedule is very

irregular because she has seizures, so I could never tie myself down to a strict schedule. The Lord showed me that I had to do things on a temporary basis. He led me to see that I had the gift of encouragement—a gift to help on a day-to-day basis.

Larry: What kinds of counseling situations do you deal with?

Nettie: My husband and I have worked together on several occasions counseling families either here at the Center or in our home. If people are referred to us, we work with them for several weeks. I have been involved by myself in crisis situations, for example, helping to find homes or apartments for people who have lived in cars for several weeks. I have worked with child abuse cases.

I have also worked with people who have come to the Center with fraudulent appeals. You see, we offer money and other types of assistance. We refer people to lawyers, to doctors, to resource people, a lot of them within our own Christian community.

We have dealt with many abused women. In Seattle there are a lot of excellent agencies that work with abused women. We refer women to these agencies, so we have to be constantly aware of what is going on in the community. We try to link them up with an agency that will deal with them in a spiritual way.

Larry: What kind of relationship do you have with others in the counseling ministry?

Nettie: Every Monday morning we have a staff meeting that we all try to attend. We study together and share prayer requests. We may even discuss some of the needs that we have run across, without violating confidences.

We encourage our counselees to attend Sunday morning services. We don't force them to come here, of course. In fact, if they have a denominational preference, we encourage them to attend evangelical churches in the community, including some excellent Catholic churches in the area. So we are constantly linking people up with church bodies.

If they come here, the staff and counselors have an opportunity to introduce them to other people within this Christian body. We hope they become involved with the body of Christ. The counselees who are part of this particular body of Christ see each other not only on Sunday, but also at other times during the week.

To build a ministry of encouragement within a Christian body, there has to be an awareness of giftedness within that body. Many people in the body have had a variety of relevant experiences—deaths in the family, problem children, runaways, etc. People who have worked through a crisis themselves are the most able to encourage others.

For example, having a handicapped child has given me many opportunities to minister to parents in the local community who have children with handicaps. I can share my faith and how it helps me deal with my handicapped child.

If you have suffered, the Bible says, you can relate more easily to those who are suffering. I have at times wondered why the Lord didn't make everything perfect for me when I turned my life over to Him. But I came to realize that if He made us spiritually mature in an instant and delivered us from everyday problems, we couldn't relate to the suffering world around us. God allows us to share common human problems so we can show others that Christ makes a difference in our lives.

We have a list of people in our church office who have had various kinds of experiences. We talk with them to find those who are willing to share with someone else who is going through a similar experience. It's amazing how much encouragement such people can be.

Christianity isn't just theory. It's practical. It says, "I've been in the situation that you're in."

One time in a counseling situation a counselee said he was so angry he could murder another person. I could say, "Hey, I know my own heart and, given the right circumstances, I could probably do the same thing. If someone were to maim my child, I might react in the same way. But there is someone in me that is greater than I am, and He moderates what I do. That's the Holy Spirit."

But my ministry also involves building relationships. The majority of the people I have been involved with have continued in relationships, even if they move away from the community.

Larry: In many counseling situations the counselee later withdraws from the relationship. Are you saying that your relationships have grown?

Nettie: I am concerned that the person not continue with me, because I really don't want to have twenty people hanging on my apron strings for twenty years. I want them to develop a relationship with Christ that will give them strength. Yet a simple relationship can easily turn into a friendship when the other person accepts Christ or you are regularly praying for him or her.

Larry: So you are really building friendships?

Nettie: I hope their best Friend will be Christ, and my relationship will be one of concern for how they are doing three or six months down the road. That involves a bit of cost. I've made phone calls in the last couple of months to Aberdeen, Portland, Coeur D'Alene—to people whose lives we've touched over the last couple years and that we are concerned about. There are some you can't touch because they get to the point where they refuse any kind of counsel. You respect that, too.

PART 1

THEOLOGICAL CORE
THE IDENTITY OF THE BELIEVER

A People of God
A New Covenant People
A Kingdom People
A Servant People
An Empowered People
A Gifted People

It's customary to approach the question of personal ministries by starting with the Bible's teaching about spiritual gifts. We have tended to look at the lists of gifts in the New Testament and to do an exposition of each one, speculating on just what the individual terms mean and how the gifts are expressed in today's congregation. Some have discussed extensively whether the "sign" gifts (such as tongues and miraculous healings) are or are not for the contemporary church.

This approach may be useful. But it also has serious drawbacks. The primary drawback is that it shifts the attention of believers away from the biblical focus of the contexts in which Scripture deals with spiritual gifts. It often leads individuals into painful speculation about their own specific gifts rather than to an understanding of how gifts are designed by God to function harmoniously in the body of Christ. Our purpose in this chapter is to focus on the more significant contextual issues, not on an analysis of the lists, or arguments for or against the sign gifts. We want to ask, "What are spiritual gifts and what is their significance in understanding ourselves as a ministering people?"

CHAPTER 6

THE NATURE OF GIFTEDNESS

The Greek word translated "gift" is *charisma*, from which the contemporary term "charismatic" comes. Arndt and Gingrich point out that the word simply means "a gift (freely and graciously given). . . ." Concerning the application of that term to "spiritual gifts," they add that it is used

> of special gifts of a non-material sort, bestowed by the grace of God on individual Christians 1 Pt 4:10 . . . Of the gift of an office, mediated by the laying on of hands 1 Ti 4:14; 2 Ti 1:6. Of the power to be continent in matters of sex 1 Cor. 7:7. Of the spiritual gifts in a special sense Ro 12:6; 1 Cor 12:4,9,28,30,31.[1]

This summary helps us see immediately that the concept of "gifts" extends well beyond either an emphasis on tongues or an emphasis on service in an "office" in the church, such as pastor or Sunday school teacher.

If we look into the Old Testament, we gain an important additional insight. *In the Old Testament the Holy Spirit is associated with all sorts of special endowments, and there is no distinction made between "secular" and "sacred."* The Holy Spirit endowed craftsmen in wood and metal with special

---

[1]W. F. Arndt and F. W. Gingrich, *A Greek-English Lexicon of the New Testament* (Chicago: University of Chicago Press, 1957), p. 887.

skill (Exod. 31:3, 6). The Holy Spirit gave Samson his unique strength (Judg. 14:6). Political wisdom was the Spirit's gift to Othniel (Judg. 3:10), and doubtless to Daniel as well. The Spirit endowed Joseph with the gifts required to manage Potiphar's household and later the whole land of Egypt (Gen. 41:38). Today this might be considered the gift of "business" or "management." When James 1:17 says that "every good and perfect gift is from above," we are helped to see that *all human excellences are rightly attributed to God.* He can use all these excellences to accomplish His purposes.

On the one hand, then, we want the *laos* of God to see and value every talent, skill, and ability as a gracious gift from God, a giftedness that can be returned to Him by serving others.

Yet when we come to those passages in the New Testament that have been traditionally viewed as the "spiritual gift" passages, we see something that is different from this general giftedness. We are not referring to a difference in source (the Spirit) or in use (for the service of God and others). What is different is the *context* and *function* of the gifts. The context in which spiritual gifts are exercised is the body of Christ. And the function or goal of the exercise of these gifts is the maturing of that body.

Misunderstanding on this point has historically led to two tragedies. First, we have failed to call all believers to use every talent and skill with which they have been endowed to carry out the revealed purposes of God in our world. We have downgraded such abilities as craftsmanship and management and wrongly uplifted the "spiritual" items from the lists in Romans and 1 Corinthians. We have led many to see as useless or irrelevant to ministry skills that are truly God's special endowments.

Second, we have so drawn attention to the *nature* of the listed gifts that we have misunderstood ministry. We have made ministry appear to be an individual thing rather than a coordinated expression of the reality of Christ's body.

To explore these issues, we need to think through together the three basic New Testament passages that deal with "gifts."

1 Corinthians 12:1—14:39

Most English translations begin 1 Corinthians 12 with the phrase, "Now about spiritual gifts. . . ." In the original language the word "gifts" is not present. Instead, the term used is *pneumatikon,* "spiritual (matters)." Many translators feel that "gifts" is the subject of the passage and so supply that term.

However, in view of the Hellenistic culture of the Corinthians and the emphasis they gave to the gift of tongues, it is more likely that Paul purposely omitted the term "gifts." Gifts are *not* Paul's focus! Instead Paul is speaking of the whole issue of *spirituality*. The Greek world viewed ecstatic experiences as an indication that a god was speaking through, or had gripped, an individual. Thus epilepsy was "the divine disease," and the oracle at Delphi would breathe in fumes and under their influence babble statements priests interpreted as the revelation of Apollo. When the phenomenon known as "tongues" appeared in the church at Corinth, many accepted the ecstatic nature of the experience as proof of its divine inspiration. It was particularly jolting to the early Christians when some, ostensibly under the influence of the Spirit, cried out, "Jesus be cursed!"

Paul's first concern is to remind the Corinthians not to build their understanding of Christian experience on ideas carried over from "when you were pagans [and] somehow or other . . . influenced and led astray to dumb idols" (1 Cor. 12:2). He assures the Corinthians that no one speaking by the Spirit says "Jesus is cursed" (1 Cor. 12:3). The *content* of the utterance, and not simply the state of the speaker, is to be considered. At this point Paul moves into an extended discussion of the work of the Spirit as He is experienced in the church.

Unity in the Spirit: 1 Corinthians 12:4–11

Paul's first concern is that the Corinthians see the Holy Spirit as the source of spiritual dynamic in the church. Gifts differ, kinds of service differ, effects differ (1 Cor. 12:4–5). But underlying all is the same Spirit, who "works all of them in all men" (1 Cor. 12:6).

Then Paul makes an especially important statement. There is some manifestation of the Spirit given "to each one" (Greek text) and the purpose of this is that each might contribute to "the common good" (1 Cor. 12:7). Clearly, then, no individual should be exalted and no gift given priority over another. Because each believer is gifted, because the Spirit is expressed in each, because the ministry of each is for the common welfare, the awe of the Corinthians at the more "spectacular" expressions of the Spirit is out of place.

At this point Paul provides one of his lists of gifts. The list here includes the message of wisdom (*sophia* emphasizes the ability to apply the truth in practical ways), the message of knowledge, faith, gifts of healing, miraculous power, prophecy, the ability to distinguish between spirits, tongues, and the interpretation of tongues. Paul did not intend this list to be exhaustive, as if these were the only ways the Spirit works through believers in the body of Christ. Instead, Paul refers to the experience of the Corinthian church. He has selected well-known spectacular and nonspectacular gifts to make his point. And so he summarizes: "All these are the work of one and the same Spirit, and he gives them to each man [individual], just as he determines" (1 Cor. 12:11).

Unity in the body: 1 Corinthians 12:12-31

Paul states his theme in the first phrase: "The body is a unit" (1 Cor. 12:12). All believers are brought into a relationship with Christ and each other in the "one body" by a work of the Holy Spirit that Paul calls baptism (1 Cor. 12:13). Every believer participates in the one body. As in a physical body, members of the body of Christ must function *interdependently.* The eye needs the ear, the ear the nose, the arm the leg, and so on. In placing believers in the body, the Holy Spirit, who has given to all believers the spiritual gifts He has chosen for them (1 Cor. 12:11), proceeds to fit the body together so that each part will function in concert. "In fact God has arranged the parts in the body, every one of them, just as he wanted them to be" (1 Cor. 12:18).

This concept of the unity of the body is taught first to help each individual realize that whatever his gift is, God has chosen it specially for him. Thus he can be satisfied rather than dissatisfied with his place. Second, the unity of the body stresses a reality often lost sight of today. Giftedness is not a doctrine of *independent* function. To say I or another has a spiritual gift does not indicate that I should go off alone to hold my own Bible class or to pastor my own congregation as "the" leader. In the context of a coordinated body, gifts are seen to be in *interdependent* relationship. It is when we work with others as teams, with each one contributing his own distinctive gifts, service, and effort, that the function of the body, and the purpose of the gifts, is accomplished. "You are the body of Christ," Paul says, "and each of you is a part of it" (1 Cor. 12:27). No wonder it is irrelevant at this point whether one is an apostle, prophet, teacher, miracle worker, speaker in tongues, or whatever (1 Cor. 12:28-30).

Unity in love: 1 Corinthians 13:1-13

Paul now inserts his famous hymn to love as the "more excellent way." His argument is not that the gifts or their expression in the body are inferior. His point is that if one is to seek a measure for true spirituality, evidence should not be looked for in the particular kind of gift an individual may have. Instead, evidence may be looked for in the love expressed in an individual's life. Love is one of the never-failing evidences of the Spirit's work in the believer (cf. Gal. 5:22). Without love, such gifts as tongues, prophecy, and faith (1 Cor. 13:1–2), and such works as giving all to the poor (1 Cor. 13:3), are empty and meaningless.

As we'll see in Paul's other studies of spiritual gifts, love is, in fact, the dynamic that holds the body together and creates the relational context in which spiritual gifts and ministry can find their full expression. The love Paul speaks of is far from spectacular. It is the simple, daily expression of Christ's concern for and valuing of the other members of the body of Christ.

> Love is patient, love is kind. It does not envy, it does not boast, it is not proud. It is not rude, it is not self-seeking, it is not easily angered, it keeps no record of wrongs. Love does not delight in evil but rejoices in the truth. It always protects, always trusts, always hopes, always perseveres (1 Cor. 13:4–7).

In the body of Christ functioning in unity is made possible by the Spirit's great fruit of love.

Unity in honor and function: 1 Corinthians 14:1–25

We have many reasons to believe that the Corinthian church was placing too much emphasis on the gift of tongues. Paul never suggests that this gift should not be exercised in the church. He does suggest that greater stress should be placed on gifts like prophecy, that have a more direct effect on the "strengthening, encouragement, and comfort" of others (1 Cor. 14:3). When the body gathers, the focus of ministry should be on edifying or building one another up, even to the extent that, unless there is a believer in the group with the gift of interpreting tongues, a tongues speaker should remain silent (1 Cor. 14:13–17). "Unless you speak intelligible words with your tongue, how will anyone know what you are saying?" he asks (1 Cor. 14:9).

There follows a passage that is probably as difficult to interpret as any in the Bible. A fair way to deal with it seems to be to keep strictly to the cultural context. Remember that in Greek culture the ecstatic experience was taken to be an evidence of divine influence. It is not surprising, then, that those whose gifts tended to be ecstatic were treated with some awe and began to take a dominant role in gatherings of the body.

Paul wrote to explain spirituality in theological rather than cultural terms. He put the gift of tongues in perspective as *one* of the gifts in the body. It testifies to a special touching of the Spirit no more than any other gift. Paul has also shown that love is a better indicator of spiritual achievement than gifts. Now he corrects the tendency to let those with the gift of tongues dominate church gatherings. He points out that the Old Testament prophesied that the age of the Spirit would involve speech in strange tongues (1 Cor. 14:21, quoting Isa. 28:11–12). This, he says, is a sign to the *laos* of God, not to unbelievers. Unbelievers might at first view such an ecstatic expression as indicating the touch of God. Yet should an unbeliever come to a gathering of the whole church and everyone speak in tongues at the meeting, the unbeliever would go away with no understanding of what had transpired. But if in the meeting a number are prophesying (which Paul defines in this passage as "speaking with understanding"), then the unbeliever will be convinced by the Word of God and be brought to worship Him.

The major purpose of this passage is to correct an excess in the practice of the Corinthian Christians and to help them better understand how the Holy Spirit works *within* the body.

Unity in worship: 1 Corinthians 14:26–39

In the concluding paragraphs Paul gives one of only two brief descriptions in the New Testament of what happened when the early church met. (The other is an even briefer reference in Heb. 10:23f.) The picture is one of coming together to *minister to each other.* In the context of mutual ministry "everyone has a hymn, or a word of instruction, a revelation, a tongue, or an interpretation" (1 Cor. 14:26). What is especially significant is Paul's next statement: "All of these must be done for the strengthening of the church" (1 Cor. 14:26). Note particularly the relationship of this statement to Paul's first affirmation about gifts: "to each [one] the manifestation of the Spirit is given *for the common good*" (1 Cor. 12:7). The impression we receive from this passage, with its careful explanation of the body, is that the "spiritual gifts" listed in 1 Corinthians *are specific expressions of the Spirit's ministry through believers for the building up of the body of Christ.* That is, those things that we have focused on in our concern with spiritual gifts have a unique focus: they are concerned with ministry *within the body of Christ,* and *not* with some general ministry or giftedness.

It is important to make a distinction here: Spiritual *gift-*

edness is a far more encompassing doctrine than spiritual *gifts*. From the Old Testament on through the New, Scripture is consistent in showing the Holy Spirit as the source of every good human endowment. All kinds of talents, skills, and abilities can be used by God to accomplish His purposes. *Thus the people of God need to learn to see themselves as ministers in every relationship and activity and should see every ability they possess within the framework of God's calling.* When we come to examine the phenomenon sermons and textbooks call "spiritual gifts," we do not look at giftedness and identity in general, but at a narrower issue. *We look at distinctive body truth—the truth that the body exists for the maturing and discipling of its members, and that the gifts deal specifically with maturing.*

While the Book of 1 Corinthians seems to suggest and support this understanding, it's important to realize that the same focus occurs in the other key New Testament Epistles.

Ephesians 3:14–5:1
A prayer for the whole family: Ephesians 3:14–20

Paul's discussion of gifts begins with a prayer. We understand this to be the case because of the phrase, "As a prisoner for the Lord, then, I urge you . . ." (Eph. 4:1). His exhortation builds on the realities dealt with in the prayer.

Key elements of the prayer explore relationships in the body of Christ. Paul begins by affirming that the church takes its identity from God. He calls God the Father, "from whom the whole family of believers in heaven and on earth derives its name" (Eph. 3:14). He is Father: we derive the name "family" from that aspect of His nature.

Paul asks for inner strengthening, so that Christians might experience the full reality of a Christ in residence in their hearts. He then prays that they, "being rooted and established in love, may have power, together with all the saints, to grasp how wide and long and high and deep is the love of Christ, and . . . be filled to the measure of all the fullness of God" (Eph. 3:17–18). The love Paul refers to here is love within the family. This is the same theme Jesus emphasized in John 13:33f., and Paul in 1 Corinthians 13. Unity in love is essential, for it is together that we grow to the full measure of our potential in Christ.

Unity in the body: Ephesians 4:1–6

Since we have been called to live and grow together as a family (Eph. 4:1), we are to "be completely humble and gentle;

117

[and] patient, bearing with one another in love" (Eph. 4:2). We are also to "make every effort to keep the unity of the Spirit through the bond of peace" (Eph. 4:3). As in 1 Corinthians, Paul again stresses the unity of the body. "There is one body and one Spirit—just as you were called to one hope when you were called—one Lord, one faith, one baptism; one God and Father of all . . ." (Eph. 4:4–5).

God's gifts to the body: Ephesians 4:7–16

In this passage the gifts are persons rather than special endowments. We are not told what endowments an apostle (Eph. 4:11) has, for instance, and we thus cannot correlate such things as faith, tongues, etc., from 1 Corinthians. This itself is an indication of the wisdom of God. If we could correlate them, we could become so involved in details that we would again miss the thrust of the passage!

What is that thrust? Simply that gifted individuals, like special endowments, are placed within the body "to prepare God's people for works of service, so that the body of Christ may be built up until we all reach unity in the faith and in the knowledge of the Son of God and become mature, attaining to the whole measure of the fullness of Christ" (Eph. 4:12–13; cf. 4:13b with 3:18b). The gifts to the Corinthians were for "the common good" and "the strengthening of the church." The gifts to the Ephesians were to "build up" the church toward maturity. This growth is said to take place, and the body to build itself up in love, when "each part does its work" (Eph. 4:16).

The context of love: Ephesians 4:17–5:1

Paul then returns to the relational context in which this kind of ministry is to take place. Having come to know Christ, the Christian is to put off the old self and former ways of life (Eph. 4:22) and "to put on the new self," which is "created to be like God in true righteousness and holiness" (Eph. 4:24). Bitterness, rage, and anger are to be replaced by kindness, compassion, and forgiveness (Eph. 4:31–32). The members of the body are to "be imitators of God, therefore, as dearly loved children, and live a life of love, just as Christ loved us and gave himself up for us as a fragrant offering and sacrifice to God" (Eph. 5:1–2).

Romans 12:1–17

Romans 12, the third basic passage dealing with spiritual gifts, begins with an exhortation to believers (Rom. 12:1–3).

In view of God's mercy, we are to offer ourselves to God to work His will out in our lives and to experience His transformation. Immediately after this exhortation Paul turns to the context in which this transformation is to take place: the body of Christ.

The unity of the body: Romans 12:3-8

Paul urges believers to see themselves within the context of the body rather than as isolated individuals. "Don't think of yourselves more highly than you ought," he says. Instead believers are to see themselves as part of a body, to which they each contribute. "Just as each of us has one body with many members, and these members do not all have the same function, so in Christ we who are many form one body, and each member belongs to all the others" (Rom. 12:4-5). Note that here as in other passages the focus is on relationships *within* the body, rather than on the relationships of individual believers or of the body to the larger community.

In this clearly focused context Paul says, "We have different gifts, according to the grace given us" (Rom. 12:6). Again a number of gifts are listed: prophesying, serving, teaching, encouraging, contributing to the needs of others, leadership, showing mercy. (Note that this list differs from the one in 1 Corinthians; this is evidence that neither list is intended to be inclusive of all gifts.) The purpose of the list is to urge believers to use responsibly whatever gifts they have.

The importance of love: Romans 12:9-17

As do the other passages on the body and gifts, this passage emphasizes living together in love. Love provides the context in which the gifts of the body function and growth takes place. "Love must be sincere," Paul writes (Rom. 12:9). He describes love in practical ways—being devoted to one another, sharing with God's people in need, hospitality, sharing the joys and sorrows of others, rejecting pride and associating with people of "low position," etc.

The chart on page 120 summarizes the similarities and differences between the three gift passages. Each context in which a list of gifts is found is a context in which Paul's subject is the body of Christ. Gifts are part of the diversity through which the unity of the body of Christ is formed and by which each believer serves as a part of that body.

The gifts themselves are from God. They are manifestations of the Spirit, given as Christ, the head of the body, has apportioned them. The teaching is that each believer has one or more gifts. What we need to realize is that in each passage

119

FIGURE 3
EMPHASES IN GIFT/BODY PASSAGES

	1 Corinthians 12–14	Ephesians 3, 4	Romans 12
Body			
unity	"is a unit" (12:12) "all . . . form one body" (12:12)	"there is one body" (4:4)	"many form one body" (12:5)
diversity	"made up of many parts" (12:12; cf. 14, 27) each indispensable (12:12)	"He . . . gave some to be . . ." (4:11)	"members do not all have the same function" (12:4)
everyone a part	"all baptized . . . into one body" (12:13; cf. 26)	"as each part does its work" (4:16)	"each member belongs" (12:5)
Gifts			
God the source	"manifestation of the Spirit" (12:7; cf. 8–11)	"given as Christ apportioned it" (4:7)	"we have different gifts" (12:6)
all possess	"to each [one] is given . . ." (12:7)		"to all the others" (12:5)
purpose	"for the common good" (12:7) "for the strengthening of the church" (14:26) "build up the church" (14:12)	"that the body of Christ may be built up" (4:12) "whole body . . . grows and builds itself up" (4:16)	
Love			
essential	"if I . . . have not love, I am nothing" (13:2)	"rooted and established in love" (3:7) "live a life worthy of . . ." (5:1)	"Love must be sincere" (12:9)
practical	12:26; 13:4–7	4:25–32	12:9–17

the purpose of the gifts is the maturing and equipping of the body. Thus each gifted believer is given "to all the others" (Rom. 12:5). Each is to exercise his or her gift for the common good, and for the strengthening of the church. Every gift is given that the body of Christ may be built up and the whole church may grow and build itself up in love.

A third focus the passage has in common with the others is on relationships between members of the one body. For the effective functioning of the body and these particular gifts, a love relationship is vital. God's people must be rooted and established in love; they are to "live in harmony with each other" (Rom. 12:16).

Giftedness

Our brief exploration of giftedness allows us to draw a number of conclusions. Each of them is significant when we are dealing with the issue of personal ministries in the local church.

Giftedness is a far more inclusive concept than the contemporary church has taught

Believers can and should see every talent and ability in perspective as an endowment by the Holy Spirit and thus be encouraged to use every ability in the service of God.

Those passages that we have traditionally studied to understand gifts make no effort to describe them

Instead, the list of gifts appear in context as *illustrations from the known experience* of believers in Rome or Corinth. The lists are not comprehensive, nor are they self-explanatory. They simply illustrate ways in which the Holy Spirit expresses Himself within the body as its members minister to one another. The focus of all the gift passages is on our identity as members of a living body.

- Because of our identity as members of a body, we see the necessity of living in unity with other believers. We must live together in harmony and unity, for no body can function when its parts are separated from one another.
- Because of our identity as members of a body, we belong to one another and are to serve and build one another up in every way possible.
- Because the body grows by "every supporting ligament" (Eph. 4:16), each of us is to affirm his identity as a minister within the body.

- Because the unity of the body is essential, we are to concentrate on developing close, loving relationships with one another. It is in the context of these loving relationships that the gifts associated with the body function.

We should not limit our attention to attempts to understand the gifts enumerated in the various New Testament lists. Instead we should focus our attention where the Scriptures focus our attention—on understanding the nature of the body as a loving community within which each one of us ministers to build up his brothers and sisters in the Lord.

The "body gifts" are designed to bring individuals and the Christian community to maturity

Every believer has a call to maturity and full commitment. Christians have a right to expect the local congregation to function in such a way that it will grow toward maturity. The primary purpose of the gathered church is not evangelism, but nurture. The gatherings of the local body as the church are to focus on the maturity of the believers. The "body gifts" have been given to make believers mature. Thus gatherings of believers should be designed to encourage members to minister to one another.

For instance, an evangelist like Billy Graham functions within the context of the body. Prayer meetings are organized, committees formed, personal workers trained, and follow-up teams developed—from the churches. In the process of the campaign many members of the body are involved at every level, and through their involvement many are trained for greater effectiveness in their own evangelism. In this way Billy Graham functions as an evangelist given to the church to "equip" the believers for their ministering work.

There are other concepts implicit and explicit in these passages. There is no notion here of any distinction in the body between "clergy" and "laity." The work of the Spirit is in all and through all. Every believer, as a member of the *laos* of God, is a minister. Leaders in the church, as servants of the servants of God, are to guide others into the exercise of their gifts so that the whole body might grow. The "superstar" approach to ministry is clearly rejected, for each member's function is vital to the growth of the body, and thus indispensible. As there is cooperation between muscles, bones, joints, and ligaments in a human body, so in the body of Christ ministry is a coordinated or team effort.

In view of these significant conclusions, debate over the place of tongues in the present age or attention to the lists of body gifts (without any recognition that they are body gifts and do not sum up the Bible's teaching on giftedness) may be more harmful than helpful. Nor is it especially helpful for individual believers to speculate about what their spiritual gifts may be. Instead we need to focus our attention as God's people on the Bible's teaching about the nature of the body of Christ. We need to live out the reality of the body in unity and love. As we live out that reality and support and minister to one another, spiritual gifts will appear. It is then, when the gifts are actually functioning in the body as they were in the Corinthian community, that our teaching can be meaningful. Then individuals in our congregations will discover through teaching and experience what their spiritual gifts are.

PROBE

▶ *case histories*
▶ *discussion questions*
▶ *thought provokers*
▶ *resources*

1. Survey at least five books dealing with spiritual gifts. Write a five-page summary of the following questions: (a) Are gifts viewed only in the context of the New Testament lists, or is a broader concept of giftedness explored? (b) How is the understanding of gifts specifically related to the teaching of Scripture concerning the body of Christ? (c) What major emphases noted in this chapter are included or ignored in the books surveyed?

2. PROJECTS: After each lesson in the study of giftedness, it is meaningful to extend the learning process with a project that is personal and practical. This opens each individual to the discovery aspect of learning something new, exciting.

   In addition, the projects help to nurture the creative side of our personalities. The projects should be diverse enough to catch the interest of all who are a part of the learning experience. The following are a number of projects that were used during the study of Giftedness at the Trinity Church:
   A. Work in your yard for one hour this week and then write up your thoughts/feelings.
   B. The birds will soon return north: select a bird you would like to attract and build a bird house. Bring your finished product to class, share your thoughts/insights with all of us, then take the "house" home and hang it. Have fun waiting for your renters!

      Some of you don't like yard work, and are not bird watchers, so here are some options for you:

C. Write a song, with words and music. Come and share it with the entire class or your Mirror Group.
D. Write a poem or a prayer to be shared.
E. Write daily in your Journal.
F. Read a biography or an autobiography.
G. Visit a sick person, a shut-in, or someone in prison.
H. Help a stranger in some way.
I. Bake a pie, a cake, or rolls and invite a friend or two in to share your treat. Share what you're learning about giftedness.
J. Arrange to take a child/shut-in to a ball game, or to a park, or a movie, etc. In some way, seek to share your faith with that person and learn about their journey with God.
K. Paint a picture of a fruit tree illustrating the seasons of the year.
L. If none of the above appeal to you, design your own project and share it with the class.

3. CASE HISTORIES

A. VERN: Vern chose to bake a cherry pie. This was to be his first experience in baking. He shared with his wife what he was going to do. She considered it a bit bizarre, but turned the kitchen over to him. He found a recipe and proceeded. All turned out well, so he called a couple of his male companions to come and share an evening with him. He reported the following:

"I was like a kid out of school! Here I was, 54 years old, and I had baked my first pie. It was fun. I opened me up to a creative side of myself that I had never before discerned. I wondered how I would share this experience with two of my non-Christian friends. It was as natural as falling off a log! For a number of years I wanted to share Christ personally with these guys, but it never seemed to happen, but on this occasion it did! One of the fellows asked, 'What in the world are you up to?' (Except he used a little different language!) I began to share how God had given gifts to His people and that I was seeking to discover my areas of giftedness in order that I might serve Him better. Then I told them, quite plainly, about God's gift of life in His Son. We talked for over two hours. We enjoyed the pie together. They thanked me for a great evening. I feel two feet taller!"

B. DOROTHY: At Trinity, Dorothy is a very special friend to many of us. God has given her a spirit of compassion, a love of giving, and ability to encourage and lift the spirits of many. Dorothy chose to bake a pie, but to do something very different than Vern. Listen to her thoughts:

"When you gave the assignment, immediately I had the urge to bake a pie for a dear friend. I wanted to surprise her, to bless her. I had this recipe for an 'Ole Fashion Raisin-Walnut Pie.' It's really yummy! Everyone loves it who likes raisins. I could hardly wait to get it baked. It was so much fun. I just knew they would love it. When I delivered the pie, my friend was so delighted. Her whole family responded to this little bit of love. As I reflected on this experience, the following thoughts surfaced: The pie was a way to express what this dear friend means to me. I was free to give without expecting anything in return. Grace. I found a deep satisfaction in just doing. I was blessed in my spirit as I watched their joy of receiving my 'Ole Fashion Raisin-Walnut Pie!' Now isn't God good!"

4. Outlines of two lessons from a series on spiritual gifts taught in a training seminar at Trinity follow. From these two lesson plans you should get a feel for the structure and some of the learning activities that can help develop giftedness in the local congregation.

Lesson 1: Spiritual Gift Seminar

> Introduction to Discerning Spiritual Gifts, How They
> Relate to God's Revealed Will, and the Believer's
> Priesthood and Service

INTRODUCTION:
- Singing together
- Prayer
- Introductory remarks concerning the course of study: Journal, projects, Mirror Group Concept, books, and Scripture passages.

Solomon, a man of unusual wisdom, a man who had the ability to observe life, both within his heart and external to himself, noted that, when men were determined to have an audience with him, then the king of Israel, they would come with some choice gift to present him. The former President Nixon exchanged gifts with Chairman Mao of Red China. It is the "thing to do" with heads of states.

Solomon noted the practice and saw in it a spiritual application. He wrote: "A man's gift makes room for him, and brings him before great men" (Prov. 18:16).

In this little statement of truth is the dynamic of a course on spiritual gifts. In this statement God gives us a key to exciting, useful, spirit-filled living. The Scriptures over and over again teach that God has given gifts to His creature, man; He has given gifted men to minister to the needs of all men, that they in turn would discern their gifts and talents and thus serve their Creator with joy.

Our gifts are designed to enable us to be sent on a mission. They are God's way of making "room" for us, and in time bringing us before men and women of greatness.

Elizabeth O'Connor in *Eighth Day of Creation,* writes that a primary purpose of the church is to help us discover our gifts and, in the face of fears, to hold us accountable for them so that we can enter the joy of creating. This is a profound observation. It underlines a desire God has put in my heart. I have always wanted to be a part of a body of believers that understood what the Word of God teaches and applied fully what they had come to understand. But only through a complete knowledge and acceptance of the biblical teaching on spiritual gifts can this happen. The more we see the gifts of the Holy Spirit in the context of the body of Christ, the greater will be our service to the world and our worship of our great, great God.

Paul wrote the Corinthian church: "Follow the way of love and desire spiritual gifts . . ." (1 Cor. 14:10). He also told them: "Now about spiritual gifts, I do not want you to be ignorant" (1 Cor. 12:1).

Peter wrote: "Each one should use whatever gift he has received to serve others, faithfully administering God's grace in its various forms" (1 Peter 4:10). And again Paul said to the church of Rome: "We have different gifts, according to the grace given us" (Rom. 12:6).

Only through a complete knowledge and acceptance of the biblical teaching on spiritual gifts can the church of Jesus Christ be strong enough and able enough to attack the evil of the world system in a unified way . . . the way Christ prayed in His high priestly prayer in John 17!

Mirror Group Concept: At this time, I will assign each of you to a Mirror Group. Tonight you will have two assignments to complete:

I. Each of you in the group will in as concise yet complete a way as possible share your testimony of faith in Christ . . . wherever you are spiritually . . . whatever your testimony is.

II. Then I want you to turn to Ephesians 4 and discuss what you believe a pastor's, an evangelist's, and a prophet's major work is in the body of Christ.
   A. Appoint a reporter;
   B. Appoint a prior (person of high rank);

126

C. Write the names of everyone in your group on a card as a prayer reminder;

D. Conclude with two to three minutes of sentence prayers, with the prior closing.

THE MIRROR GROUP CONCEPT: Proverbs 18:16

INTRODUCTION: Pages 55–56, *The Church at the End of the Twentieth Century* (F. Schaeffer). The Mirror Group Concept is designed to highlight the body aspect of Christ's church.

It is designed to seek authentic community with those within that unique body. The gifts help develop a sense of community, of being one in Christ through many members!

The Mirror Group Concept is designed to allow everyone to have an opportunity to share . . . not just the gregarious.

For example, Jesus taught the Mirror Group Concept; He selected only twelve to be with Him. He said things like: "For where two or three come together in my name, there am I with them" (Matt. 18:20).

This suggests to me that God can often work in special ways within the small group in contrast to the larger group (Matt. 18:18f.).

James wrote: "Confess your sins [not your wife's or your husband's; there need be no betrayal!] to each other and pray for each other so that you may be healed" (James 5:16). Selfishness, pride, and ignorance will keep this from happening. But God said to confess . . . and to each other . . . (elders).

"How can we become more faithful in praying for those in our Mirror Group?" someone asked last week. Be creative: Write names on a card . . . Put the card in an obvious place . . . Call each other toward the end of the week . . . Pray over the phone. Agree to get together . . . for a work-fellowship time.

JOURNAL

Why a journal? This will serve as a very important part of the discovery process. I urge every one of you to make daily entries in your journal. Please remember that this is not a diary, but more of an "idea notebook" to stimulate growth in both mind and spirit. God is concerned that we think about certain experiences He gives us, so that we will not quickly forget the lessons that He intends us to learn from these life experiences lest we miss His best in time for us. Writing tends to concretize our thinking, help us identify our weaknesses as well as our strengths, and help us discover our gifts. Concern yourself with the following Scriptures: Deuteronomy 6:9f.; Habakkuk 2:1f.; Exodus 24:4; Luke 1:1–4; Matthew 4:1–11; 1 Corinthians 10:11; Romans 15:4; 1 John 1:4; 2 Peter 3:1f.

PROJECTS

During our course of study there will be an opportunity to participate in a number of projects. These projects are also designed to enable us to enter into the discovery process. Whenever projects are assigned, there will be a number of options from which you can select. It is important at these times to make your selection and to be faithful in completing the project you select. More information will be given concerning the projects as the course develops.

SCRIPTURE REFERENCES

Romans 12
Matthew 25
1 Corinthians 12, 13, 14
Ephesians 4
1 Peter 4:7–11
1 Timothy 4:11–16

2 Timothy 1:3–7
1 Corinthians 1:3–7
1 Corinthians 1:4–9
Romans 11:29
Romans 6:23
Romans 1:1–12

Matthew 4:16
James 1:16–18
Proverbs 18:16
Proverbs 25:14
2 Corinthians 2:14–16

SUGGESTED BOOKS

Elizabeth O'Connor, *Call to Commitment*
Elizabeth O'Connor, *Eighth Day of Creation*
Agnes Sanford, *The Healing Gifts of the Spirit*
Ray Stedman, *Body Life*
Robert E. Coleman, *The Master Plan of Evangelism*
Standard commentaries on Romans, 1 Corinthians, Ephesians, 1 Peter

Biographies and autobiographies of men and women of the faith:
J. C. Pollock, *Billy Graham*
A. T. Pierson, *George Mueller of Bristol*
Brother Andrew, *God's Smuggler*
Bob Harrison, *When God Was Black*

SUBJECT MATTER to be covered in the spiritual gift series:
How to discern your gift or gifts
How the body's needs and the believer's gifts are related

A Gifted People

Gifts: God's key to honest, holy living
Spiritual growth through the use of your gifts
Hurdles to be hurdled
The joy of creating in God's world: your priestly work
A journey into reality
The difference between natural talents and spiritual gifts
Gifts and the Great Commission

• • •

Lesson 4: Spiritual Gifts
    The Difference Between Gifts *(Charismata)*, Ministries
      (Diakoniai) and Experiences *(Energemata)*

INTRODUCTION: In lesson 3 we looked at the most important concept to be grasped if we are going to develop an adequate theology concerning biblical teaching about our spiritual gifts. First, we noted that Paul was concerned that we not be "ignorant" about the whole subject of spiritual gifts *(pneumatika)*. Paul suggests that to be ignorant in this important area of revelation is to be insensitive to the ministry of the Holy Spirit (1 Cor. 12:1–3). Second, we observed that the character of inspiration and revelation is not to be judged by its form, that is, prophecy, tongues, healing, teaching, etc., but by its *tendency*, or its *propensity*.

Illustration #1:   If the tendency of the utterance or effect amounts to saying, "Jesus be cursed!" then it is not divinely inspired. The Spirit of God always glorifies the Son (John 16).

Illustration #2:   If the tendency of the utterance, etc., amounts to saying, "Jesus is Lord!" then it is divinely inspired. It is our task to be alert to the ministry of the Holy Spirit.

Following this, we looked briefly at the three key words in this study:

                    Gifts *(charismata;* 1 Cor. 12:4)
                    Ministries *(diakoniai;* 1 Cor. 12:4)
                    Experiences *(energemata;* 1 Cor. 12:6)

Tonight we will continue the research on these three word-concepts so that we can build a very firm and biblically sound foundation for the remainder of this study.

129

THEOLOGICAL CORE

1 CORINTHIANS 12:1f.: VARIETIES OF GIFTS
(12:4—CHARISMATA)

In 1 Corinthians 12:7 Paul tells us that "... to each one the manifestation of the Spirit is given for the common good." The word "manifestation" is from the Greek word *phaneros* meaning "open to one's sight, visible, manifest." The root of this word is *phos*, meaning "light" (Matt. 5:16).

Therefore, these gifts and ministries and experiences are not hidden, but are open to observation. Thus we have the body of Christ, we have the various projects, and we have the journal to enable us to become more observant of what God has given to His church.

Since Paul teaches that these manifestations are in three dimensions, let us look at some illustrations and charts that will help us get a mental picture of this truth ... that it might "shine" *(phaino)* in our hearts and minds! Let us look at a comparison, a very apt one, I believe, THE TRINITY.

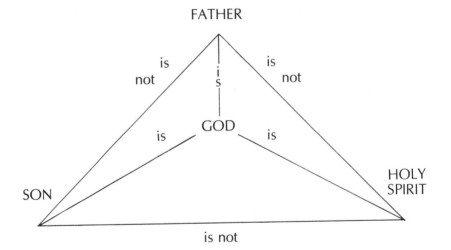

There is only one God (Deut. 6; Mark 12), yet He is revealed in three persons. If you divide the teaching of the Trinity without again uniting it, you pervert the truth of God. This is the work of *every major cult* in the world.

I discern that the same truth is relevant to the biblical concept of gifts. The gifts of God are triune in nature. We can look at the various parts and must study the truth of it, but we must always see them in their relationship to each other. Otherwise we pervert the core truth.

1. Picture the interrelationships of the three orders of gifts.

GIFTS	MINISTRIES	EXPERIENCES
Aptitude	Ordination	Word effected (result)
Creative powers	Administrations	Operations
Distribution	*Recognition*	*Contribution*
(1 Cor. 12:11)	(1 Tim. 4:14) (Order)	(1 Tim. 4:15) (2 Tim. 4:5)
1. By the Holy Spirit	1. When ordained by elders (church)	1. To the body of Christ To the world
2. WHEN? At the moment of salvation	2. WHEN? At the time of ordination the body recognizes the gifted one.	2. WHEN? When "gift," "ministry," and "the Holy Spirit" work together.
3. HOW MANY? Seven powers, gifts, aptitudes	3. HOW MANY? Infinite number	3. HOW MANY? Infinite number
4. Gifts of the first order (Rom. 12)	4. Gifts of the second order (Eph. 4)	4. Gifts of the third order (1 Cor. 12:7)

THEOLOGICAL CORE

(Keep in mind that the following is *only* an illustration of this principle; there are not enough books to print all the options!

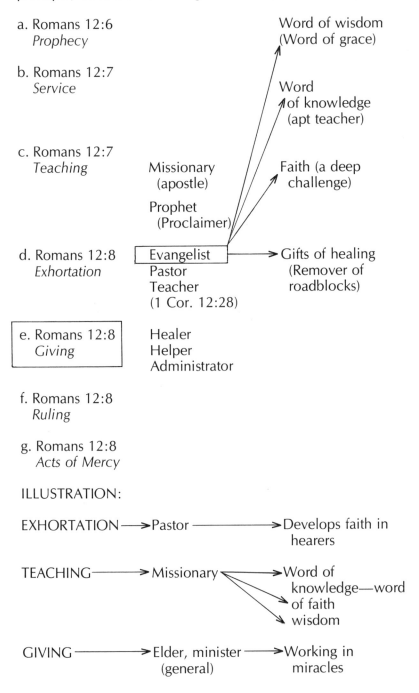

a. Romans 12:6
  Prophecy

b. Romans 12:7
  Service

c. Romans 12:7
  Teaching

Missionary (apostle)

Prophet (Proclaimer)

Word of wisdom (Word of grace)

Word of knowledge (apt teacher)

Faith (a deep challenge)

d. Romans 12:8
  Exhortation

Evangelist
Pastor
Teacher
(1 Cor. 12:28)

Gifts of healing (Remover of roadblocks)

e. Romans 12:8
  Giving

Healer
Helper
Administrator

f. Romans 12:8
  Ruling

g. Romans 12:8
  Acts of Mercy

ILLUSTRATION:

EXHORTATION ⟶ Pastor ⟶ Develops faith in hearers

TEACHING ⟶ Missionary ⟶ Word of knowledge—word of faith wisdom

GIVING ⟶ Elder, minister (general) ⟶ Working in miracles

CONCLUSIONS:

The Bible uses the word "gifts" and the word "gift" in a number of very different ways. It is the work of the student (believer) to discern the difference in the usage by studying the *context* in which it is used. This is hard work, but it is absolutely necessary if we ever hope, once again, to see the body of Christ as a whole experiencing the blessing of the "abundant life" that Jesus promised.

Take note:

A. We can be committed to Christ, the Giver of every "good and perfect gift," and still not be committed to His many gifts. This is traditionalism.
B. We can be committed to seeking the gifts of Christ to His body and fail to serve either God or man. This is cultishness.
C. We can learn the truth about the Giver and His gifts to the body, and in the power of the Holy Spirit serve both God and man with greater joy and effectiveness. Remember: The Giver has chosen to give gifts. The gifts, therefore, are to bring glory to our God and Savior. This is discovering a living faith.

MIRROR GROUPS:

1. Introduce new members into the group.
2. Pray as friends, each taking part.
3. Share what God is teaching through your journal projects. (Please learn to be brief, yet complete.)
4. Prior: Make a list of those who will share (this helps to speed up the process).
5. Seek to help those who are having a problem grasping the ideas that are being shared.

PROJECTS:

1. Complete the first two that you chose to do first (check your notes).
2. Options for the week: bake a pie, a cake, or rolls, and invite a friend or two in for an evening of fellowship.
3. Arrange to take a child to a ball game, boating, to a movie, or for a hike in the woods. In some way share your faith with that child.
4. Paint a picture of a fruit tree in the winter, spring, and late summer.

5. This chapter has stressed the mutuality or "body context" of ministry. Even those in "professional" ministry are to live interdependently and function interdependently with others in the *laos,* who are as fully "ministers" as they. Yet this is often a difficult challenge for those trained for "full-time" ministry.

THEOLOGICAL CORE

Jack Wood, whom we met earlier, continues his story in the following paragraphs and shares the results of his struggle. His wife, Mary Lou, shares her views also. Each helps us see something of the attitudinal change and emotional turmoil that is involved in working toward the development of a *laos* that is functioning according to the biblical view of spiritual gifts.

JACK WOOD

God began to show me that the biblical pattern of leadership was a group of elders. Eldership was a new word to me. My background taught me that the leaders of the church were a pastor and deacons, with the church operating as a democracy. There were often ugly political power struggles. There were contests between the pastor and the board of deacons, and a triangle between the membership and the pastor and the board of deacons. The result was many scars and hurts.

It was not easy for me, therefore, to learn to trust an eldership or a group of leaders or to subject my recommendations to a group. I had been in contests with boards all my life, and I had had a lot of negative experiences with the "democratic" political process. I agreed with my elders that no decision would be implemented without the agreement of every elder. We concluded that the Lord did not want His church to follow Robert's *Rules of Order* or operate in a "democratic" way. We were sure the Holy Spirit was to direct us, and we waited on Him and sought the mind of God. If one of the eight elders disagreed with a recommendation, it was rejected.

I was surprised at the harmony and unity that resulted. Little by little I began to trust in the board of elders and feel more secure. I had always thought that freedom was getting away from those guys and being independent, making decisions on my own. I never thought freedom would result from the security of being surrounded by men who love me.

God had to take me through a process, and right in the middle of my depression I had these men come to me and say, "Jack, we love you and we really feel like you need a break. How would you like a sabbatical? A paid vacation for a year, or an open-ended one?" This was overwhelming! God was trying to say to me, "Hey, learn to trust. Learn to trust these men. They have your welfare at heart and they are not going to string you up by your toes and hang you from the church steeple." So I went on a sabbatical!

I now feel secure about not having a quasi-dictatorial power to make decisions on my own. I am beginning to realize that the input, wisdom, discernment, and gifts of my elders through the

Holy Spirit are so desperately needed to balance mine that I am now afraid to make any decision without them.

I haven't arrived yet. I'm still learning to relax when I can't be independent and say, "This is *my* church," or "I sat on this egg and hatched it." It was hard because I had, as a matter of fact, hatched this congregation from an egg; it was my "chick" from the very beginning. My attitude was bad, and I got very protective. It was hard to give up the reins to the people and say, "This is your responsibility." When we first began to talk of the death of the clergy and of the priesthood of all believers, I could see why it was so hard for some people to comprehend. I knew it was something that the Holy Spirit had to bring to pass. At first it was just words, no reality. But God told me to say the words until the reality was mine. Gradually He brought me into a priesthood of all believers and an acceptance of a plurality of leadership.

I'm not really sure why I was so busy as a pastor. I always thought it was because I was a really needed person, that the Lord needed me, that He had given me the gift of love, that I had a shepherd's heart, and all the rest. I don't deny that even now. He has given me a shepherd's heart and a deep love for people. But most of my activity was in response to people's expectations. I wasn't strong enough to say no. And my ego needed to be gratified, too.

But I found that Christ was capable of running His church and meeting people's needs, without my help. I learned that He wanted me to leave my magic wand, stop waving it over people's heads, stop saving the world, stop feeling so responsible. I realized He is the Good Shepherd, and He doesn't need so much help. I am still too busy to this day.

At first I got heavily into counseling. So many people were coming off the street that the counseling load became overwhelming. Then the Lord said, "Hey, there are people out there who are just as capable as you are, if not more so. Stop limiting My grace." He began to send people from among the body. All the people who are on the staff now, either volunteer or paid, are from the body itself. We have never gone outside our body to find leadership. The ministry has been here—it was just a matter of recognizing it! We don't appoint anyone—the Lord appoints them through the Holy Spirit. We are here to discern their appointment and recognize the ministry they have.

So what we have been doing is watching the Lord bring forth leadership, ministry, in the body. We are very careful not to appoint anyone, set anyone up, or put anyone down. We make room. We believe that a man's gift makes room for itself.

Right now, I do considerable counseling. But I am finding

more and more that my role is ministering to those who minister to others. In other words, I feel my first responsibility is to the elder-ship, the elders' first responsibility is to the group leaders, and the group leaders' first responsibility is to the saints.

MARY LOU WOOD

One thing that is important before any ministry can take place is for each of us to recognize our need to be ministered to. As a pastor's wife I had a real problem with this idea. I thought I had to have all the answers. I thought that was expected of me. No matter what was actually going on in my life, I was to project complete-ness to the members of the congregation.

So it was really a hard thing for me, a matter of pride, I sup-pose. I had been taught by every pastor that we worked with that this was the role I was to play. I had the answer, and I was never to show weakness. I can remember one time when Jack was an assistant pastor—it was our first position—when a person walked up to me and said, "Mary Lou, what is wrong today?"

I said, "You know, I'm just feeling tired."

The pastor overheard us, and he brought both my husband and me into his office and reprimanded us—all because I had ac-knowledged that I was tired.

I became an effective minister to others. But I was not receiv-ing at all.

It has only been in the last year that the Lord has begun teach-ing me that I need to be ministered to. I'm learning that there are other gifts within the body, and just because one person has a gift I don't have I don't need to be uneasy about it. Rather than feeling uneasy, I can be blessed by that person's gift if I accept it. It can become part of my life if I simply acknowledge that it is there. That is really special. I shared with you, Larry, that one day when I was reading your book, I suddenly laid it down and said, "Lord, re-member all those neat things that I used to do for You?" I was such a doer, Larry. And the Lord began to laugh. I could hear Him laugh, and say, "Mary Lou, you did such a super job of tying fruit on the branches!"

If someone else had said that to me it would have hurt, but He did it with such humor and gentleness that I said, "You're right, Lord." We laughed together. And He said, "Didn't you notice that it withered the next day?" I told Him I had noticed that no matter how hard I tried, it always seemed to wither. He said, "If you will come and abide in Me and let Me produce the fruit, not only will it not wither, but there will be enough fruit for others to enjoy."

This is my ministry. You may produce one type of fruit and I another, but if we come together in the body I can enjoy the fruit of your ministry and you can enjoy the fruit of mine.

We are not touchy or edgy about this. We don't feel threatened. So it can grow, and we become whole people.

Just the other day I was having a rough day. There was no one here, so I called a friend in the church and told him I was having a rough time. I felt as if something in me needed prayer, but I wasn't able to put my finger on it. I asked him if I could come over and have him and his wife pray for me. Even before I put my feet out of the door, peace came to me, and I knew that by subjecting myself to their ministry God was pleased. He was wearing down the pride in me and releasing the falseness that I had put there so long ago.

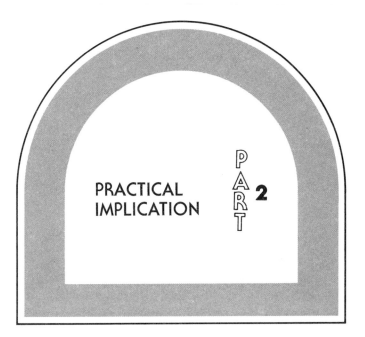

PRACTICAL
IMPLICATION

PART 2

PART 2

PRACTICAL IMPLICATION

Identity Implications
Communicating Vision
Building Relationships and Community
Making Disciples
Equipping
Extending Freedom
Understanding Leadership

IDENTITY IMPLICATIONS

History and culture, not theology, are the source of many of the practices we find in the contemporary local church. This is true whether we explore educational ministry[1] or leadership practices.[2] It is also true in the area of the personal ministries of the people of God. An artificial and wholly inaccurate division of the *laos* into a "full-time ministry" and a part-time or passive laity is deeply entrenched.

As a result, a number of unbiblical practices exist in our churches. Ministries that are open to the laity are almost exclusively service in one of the agencies or programs of the local church. Church structures institutionalize control of the laity rather than develop personal responsibility in them. In general, these practices have not been evaluated theologically. They have simply been accepted as the way the church does (and therefore should) operate in our society.

It's natural to accept practices and values that have grown up over the years and that reflect the culture in which we live. Most of us will sense something "right" about practices that have been part of our experience for so long. And there is, of course, no reason to challenge traditions just for the sake of change.

CHAPTER 7

On the other hand, Scripture warns against conforming to the pattern of this world (Rom. 12:1–2). We are a people who have been called to evaluate our practices, our values, and our assumptions by the light provided in God's revelation. The Word of God stands in judgment over every human society and culture, and it is only by the Word that we gain a perspective to make adequate evaluations. This fact underlies Paul's prescription for renewal: "Be transformed," he writes, "by the renewing of your mind." The Greek word translated "mind" is *nous*. While seldom used in the New Testament (some thirty-six times in one form or another), it is nevertheless a significant term. In the noun form, *nous* speaks of the faculty of religious judgment or insight.[3] It was the *nous* Christ opened after His resurrection when He walked with His disciples and communicated the real meaning of the Scriptures associated with His death (Luke

---

[1]See Larry Richards, *A Theology of Christian Education* (Grand Rapids: Zondervan Publishing House, 1975).

[2]See Larry Richards, and Clyde Hoeldtke, *A Theology of Church Leadership* (Grand Rapids: Zondervan Publishing House, 1980).

[3]See the article on "Reason" in Colin Brown, ed., *The New International Dictionary of New Testament Theology*, 3 vols. (Grand Rapids: Zondervan Publishing House, 1976–1978), 3:126f.

24:45). The New Testament expectation is that a right understanding of God's truth leads to a renewed perspective or outlook. Our outlook will involve facts, values, and attitudes necessary to bring our approach to life into full harmony with God's revelation of reality. The goal of the renewed *nous* is always that, by evaluating from His new perspective, we might be "able to test and approve what God's will is" (Rom. 12:2). This means we are to let God's revelation stand in judgment over our ways of life. Through the vision of reality presented by God, our own outlook is to be transformed. The transformed outlook provides us with a grasp of the will of God, and we are to follow the vision obediently, to test and approve God's will that *will* prove to be "good, pleasing and perfect" (Rom. 12:2).

Our goal in exploring the structures of congregational life, then, is never to be critical or negative. It is always to evaluate. We are charged by God to resist mindless conformity to *any* tradition and to distinguish between practices that are patterned after this world and those that are patterned on eternal realities. In a very real way it is the task of theology to explore those eternal realities that help us evaluate our life in the world. This is why in order to evaluate we must first define theologically (that is, by God's revelation of reality) the issues involved in the area to be explored.

The first part of the present text sought to define core theological truths that must be considered if we are to have God's perspective on personal ministries and giftedness. With a theology thus defined, we can now suggest some of the implications. *Then* we have a basis both to evaluate present practices and to develop ways of living together as Christ's church that better express God's plan for His body.

REVIEW OF CORE THEOLOGY

We began our study by exploring what it means to be the people *(laos)* of God. We saw that the term "people" in the Old Testament spoke of a special relationship between Israel and the Lord. Israel found her identity in this relationship. God was understood and known as the "God of Abraham" and the "God of our fathers." This designation and the relationship of belonging it portrays was formalized in unbreakable biblical covenants that God made with Abraham and his descendants.

In the New Testament the *laos* of God are still portrayed as a covenant people. In Christ Jews and Gentiles alike are called out from the nations *(ethnoi)* to become a people *(laos)* called by His name (Acts 15:14). The relationship with God expressed in the phrase "His people" is inclusive: it refers to the whole people, not just a special class or group of believers. In Israel prophet, priest, and common man were alike enfolded in the covenant. All found their identity in that relationship with the Lord. In the church, too, we share an identity: "Christ is all, and is in all" (Col. 3:11). *There is no division by class or status among the people of God.* The whole community of faith shares a single calling and identity.

To better understand the relationship we now have with God as His *laos,* we looked at the new covenant. The Scriptures show us that God's people have always lived in a covenant relationship with Him. Identity as God's people is established on the basis of God's promises and commitments, not on our own works or efforts. In the Old Testament the promises to Abraham and his descendants included the initiating Abrahamic covenant, the land covenant, and the Davidic covenant. In addition there was a different kind of covenant, the Mosaic or Law covenant. This was not a covenant of promise. It was a conditional covenant, showing each generation of Old Testament believers how to live in harmony with God's will and to experience the benefits promised the people of God under the other covenants. In addition, Israel was promised that one day God would make a new covenant to replace the Law covenant. The new covenant would be a promise covenant like the others.

That new covenant, rooted in the Abrahamic covenant of promise, was instituted by the death of Christ. Under it all who trust Christ now come into a covenant relationship with God, a relationship that rests on His own promise and the oath made at Calvary. Under that covenant, God has committed Himself to write His law on the minds and hearts of His people. The Spirit will write *upon all* the very character of Christ.

The Book of Hebrews shows that our new covenant benefits are guaranteed by the high priestly work of Jesus. In His sacrifice of Himself He provides full forgiveness for the people of God. This ever-living High Priest guarantees access to God for all His *laos.* Through His once-for-all sacrifice we, as a forgiven people, are cleansed and perfected. In 2 Corinthians Paul argues that the new covenant relationship means that the *laos* of God will incarnate the living Jesus in the world! As we "are being transformed into his likeness with ever-increasing glory" (2 Cor. 3:18), the life of Jesus is "revealed in our mortal body" (2 Cor. 4:11).

Under the new covenant every believer lives in the very presence of God and has full and immediate access to Him. By

145

the Spirit's transforming work Jesus is revealed in each person, and He continues to be present in our world in this contemporary incarnation. It is of particular significance that these new covenant realities express the identity of *every* believer. These great blessings and responsibilities are not limited to the clergy or to some ministering class. New covenant identity and incarnational ministry are the heritage of every one of the *laos* of God.

Kingdom people

But the reality underlying the Bible's picture of who we are cannot be adequately expressed even by such a magnificent concept as the new covenant. Scripture adds other dimensions. Among them: We who are the *laos* are also a kingdom people!

The entire universe is in one sense the kingdom of God, and He exercises sovereign rule. To say that "God is the King of all the earth" (Ps. 47:7) is to recognize that basic reality.

At the same time, the concept of kingdom in Scripture has a more specific application. In the more specific sense it speaks of God's active involvement in and control over life on earth. When this view of the kingdom is presented, (1) *the presence of the King is implied,* and (2) *a fruit of the kingdom is expected.*

In the Scriptures this kingdom has past, future, and present aspects. It is future in that the prophets' vision of the Messiah's rule will be fulfilled at the return of Christ. It is past in that when Jesus was present on earth, the kingdom of God was among men in the person of the King. It is present in that Jesus the King is present now in the persons of the citizens of His kingdom.

In both future and past expressions of the kingdom on earth, its presence is demonstrated by the power of the King over those things that hold mankind in bondage. It is also demonstrated by the use of the King's power in the cause of the needy. Where the kingdom finds expression, Jesus is present, and He goes about the kingdom mission of relieving human suffering and oppression, caring for the poor and needy, and touching the outcasts of society with love. Citizens of Christ's kingdom are to produce this kingdom fruit!

The exciting contribution kingdom teaching makes to our understanding of the *laos* of God comes as we realize that we *have been* "brought . . . into the kingdom of the Son he loves" (Col. 1:13). Through His incarnation in His new covenant people Jesus *is* present in the modern world. And the kingdom exists wherever the King is present. Thus the kingdom is present in all believers. Because Jesus lives in all, all are now called to bring forth the kingdom fruit, justice and righteousness.

Servant people

This picture of the kingdom ministry leads us to another aspect of our identity as the *laos* of God. We are to understand ourselves as a servant people. Again the Old and New Testaments are in full harmony. Israel was called the servant of God, a term that speaks of relationship and mission. Israel failed in its mission to reveal the holiness of God to the nations. It was disobedient to the historic Law revelation of God's will for His people. So the Old Testament, while it affirms God's continued commitment to His unprofitable servant, Israel, prophesies that an individual known as the "Servant of the Lord" will come. This individual will fully accomplish the Father's will. He will be obedient and through His obedience accomplish His mission, even though obedience leads Him to suffering and death.

When Jesus of Nazareth appeared He was revealed to be the Messiah-Servant. Jesus accomplished His mission of redemption and forgiveness. And He called to Himself a people to serve others as He had served them. Thus the New Testament models the attitude and commitment of Jesus' *laos* on His own servant ministry. Jesus emptied Himself. Like Him we are to remain humble, willing to set aside our interests for the sake of others. We are to find greatness by serving as He served. Jesus was completely obedient to the will of God. We are to be obedient and through love-motivated obedience find meaning for our lives in serving those within and outside the *laos*.

The calling of the people of God is a high calling. The responsibilities are overwhelming. Thus it's vital to see in Scripture that the *laos* of God are more than a new covenant people, kingdom people, and servant people. We are also an empowered people. God's Holy Spirit, always the agent of enablement, has taken up residence in the life of each believer. Jesus relied on the Holy Spirit while He was on earth as the source of His power for teaching and miracle working. Christ taught that we would continue His ministry when the Spirit came. After the Resurrection Jesus promised to send the Spirit to those who believe in Him. He promised that the Spirit would be in them. The Spirit within will teach, guide, enable, and be the living link between the believer and the Godhead.

The later New Testament documents show the Spirit at work in the early church. He took an active role in directing individuals, groups, and the body as a whole. The Epistles teach us that the Spirit serves as the voice of God to the *laos*. Christ, the head of the church, exercises His Lordship through the Spirit. By the Spirit our Lord directs the body. The Spirit is also the agent of transformation. It is through His work that we progressively mature toward Christ's likeness.

In the last chapter we further explored the work of the Spirit in the *laos* of God. We saw that He is portrayed in Scripture as the One who endows men and women with special talents and abilities to be used in the service of God and others. *Giftedness* involves every quality and talent we possess. All is to be committed to God for Him to use to accomplish His purposes in our world. In this broad sense giftedness encompasses every potential of every believer in whom the Spirit dwells.

The New Testament adds a distinctive aspect of giftedness. This involves the existence of special *body gifts*, which are used within the *laos* of God to build up and mature believers in the Christian community. The body gifts listed in Scripture (Rom. 12; 1 Cor. 12; Eph. 4) are not inclusive. The lists illustrate ways in which members of the body minister to other believers to strengthen them. In fact, the lists are *not* the focus of the New Testament passages in which they are found! The focus is the nature of the church as a body, in which each individual, equipped by God in different ways, contributes to others.

It is particularly significant that the body gift passages do not emphasize the gifts listed, as though we were to analyze and understand each in detail. Instead, the reality of the body and the significance of the body's dependence on each part to function effectively is stressed. In addition there is a common emphasis on love between the members of the body. Love provides the relational context in which God's gifts are exercised. Love also maintains the unity of the body so that the members can function in a cooperative way.

In all of these explorations into Scripture in search of our identity as the *laos* of God, *a major and repeated emphasis is the full participation of each one of the laos.* Each believer has access to God under the new covenant. In each believer Christ incarnates Himself as the Spirit writes the Word on heart and mind. Because the King is present within each believer, we each live as citizens of the present kingdom of God. Because the King is present in each of us, each is to bear the kingdom fruit. In addition, we are to understand ourselves as a servant people, and each one of us is called in Christ to servanthood. We are each to live in responsive obedience to God and so serve our fellow men.

To make it possible for us to live this demanding life, God has given everyone who believes in Jesus the gift of the Holy Spirit. The Spirit lives within as our source of power, as the transformer of our personalities, and as the living voice by which Christ exercises His lordship over individuals and congregations. The Spirit in us is the giver of our talents and abilities. He is able to use all that we are to make our contribution to God's purposes. In addition, every one of us has been given a "spiritual gift" with which he or she is to minister within the body. When each part of the diverse body is functioning properly, it grows in love by what every member supplies.

We can only conclude that as each one of the *laos* is a full participant in the identity that underlies all ministry, *each part of the body of Christ in our local congregations must be guided to live out its identity in ministry!* Any biblical approach to ministry in the church of Jesus Christ must be rooted in the conviction that we *are* a ministering people . . . each and every one.

BUILDING A MINISTERING PEOPLE

How do we develop spiritual giftedness in the local church? How do we build a people whose lives express their identity as the people of God? In the rest of this text we want to examine what can be done in local congregations to help believers discover their potential and their divine calling.

The things that we will develop are drawn directly from the theological core already examined and will be applied in practical ways. In each chapter we will draw heavily on the experience of Gib Martin at Trinity, but also on the experiences of other congregations in various parts of the United States. In many ways the approaches and the lifestyle sketched here will not "fit" many contemporary theories about how churches should be organized and run. However, we believe the patterns presented are consistent with Scripture and are in harmony with a biblical theology of the *laos* of God. Contemporary theories (and the concepts presented in this text) should always be scrutinized and placed under the judgment of the Word of God. Each of us remains responsible to God for how we respond when we recognize either truths that reflect a renewed mind or errors that reflect conformity to the world's ways of thinking.

PRACTICAL IMPLICATION

But what are specific areas with which we need to be concerned in the local church if we are to develop a ministering people? At least seven areas of concern are suggested by our exploration of a core theology.

1. *We must communicate a vision of the purposes God seeks to achieve through His people*

All too often Christians have a severely limited perception of the purposes God seeks to accomplish through the church. "Evangelism" and "nurture" are, of course, always listed. But most churches ignore many areas of ministry and mission that are revealed in kingdom teaching . . . or treat them with suspicion as part of a "social gospel."

The Old Testament reminds us that "where there is no revelation, the people cast off restraint" (Prov. 29:18). Both the Old and New Testaments are full of revelations of God's concerns and purposes. Unless we teach them and have some sense of the needs that God intends to meet through the incarnation of Jesus in the body of Christ, many believers will miss their mission and be unaware of opportunities they have to serve God and others.

When we explore this area, we will see what some of these revealed purposes are, how they can be and are being accomplished by believers, and how the individuals in a local congregation can be guided to catch a personal vision from the Lord.

2. *We must build a community of love in which close personal relationships are nurtured*

We've seen in our exploration of a core theology that all passages dealing with body gifts stress the importance of loving relationships between Christians. The loving community is the context in which spiritual gifts are exercised.

The relational context of ministry also leads us to explore the noninstitutional nature of giftedness. Gifts—in the more limited body gift sense and in the broader sense of giftedness as a general endowment of the Spirit—are to be given expression in the context of close personal relationships. The church has made the mistake of institutionalizing service. Even such natural ministries as teaching are perceived as taking place at a certain limited time and place and in a formal organized way. But church programs all too often *limit* rather than *encourage* the development of personal relationships. Yet the relational context is significant and often determinative of the impact of ministry.

150

One of the challenges that a church that wants to build a ministering people must face is to develop a community of love as the context for the exercise of body gifts, and to build significant relationships with the surrounding community for a continuing ministry to the world.

3. *We must learn to make disciples and not simply church members*

One of the truths emphasized by the presence of the Spirit in the life of the believer is transformation. This is also stressed in biblical teaching about body gifts. We are called to minister to one another so that the *laos* of God may grow to maturity in Christ.

The incarnational emphasis in both new covenant and kingdom teaching helps us realize how vital growth toward Christlikeness is for a ministering people. Both these doctrines present Christ in His present incarnation among the *laos*. To represent Jesus in the world, it is utterly essential that believers grow toward Christian maturity.

This helps us realize that discipleship—leading believers toward maturity and full commitment—is more significant than it is normally considered to be in the church. A congregation that seeks to become a ministering people and thus to be in reality what it *is* theologically as the *laos* of God will need to give specific attention to the discipling process.

4. *We must guide the people of God to become servants of one another and the world*

Ministry is essentially a response to the needs of others, whether those needs are individual, corporate, or societal. The Christian is called to become involved with others in their needs and to express caring in significant ways.

Yet often churches are so designed that in practice they *isolate* Christians from those in need, and particularly from the tragedies that occur in society. To guide the people of God into servanthood—or, more accurately, to bring them into relationship to human need so that each individual can hear the call and voice of God the Spirit—is another vital task for the local congregation.

5. *We must provide training in ministry so that members of the body will be effective in their service*

Discipleship focuses on building toward maturity and personal commitment. Special attention in discipleship needs to be paid to the *inner growth* of believers.

But as the Spirit calls believers to various ministries, and gives and shapes their vision, there must also be an equipping for the ministry. Equipping and training need not be through "professional" classes. Training will, in fact, seldom involve such classes. What is needed are ways to provide guidance and support so that people will be successful in the ministry to which they have been called. Such training will often include the theological principles on which the ministry must be constructed, training in skills and methods, and also counseling and supervision as the ministry is launched.

The kinds of support provided for believers involved in personal ministries are a significant issue the local church must face.

6. We must extend freedom to the people of God to respond to the voice of the Spirit

This concept is complex and yet very significant. On the one hand it means developing an awareness in the congregation that God speaks to and leads each member. Each Christian needs to learn how to hear the voice of God and respond to His leading. This is a necessary part of the equipping of the people of God for ministry.

It must also be recognized that the way ministry is institutionalized in most churches leads to the replacement of the voice of God by control by a committee or a professional leader. To protect a supernatural dynamic, those conducting a ministry to which the Spirit of God has called them should be given full responsibility for it. They "own" their ministries; leaders do not give "ownership" to the church, as though ministries should be programs of the church and under its control.

Thus a distinctive organization, as well as a people made sensitive to the voice of God, is a part of building a ministering people.

7. We must come to a better understanding of leadership in the body of Christ

Within the context of a people, each of whom is a full participant in Christ and a full participant in ministry, a fresh understanding of the nature of spiritual leadership must be developed.

Traditional concepts of the role of spiritual leadership and the authority of leaders are rooted in clergy-laity distinctions that Scripture does not support. How leaders can function as one with other members who are also full participants in

152

Christ is another area that needs to be explored.

In short, then, our exploration of a core theology has led us to a number of practical issues. We are forced to think about the local congregation and ask, "How can these vital truths of the Word of God be best enfleshed in the life and ministry of the local church?"

PROBE

▶ *case histories*
▶ *discussion questions*
▶ *thought provokers*
▶ *resources*

1. Review chapters 2–6 and determine which *one* truth explored is the "most significant" to you for the building of a ministering people. Then, *without looking ahead,* write a five-page paper exploring how that truth might be implemented in your own local congregation. Have two parts to your paper. The first part should focus on "the ideal." Tell how a full experience of your ideal church would find expression in your congregation. The second part should focus on "ways to reach the ideal." Suggest any changes that would need to be made in your congregation to reach your ideal.

2. Look at the following by Steve Turner. What is he saying? Do you agree or disagree? Why?

How to Hide Jesus

There are people after Jesus.
They have seen the signs.
Quick, let's hide him.
Let's think—carpenter, fishermen's friend,
disturber of religious comfort—
let's award him a degree in theology,
a purple cassock and
a position of respect.
They'll never think
of looking here.
Let's think, his dialect may betray him,
his tongue is of the masses.
Let's teach him Latin,
let's educate him in Middle English,
they'll never think of listening in.
Let's think—humble, man of sorrows,
nowhere to lay his head.

153

PRACTICAL IMPLICATION

We'll build a house for him,
somewhere away from the poor.
We'll fill it with brass and silence.
It's sure to throw them off.

There are people after Jesus.
Quick, let's hide him.

3. Case History

How competent are the people of God when given responsibility for the ministries to which they are called? Does giftedness express itself in *competent* ministry, or is the fear many feel of an "uncontrolled" (and thus sloppy) ministry warranted?

Many of the concepts that will be explored in the last part of this text are embodied in the following case history. It tells of the development of an R & R (Renewal and Refreshment) ministry at Trinity. The case history report, for you to examine in a Case Study Conference, is shared by Sharon Moss.

SHARON MOSS

A number of women saw a need for mutual discipleship among the women of Trinity. They saw that we didn't have many older women who could be disciplers and realized that a solution required more than matching one woman with another. I think this conclusion was reached about the time Gib Martin was starting discipleship groups with men, and the women said, "Hey, we need something like that."

These women also realized that our Bible Study Fellowship, good as it was, was not for all the women in our body. For example it met once a week all year long in the daytime, so working women couldn't attend. Some of us felt the "fellowship" was inadequate, too. What we were looking for was women discipling women in more than just Bible content. Our goal was contacts with women who would hurt when we hurt, women who cared for us, women who would become our close friends.

The leaders at the beginning were six or seven women. Several of them have since moved away. Initially the program did not have enough direction. The council that organized it did not do much at first other than put people in groups and listen to problems. So the groups became successful or unsuccessful according to the chemistry of the group. I became involved in the council at the end of its second year. Then Jan moved away and Lorane and Susan had small children and ceased to be active. That left Myrna, Jean, Marybeth, and me. That summer the four of us sat down and talked about the groups. Several of us had been blessed by Ralph's ministry and teaching about the church. Myrna, Ralph's wife, had been in our body that spring and shared her study of the character of God and how it related to women. We felt we needed to develop a curriculum for that type of study. There needed to be a focal point in the groups that was really solid. So we decided that we would study a book called *Knowing God*, by J. I. Packer.

At the end of that year we had far fewer problems than we had had before. There was a focal point, and we had our leaders' training session in which we taught some things about group dynamics. That summer as we were thinking about what to study, the Lord brought to several of our minds the Book of Romans. At the end of Packer's book he said a good continuation to this study would be the Book of Romans. We studied eight chapters a year for two years and got through the whole book.

Then we felt that we needed to zero in on our personal prayer life. We are going to study prayer for two months, the Psalms for three months, and Proverbs for three months. We have it all outlined and we spent a lot of time in bookstores looking through commentaries and study guides. The "we" is the leadership council; at this point there are only two of us left—Jean and Marybeth just had babies. It started out with more people, but if you have too many people it is difficult to make a leadership council function effectively.

The primary role of the council is to develop materials, and we spent hours preparing them. Now we meet as a group. We are not just theorizing about how all the groups should function—we are a group. We go through all the materials for the next month with the leaders. The idea—and it was pretty faithfully implemented—was that the leaders were to be prepared before they came.

Last year I think there were about forty women in the Renewal and Refreshment group. I anticipate that it will be larger this year. We expect many of last year's women to return, and everyone who has spoken with me so far is a new person.

Our council has an elder representative, Tom. He has been invited and has come to several council meetings. He has listened to the process that we go through and knows what we are studying. He came to one of our meetings at the end of last year when we had a sharing time in which people told what God had done in their lives. There has been no other administrative involvement. We have taken care of our own money. I have had the freedom to say, "I need some materials," and the cost has been covered. The elders have not exercised any authority as such, although they have it as far as we are concerned. We would waste their time if we encouraged them to become too involved. Why should they do that when there are many other, more important things they need to do?

155

PRACTICAL IMPLICATION

The year I came in as a full council member was the year a lot of people dropped out. That year it was a team effort in many ways. What we would do is alternate responsibility in the leaders' session. So that year leadership was shared equally. The year before last—our first year in Romans—I moved into a place of leadership because I had studied Romans before and no one else had. I had taken an excellent course in Romans at Campus Crusade headquarters in Arrowhead Springs, so they started to depend on me. I knew how to go into a bookstore and confidently make choices about commentaries, Bible dictionaries, etc. As we worked together, I emerged in a leadership capacity. Part of it was that I had prayed and asked the Lord to give me a ministry, but I didn't want it to be outside my home because of the children. As it worked out, almost all of our meetings have been held in my home.

A council still exists. In fact, what was really special was that whenever I was under pressure, Jean could pick up the ball. The same thing happened when Jean was too busy.

Jean and I found that we have developed a special interplay. It was interesting to see how we alternated. Each of us had strengths in developing certain questions, and there would be times when Jean came up with an excellent idea and mine was mediocre. Then the next time my idea would be great and hers would be mediocre! But there was never a time when one of us insisted, "I think my idea is a good one." When we got together, we always knew which idea was best. There was no sense of competition. It was very natural, very comfortable.

This year it is a little different. Candy has moved in to help. We know each other but are not close friends, so one of our prayers is that that kind of friendship will develop. At this point I don't know that if I "drop the ball," she will pick it up. There isn't that sense of unity yet, so I feel more of the weight of responsibility. Candy and I will probably meet during the day. Then Cindy and I will meet in the evening and go over the material. That will give me input from more than one source.

We don't feel as if we have any resource people. The buck stops with us. I don't feel as if I can go to the board of elders and get all the help I want. We tried to enlist Ralph Alexander's help. He wrote that he had a heavy schedule for the fall. We felt he could give us a lot of background on the Psalms. The letter was a real disappointment, but it threw me back on the Lord.

4. What kinds of study materials and plans can be developed without "professional" training? Here is an overview of the study approach developed by the women of the Renewal and Refreshment council at Trinity.

Identity Implications

THE MINISTRY OF RENEWAL AND REFRESHMENT

The Renewal and Refreshment Ministry was begun six years ago by a group of women who were concerned about the need for women in our church body to be discipled. The concept "Renewal and Refreshment" was built out of a desire to find growth in mutual discipleship relationships through Bible study, committed relationships, and the development of gifts, fellowship, and commitment throughout the entire church family.

Some fundamental principles were drawn from Hebrews 10:23–25; 2 Corinthians 2:14–16; and Titus 2:3–5. We found an underlying purpose in 1 Corinthians 10:31: "Whatever you do, do it all for the glory of God."

Although the ministry is still being shaped, certain policies have guided the groups over the past few years:

COUNCIL
1. Content—the council will provide a resource of study materials from year to year, to be used during the year's study time.
2. Training—The council will provide opportunities to prepare "for works of service, so that the body of Christ may be built up" (Eph. 4:12; 2 Tim. 2:15; 3:16–17).

GROUPS
1. *Confidentiality*—All personal sharing done by an individual within the group is to be an expression of what God is doing in her life. This includes prayer needs, joys, sorrow, victories, etc. (Col. 2:2; Prov. 6:19). It is to be kept strictly confidential, not shared with anyone outside the group.
2. Groups will follow the format designated by the council unless council approval is given for any changes.
3. The group will include not less than four and not more than eight women, including the group leader.
4. Women must arrange for baby-sitting for their children before the group meetings.

LEADERS
1. A leader is asked to commit herself to one year (nine months) of R and R ministry.
2. Leaders are expected to be examples (1 Tim. 4:12) for the members of their group (for example, through letters, phone calls, personal contacts, etc.), thus stimulating all members to love and good deeds (Heb. 10:23–25).

GENERAL SUGGESTIONS FOR STUDY:

Approach each study session as a time when God wants to speak to you. Going to Him in prayer before beginning to study is a crucial step. Ask the Holy Spirit to guide you into the truth and protect you from error. Ask Him to clear your mind of possible distractions. This may involve some specific steps on your part, such as committing areas of stress or concern to Him and allowing Him to free you from them. It also may involve getting out a piece of paper and writing down the things you need to do so that you can put them out of your mind. It might involve unplugging the phone, getting up before the rest of the family, or postponing a less important (but maybe not less urgent) activity or duty.

Keep in mind that not every study session will be as profitable and stimulating as every other. Some aspects of the total study program for each chapter will appeal to you more than others. Each step, however, has been included with the goals in mind of gaining a life-changing understanding of the Book of Romans and of refining Bible study skills. Don't forget that frustration and lack of understanding are valuable steps in the learning process.

There will be questions or problems for which you will not find satisfactory answers. This should not discourage you from studying but should simply help you keep a good perspective. Scholars have debated some of the issues raised in Romans for centuries. However, we can rest assured that God will not keep from us any truth that is basic to our salvation and maturity. Also, there are things that will become more clear to each of us as we progress in our study and have the advantage of retrospect and a more complete picture of what Paul's message is.

Perhaps the best checks against errors in our thinking or understanding are: 1) approaching the study in an attitude of prayer, 2) maintaining a teachable spirit, 3) keeping in mind that God does not violate His own character or principles nor does His Word contain contradictory doctrine, and 4) consulting the writings of established Bible scholars for their insights.

One additional suggestion for your study is to keep a notebook of all your work as well as handouts received. This will help you stay organized and keep your materials available for reference.

METHODS FOR STUDY

The basic methods we will be using in our approach to the Book of Romans are:

Week 1 Inductive study

Week 2 Study using prepared questions from Neighborhood Bible Study series and other resource material

Week 3 Further opportunity for study using materials from Week 2 with emphasis on personal application and areas of special interest to individuals

The goals that guided the choice of study methods are gaining a life-changing understanding of the Book of Romans and refining Bible study skills.

Begin your study of each chapter by using an inductive approach. This is the process of looking at a passage of Scripture itself to discern what it says and means, and of drawing conclusions and generalizations from the findings. This is different from deductive study, which is the process of starting with generalizations and using the Bible to support them.[4]

The specific aims of inductive study are

1. To learn to study Scripture without having to depend on others and what they have written or said;
2. To stimulate you to do further study of areas you don't understand or in which you want deeper understanding;
3. To acquire a basic grasp of the content and progression of the chapter.

To assist you in the process of inductive study we have put together a plan that will familiarize you with the chapter. (Note: During the *initial* stages of the inductive study, it will be most beneficial to you if you do not use commentaries and other resource material.)

Day 1

Pray that you will have a clear head and heart as you begin.

Read through the chapter *quickly.*

Read through the chapter *slowly,* using the Swedish marking system in the margin to indicate the following:

---

[4]Oletta Wald, *The Joy of Discovery in Bible Study* (Minneapolis: Augsburg Publishing House, 1975), p. 6.

? things you don't understand
√ penetrating thoughts that stimulate thinking, bring special meaning or conviction to you
* new insights or ideas

Write out your questions, insights, and observations.

Day 2
Read the chapter through in three different translations. (Purpose: thoughtful and prayerful observation.) Note the differences in phrasing and wording that are evident.

Day 3
Build a vocabulary list, picking out key words or words for which you have no working definition. Look up meanings for these words in a Bible dictionary or regular dictionary. Begin to visualize the meaning of the words in the context of the chapter.

Day 4–6
Begin answering the questions in *Neighborhood Bible Study,* using your commentaries. This is *optional* and these answers will not be used until the second week's discussion.

You might be wondering about the value of writing down your observations and questions and are possibly asking if it isn't enough just to make mental notes. Why spend the time writing them out on paper? Oletta Wald makes the following comment in this regard:

It is indeed possible to read Scripture and mentally make observations and ask yourself questions about meanings, but writing requires more discipline in thought and concentration. Most of us are rather superficial in our thinking unless we force ourselves to write our thoughts on paper. We are told that "writing makes an exact man."[5]

TOOLS FOR STUDY

One of the primary goals for this study is that we learn how to go to Scripture to discover truth for ourselves. It is very easy to forget that God's Word itself is living, active, powerful, and transforming (Heb. 4:12; John 17:17). Commentaries are man's words about the Word. This is not to discount the many valuable study aids but simply to caution us to "keep books about the Bible carefully subordinate to the biblical text."[6]

Some of the information on the types of study aids available has been reworded to fit the needs of our study of Romans.[7] The specific books listed are those we consider to be of value for the study.

Discovery Aids
1. *Concordances.* A good concordance lists each occurrence of every word in the Bible. The best concordance is an exhaustive one that enables you to trace each word of the English text back to its Greek or Hebrew original. Many Bibles contain their own small concordance.

   Young's Analytical Concordance to the Bible
   Cruden's Complete Concordance
   Strong's Exhaustive Concordance of the Bible

---

[5]*The Joy of Discovery,* p. 12.
[6]Lawrence O. Richards, *Creative Bible Study* (Grand Rapids: Zondervan Publishing House, 1979), p. 250f.
[7]*Creative Bible Study,* p. 205.

PRACTICAL IMPLICATION

2. *Versions and translations.* When searching for meaning, it is helpful to compare various translations of the biblical text. Strict translations attempt to give the translation of the original Greek and Hebrew texts with as little as possible interpretation for cultural adaptation; paraphrases, on the other hand, attempt to express the meaning of the original in contemporary English. The use of both translations and paraphrases is recommended, but one should work primarily with one basic, accepted translation, using other translations and paraphrases for reference.

> *King James Version.* Translated nearly four hundred years ago. Limited by outdated vocabulary and writing style and by inadequate resource material for translation work.

> *New American Standard Bible.* A revision of the American Standard Bible of 1901 by a team of fifty-eight evangelical scholars with the latest manuscripts. Completed in 1963. Like the ASV, the NASB is noted for its literal translation from the original to the English. It is one of the best modern versions for serious Bible study and rated by many to be one of the most accurate.

> *Revised Standard Version.* The RSV is the work of a committee of thirty-two scholars sponsored by the National Council of Churches and was completed in 1952. It retains the good qualities of the KJV but takes modern scholarship into account. On the whole an excellent translation, although frequently criticized as reflecting the liberal bias of its translators.

> *The New English Bible.* This translation was completed after twenty-four years of labor by a panel of British scholars in 1970. It is a fresh, stimulating rendition of the biblical text, and is based upon the most accurate and up-to-date findings in all related fields of knowledge.

> *New International Version.* This Bible was begun in the 1960s by a group of nearly one hundred evangelical translators and was completed in 1978. It is designed to be the Bible for both public and private use, for the person who is a member of a church and the one who never attends. It is rated as excellent by many scholars. It combines accuracy to the original with sensitivity to modern usages (uses "you" and "your" throughout for God). Some feel it may become the all-purpose translation for evangelical churches in spite of the many other translations available.

> *Phillips New Testament in Modern English.* One of the first of the modern paraphrases and in some ways still the best. Considerable liberty has been taken with the original text to make the content come alive.

> *The Living Bible.* This is a paraphrase done by Kenneth N. Taylor and designed for family reading to communicate the message of the Bible to all ages. It is not a good "translation," yet its strongly evangelical bias is true to the larger import of Scripture. Readability is its main merit.

> *The Amplified Bible.* A helpful study tool that provides the English equivalent to Hebrew and Greek words by supplying many synonyms for the purpose of indicating shades of meaning that are often concealed by the traditional word-for-word method of translation.

Identity Implications

Background Aids

The Bible reflects the customs and political and economic setting of the periods in which it was written. Often they are confusing or difficult for the twentieth-century Christian to understand. The teaching of the Bible will become clearer when its historical background is understood. A variety of reference works are available to provide this background information.

1. *Bible Handbooks.* These provide background information of all sorts on the Bible and its world and some of them give a concise comment on the entire text of the Bible.

    Merrill F. Unger, *Unger's Bible Handbook*
    H. H. Halley, *Halley's Bible Handbook*

2. *Bible Surveys.* Surveys of the Old and New Testament attempt to place the text in its historical setting and normally include outlines and analyses of the individual books of the Bible.

    Merrill C. Tenney, *New Testament Survey* (pp. 303–308 for Romans)
    Walter M. Dunnett, *New Testament Survey*
    Henry C. Thiessen, *Introduction to the New Testament* (pp. 219–227 for Romans)

3. *Bible Dictionaries.* These reference tools include brief articles on places, persons, and things in the Bible. Since a distinctive theological viewpoint is reflected in most works of this sort, it is suggested that you obtain one that is published by an evangelical publisher.

    William Smith, *Smith's Bible Dictionary*
    Merrill F. Unger, *Unger's Bible Dictionary*
    J. D. Douglas, ed., *The New Bible Dictionary*
    Merrill C. Tenney, ed., *Zondervan Pictorial Bible Dictionary*
    Everett F. Harrison, ed. *Baker's Dictionary of Theology* (dictionary of theological terms)
    W.E. Vine, *Expository Dictionary of the New Testament Words*

Interpretation Aids

Interpretation aids help you understand what you read in Scripture. They characteristically tell you what others believe the Scripture means or teaches. Reading books in this category, as mentioned above, should never become a substitute for a personal study of Scripture itself and should never be a shortcut to understanding the meaning of Scripture. These books should be used after a person has initially studied the passage and has come to a tentative interpretation of Scripture through personal search and discovery.

Commentaries. There are a variety of commentaries. The ones of greatest value are the single book commentaries. They include an extended discussion of the background of a book and carefully try to follow its main theme.

    J. Vernon McGee, *Romans,* 2 vols.
    William R. Newell, *Romans Verse By Verse*
    James M. Stifler, *The Epistle to the Romans*
    Alan F. Johnson, *Romans: The Freedom Letter,* 2 vols.
    Everett F. Harrison and Charles F. Pfeiffer, eds., *The Wycliffe Bible Commentary*

Note: See *Romans: The Freedom Letter* by Johnson and *Romans* from the Neighborhood Bible Studies for further bibliography on the Book of Romans.

PART 2

PRACTICAL IMPLICATION

Identity Implications
Communicating Vision
Building Relationships and Community
Making Disciples
Equipping
Extending Freedom
Understanding Leadership

COMMUNICATING VISION

The concept of "vision" seems foreign to us at first. It is vague, almost ghostly, and indistinct. Yet Scripture tells us that in the age of the Spirit, marked by the empowering of men and women for ministry, "your young men will see visions." Most simply, this term in Old and New Testaments identifies *a word from God and its interpretation*. The reason that "without a vision the people perish" is that, apart from God's guidance understood and applied, purpose and motivation are lost. No wonder Habakkuk, confused about what God was doing in the Judah of his day, determined to stand watch and see what God would reveal. When the Word came from God Habakkuk was told, "Write down the revelation [vision] and make it plain on tablets so that a herald may run with it" (Hab. 2:2).

Such a word from God, interpreting the times and giving direction to God's people, is essential.

This seems to be the significance of the promise that in the present age visions and dreams will be given. Under the new covenant the whole *laos* now have personal access to God. *All possess the Spirit, and thus each can hear God's voice.* To each generation, to each congregation, God gives words of vision to provide a fresh, personal sense of purpose and a direction for ministry.

It is important to realize that the vision spoken of in Scripture is God's vision. *Visions communicate God's goals and purposes to His* laos *to guide them.* We are to respond to God's vision when He shares it with us. Our personal ministries are to be in full harmony with His purposes.

In this chapter we want to sketch what the New Testament reveals of the vision God has for the people of Christ, and then see how His vision can be seen by members of a local congregation.

GOD'S VISION FOR HIS PEOPLE

The Old and New Testaments are rich in the revelation of God's vision. Without question, God is currently carrying out many of His purposes through the body of Christ. As Ephesians tells us, "through the church, the manifold wisdom of God should be made known to the rulers and authorities in the heavenly realms" (Eph. 3:10). The wisdom of God is far too manifold, complex, and multifaceted to be adequately summarized by our traditional statements of His purpose for the church: evangelism and nurture. God's vision involves a total display of His wisdom and purposes.

PRACTICAL IMPLICATION

The multifaceted nature of God's vision makes it difficult to organize what has been revealed into logical categories. It is better simply to scan a few that we discover in reading through the New Testament and, as a representative of the Old Testament, Isaiah.

God's vision of a restored humanity

Sin warped and twisted mankind, distorting individual personalities and society. In Christ there is full restoration. "He who has been stealing must steal no longer, but must work, doing something useful with his own hands, that he may have something to share with those in need" (Eph. 4:28). The old ways "you used to walk in" are rejected so that a renewed self might be "put on" (Col. 3:7, 10). "Make it your ambition to lead a quiet life, to mind your own business and to work with your hands, just as we told you, so that your daily life may win the respect of outsiders and so that you will not be dependent on anybody," the apostle writes (1 Thess. 4:11–12). At one time all of us lived in the kingdom of the enemy and the spirit of evil in one way or another was at work in us. Then our lives concentrated on "gratifying the cravings of our sinful nature and following its desires and thoughts" (Eph. 2:3). Now, made alive in Christ, we are to live transformed lives, as Jesus Himself is gradually formed in us (Gal. 4:19).

God's vision of a people who live good lives

Evangelicals have been suspicious of the idea of "doing good." Yet it's clear in Scripture that God has a vision for a people who *are* "do-gooders." "Live such good lives among the pagans," Peter says, "that though they accuse you of doing wrong, they may see your good deeds and glorify God on the day he visits us" (1 Peter 2:12). Paul adds, "Let us not become weary in doing good. . . . As we have opportunity, let us do good to all people, especially to those who belong to the family of believers" (Gal. 6:9–10). We are, in fact, a people who are "created in Christ Jesus to do good works, which God prepared in advance for us to do" (Eph. 2:10). No wonder there is so much emphasis in Scripture on common goodness and "seeking . . . the good of many" (1 Cor. 10:33), thus expressing in our lives the goodness that God planted within us in Christ (cf. Matt. 6:1; 12:35).

A life committed to doing good demonstrates the wisdom of God (James 3:13), who has chosen us to be a people who clothe themselves "with compassion, kindness, humility, gentleness and patience" (Col. 3:12).

God's vision of a people who do His word

God has a vision for a renewed mankind that lives by the reality expressed in His Word. Thus He emphasizes coming to know the Scripture, *that we might do it.* "Do not merely listen to the word, and so deceive yourselves," James warns (James 1:22). God's blessing is for the person who looks intently into the Word "and continues to do this, not forgetting what he has heard, but doing it—he will be blessed in what he does" (James 1:22f.). He is to live, then, as an obedient child (1 Peter 1:14) and so "live the rest of his earthly life" for "the will of God" (1 Peter 4:2). No wonder Jesus taught that the foundation of a believer's life is not a mere *hearing* of the Word but a doing of it (Matt. 7:24–27). As John later writes, "If anyone obeys his word, God's love is truly made complete in him" (1 John 2:5; cf. 5:3).

God's vision of a holy people

The theme of holiness and righteousness appears over and over in both testaments. Before the creation God "chose us" in Christ that we might be "holy and blameless in his sight" (Eph. 1:4). We are thus to live "so that [we] may become blameless and pure, children of God without fault in a crooked and depraved generation, in which [we] shine like stars in the universe as [we] hold out the word of life . . ." (Phil. 2:15f.). God wants His *laos* to be "pure and blameless until the day of Christ, filled with the fruit of righteousness that comes through Jesus Christ—to the glory and praise of God" (Phil. 1:10–11).

It's helpful to realize that this is an *active* holiness, not a passive one. Thus in Romans Paul teaches us that we are to surrender to God and through obedience offer ourselves "to obey him as slaves . . . to obedience, which leads to righteousness" (Rom. 6:16). Holiness means to "say 'No' to ungodliness and worldly passions, and to live self-controlled, upright and godly lives in this present age" (Titus 2:12).

God's vision of a people concerned with justice

Concern with justice is one aspect of active righteousness. Society, as well as the individual, is warped by sin. While we will not see a full transformation of society until Christ reigns, we are not to ignore injustice today. Here the Old Testament speaks with special clarity: "Learn to do right! Seek justice, encourage the oppressed. Defend the cause of the fatherless, plead the case of the widow," Isaiah begins his exhortation to Judah (Isa. 1:17). Throughout the Bible this same emphasis is maintained. God announces woe because of "unjust laws" and "oppressive decrees" and because sinners "deprive the poor of their rights and rob my oppressed people of justice" (Isa. 10:1–2). The *laos* of God are commanded to "maintain justice and do what is right" (Isa. 56:1). This is far more important to God than the performance of religious duties:

> Is not this the kind of fasting I have chosen:
> to loose the chains of injustice
>   and untie the cords of the yoke,
> to set the oppressed free
>   and break every yoke?
> Is it not to share your food with the hungry
>   and to provide the poor wanderer with shelter—
> when you see the naked, to clothe him,
>   and not to turn away from your own flesh and blood? (Isa. 58:6–7).

No wonder Jesus condemned the Pharisees, who claimed to be God's people, "because you give God a tenth of your mint, rue, and all other kinds of garden herbs, but you neglect justice and the love of God" (Luke 11:42). Compassion for the outcast and the oppressed is always associated with what the Bible calls a "pure and faultless" religion (James 1:27; cf. also 1 Tim. 5:3; Matt. 20:29f.; 25:31–40).

God has a vision of a people who meet the material needs of others

Associated with the divine concern for justice is a matching concern for the poor and needy. This is reflected in a variety of ways and stated strongly. "Suppose a brother or sister is without clothes and daily food," James says (James 2:15). Good wishes are irrelevant if one "does nothing about his physical needs" (James 2:16). John says, "If anyone has material possessions and sees his brother in need but has no pity on him, how can the love of God be in him?" (1 John 3:17).

Meeting needs within the body is a theme that underlies the New Testament teaching on giving (2 Cor. 8:8; 1 Cor. 16). In essence, we are to "share with God's people who are in need" (Rom. 12:13; cf. Rom. 15:26f.), so supplying the whole body with required resources.

In actuality, concern for others in need extends beyond the fellowship of believers, although there is to be a special emphasis on the sharing of possessions within the church (cf. Acts 4:32f.). God's compassion extends to strangers and even enemies. According to Jesus' story of the Good Samaritan, *anyone in need* is the neighbor whom we as God's people are called on to love (cf. Luke 10:25–37).

God has a vision of a people freed from materialism

An anti-materialistic theme recurs often in Scripture. Jesus spoke of a freedom from worry that comes when God's people realize that their "heavenly Father knows that [they] need them" (Matt. 6:32). Freed from the pagan's dominating concern for the material world, the believer is to "seek first his kingdom and his righteousness," sure that "all these things will be given to [him] as well" (Matt. 6:33; cf. 6:25–34; Luke 12). Yet materialism involves far more than a concentration on possessions. It also involves a change in values. In the body of Christ there is to be no partiality based on a believer's wealth or poverty (James 2:1f.). In addition, freedom from materialism means deliverance from covetousness, which James associates with the "fights and quarrels" that break out among people (James 4:1f.).

It is clear to Paul that

> godliness with contentment is great gain. For we brought nothing into the world, and we can take nothing out of it. But if we have food and clothing, we will be content with that. People who want to get rich fall into temptation and a trap and into many foolish and harmful desires that plunge men into ruin and destruction" (1 Tim. 6:6f.).

It is not wrong to be rich. But the rich are to share the non-materialistic values of other believers: "to do good, to be rich in good deeds, and to be generous and willing to share" (1 Tim. 6:18). With these values comes freedom for the believer to invest his resources in meeting the needs of others.

God has a vision of a loving community

The church as the family of God is to be a loving community in which the character of God is revealed. Many passages in Scripture emphasize the necessity of loving one another as Christ loved us (e.g., John 13:34). Such exhortations reflect one of God's basic purposes. Peter speaks of loving "one another deeply, with all your hearts" (1 Peter 1:22). John links loving our brothers to living in the light (1 John 2:9f.). Over and over Paul's letters repeat the same theme. "The only thing that counts is faith expressing itself through love" (Gal. 5:6). We are to "serve one another in love" (Gal. 5:13). Paul praises the Thessalonians for the fact that "you do love all the brothers throughout Macedonia. Yet we urge you, brothers, to do so more and more" (1 Thess. 4:10).

In a world that is marked by alienation, selfishness, and

169

shattered relationships, Jesus' kind of love, revealed in relationships between members of the body of Christ, is a compelling invitation to hope (John 13:34).

God has a vision of a praying people

Prayer is more than an expression of dependence on God; it is an avenue of fellowship and communication. Scripture is clear that God's people are to be a praying people. Jesus Himself often retreated to spend time with His Father in prayer. In the Upper Room, Jesus encouraged believers to pray (John 14:27f.). "Do not be anxious about anything," Paul teaches, "but in everything, by prayer and petition, with thanksgiving, present your requests to God. And the peace of God, which transcends all understanding, will guard your hearts and your minds in Christ Jesus" (Phil. 4:6–7). Prayer for others is also an important aspect of the ministry of believers. "I urge, then, first of all, that requests, prayers, intercession and thanksgiving be made for everyone . . ." (1 Tim. 2:1).

Paul's own prayers for believers provide a beautiful pattern for a prayer ministry. He focuses his requests for those in the body of Christ on their need for spiritual growth and health and a vital life in Christ (cf. Eph. 1:15f.; 3:14ff.; Col. 1:9ff.; etc.). There *is* power in prayer. His people are to tap and experience it.

God has a vision of a people who live in hope

Hope is one of those precious gifts that sin has torn from the hearts of men in the world. Yet hope is to be ours in Christ. "In his great mercy he has given us new birth into a living hope through the resurrection of Jesus Christ from the dead," Peter says (1 Peter 1:3). Similarly, Paul says, "I pray also that the eyes of your heart may be enlightened in order that you may know the hope to which he has called you . . ." (Eph. 1:18).

With hope we are able to endure the trials that destroy others. Even when we suffer for doing right, we recognize the lordship of Christ in the situation (1 Peter 3:14f.). Others observe us and wonder. Thus hope opens the door to a sharing relationship with God, and we are to "always be prepared to give an answer to everyone who asks [us] to give the reason for the hope that [we] have" (1 Peter 3:15).

Even suffering and trials are part of the vision of God for His people, for in these experiences the qualities of hope and joy become visible to others as evidence of the reality of Christ (cf. 1 Peter 1:6; 2 Cor. 1:5; 1 Peter 4:13).

170

God has a vision of a people who live under authority

The world in which we live has, because of sin, set up various kinds of authority to control sin's expression. These authorities are not themselves free from sin. Thus injustice is often expressed and even institutionalized by authorities that were established by God to protect against injustice. Men rebel against authorities for many reasons—because an authority acts oppressively, because even authority exercised rightly is onerous, etc.

Yet God has shaped a people who look beyond human authority and see a sovereign Lord. Seeing Him, the *laos* lives righteously even in oppressive situations. "Everyone must subject himself to the governing authorities," says Paul, who argues that "he who rebels against the authority is rebelling against what God has instituted" (Rom. 13:1f.). Peter puts it this way. "Submit yourselves for the Lord's sake to every authority instituted among men" (1 Peter 3:13). His argument on this point is extensive: "It is God's will that by doing good you should silence the ignorant talk of foolish men. Live as free men, but do not use your freedom as a cover-up for evil; live as servants of God. Show proper respect to everyone: Love the brotherhood of believers, fear God, honor the king" (1 Peter 3:15–17).

Even the institution of slavery, part of the society of the New Testament period, did not warrant rebellion. "Slaves, submit yourselves to your masters with all respect, not only to those who are good and considerate, but also to those who are harsh." In such a situation we can follow Jesus' example, for He "entrusted himself to him who judges justly" (1 Peter 2:18, 23).

It is not always easy to use the freedom to live within the framework of authority that exists in a particular culture or society. No wonder this theme is often repeated and Paul tells Titus to "remind the people to be subject to rulers and authorities, to be obedient, to be ready to do whatever is good" (Titus 3:1). A people who trust the sovereign God to work out His good will within the limitations imposed by existing authorities are a unique witness to the Lord.

God has a vision of a people involved in spiritual warfare

During Jesus' life on earth, warfare with satanic forces was open and often violent. It is typically less open today, and thus many Christians are unaware of such invisible realities. But Scripture urges us to recognize the nature of our warfare and to rely on spiritual resources to overcome the enemy in our invisible war. Paul writes to the Ephesians, "Put on the full armor of God so that you can take your stand against the devil's schemes. For our struggle is not against flesh and blood, but against the rulers, against the authorities, against the powers of this dark world and against the spiritual forces of evil in the heavenly realms" (Eph. 6:11–12). He writes to the Corinthians that "though we live in the world, we do not wage war as the world does. The weapons we fight with are not the weapons of the world. On the contrary, they have divine power to demolish strongholds" (2 Cor. 10:3f.). Peter describes Satan as one who "prowls around like a roaring lion looking for someone to devour." "Resist him," he adds, "standing firm in the faith" (1 Peter 5:8f.).

Satan, who has blinded the eyes and darkened the understanding of those captive in his kingdom, is an enemy against whom Christ still battles in His body on the earth.

God has a vision of a people who do not judge others

The heart of the gospel is the message that God accepts us as we are, forgiving us in Christ, and through Christ working His own transformation in our personalities. Paul points out that the message of reconciliation is just this, "that God was reconciling the world to himself in Christ, not counting men's sins against them" (2 Cor. 5:19).

In the Christian community we are to model just this attitude toward one another—and even toward the world. When a brother sins he is to be restored "gently," and we are to carry his burden rather than burden him with guilt (Gal. 6:1f.). James makes it clear we have no right to judge. "Anyone who speaks against his brother, or judges him, speaks against the law and judges it. When you judge the law, you are not keeping it, but sitting in judgment on it. There is one Lawgiver and Judge . . . who are you to judge your neighbor?" (James 4:11f.).

Paul develops this theme at length in Romans. We are not to pass judgment on "disputable matters." After all,

> who are you to judge someone else's servant? To his own master he stands or falls. And he will stand, for the Lord is able to make him stand. . . . Christ died and returned to life again so that he might be the Lord of both the dead and the living. You, then, why do you judge your brother? Or why do you look down on your brother?" (Rom. 14:1, 4, 9f.).

Paul had explained earlier in Romans that pagans who are aware of sin have only two ways to deal with it. They go about with "their thoughts now accusing, now even defending them" (Rom. 2:15). In Christ there is an honest confrontation of sin and failures . . . but condemnation is ruled out by a God who deals with sin by forgiveness! Thus by rejecting judgmental attitudes and behaviors the believer models God's own forgiveness—in the church and in the world.

God has a vision of a worshiping people

The Book of Psalms gives us many expressions of worship from God's people and sets a pattern for our own worship. Worship, as attributing worth to God for who He is by nature, also played an important part in the life of the early church. Many recorded New Testament prayers begin by a recalling and affirming of who God is (Acts 4:24–30).

Jesus said that worship is one of God's purposes for His people. He explained to one person that "the Father seeks" those who will worship Him "in spirit and truth" (John 4:23). In Philippians Paul speaks of believers as "we who worship by the Spirit of God" (Phil. 3:3), showing the intimate relationship of the Spirit's presence within us and the ministry of worship.

God has a vision of a witnessing and missionary people

The mission of bringing the message of Jesus to the lost is a vital one and is mentioned over and over again in the Scriptures. Paul speaks of his privilege "to be a minister of Christ Jesus to the Gentiles with the priestly duty of proclaiming the gospel of God" (Rom. 15:16). He shares his "ambition to preach the gospel where Christ was not known" (Rom. 15:20). We too are to seek the good of others, "so that they might be saved" (1 Cor. 10:33). So, Paul says, "the important thing is that in every way . . . Christ is preached" (Phil. 1:18).

God has a vision of a ministering people

All Christians are now believer-priests, and each is given the privilege of ministry to others in the body of Christ. The New Testament pictures a people of God indwelt by the Spirit who "teach and admonish one another with all wisdom" (Col. 3:16). This theme is emphasized in the body gift passages that we have explored. But it is also repeated elsewhere. "I myself am convinced," Paul says to the Romans, "that you yourselves are full of goodness, complete in knowledge and competent to instruct one another" (Rom. 15:14). Thus "each one should use whatever gift he has received to serve others, faithfully administering God's grace in its various forms" (1 Peter 4:10).

PRACTICAL IMPLICATION

God has a vision of a servant leadership

Scripture makes it clear that leadership in the church is distinctly different from secular leadership (cf. Matt. 20:24–28). God's goal is for a leadership that moves others through spiritual power and authority, not by secular coercive or authoritarian approaches.

The people of God are to recognize the qualities that make spiritual leadership dynamic (cf. 1 Tim. 3:1ff.). "The Lord's servant must not quarrel," Paul writes to Timothy, "instead, he must be kind to everyone, able to teach, not resentful. Those who oppose him he must gently instruct, in the hope that God will grant them repentance leading them to a knowledge of the truth" (2 Tim. 2:24). Leadership in the church is to reflect Christ, serving "not because you must, but because you are willing . . . not greedy for money, but eager to serve . . . not lording it over those entrusted to you, but being examples to the flock" (1 Peter 5:2f.).

Leadership that ministers by example and modeling, rather than controls by command, follows God's own way of dealing with us.

God has a vision of a people who will be lights in the world

One impact of sin on society is to so warp our perception that evil may go unrecognized. It is against this background of disguised evil that Scripture speaks of the *laos* of God as lights in the world. "You are the light of the world," Jesus said to His followers. "Let your light shine before men, that they may see your good deeds and praise your Father in heaven" (Matt. 5:14, 16).

The people of God serve as light when they live godly lives. By their goodness they expose evil for what it is. John explains, "This is the verdict: Light has come into the world, but men loved darkness instead of light because their deeds were evil. Everyone who does evil hates the light, and will not come into the light for fear that his deeds will be exposed" (John 3:19f.). Paul adds, "You were once darkness, but now you are light in the Lord. Live as children of light (for the fruit of the light consists in all goodness, righteousness and truth)" (Eph. 5:8–9).

God has a vision of a people who associate with sinners

This may be a shocking concept to many. It shocked the Pharisees of Jesus' day. Yet when they attacked Jesus for His associations, Jesus explained, "It is not the healthy who need a doctor, but the sick. But go and learn what this means: 'I desire mercy, not sacrifice.' For I have not come to call the righteous, but sinners" (Matt. 9:12f.).

In the prayer recorded in John 17, Jesus speaks of sending us into the world as He was sent into the world. He did not come to condemn (cf. judging, above, and John 3:17f.). We, like Him, are to live love among the lost so they might sense God's love in us. Paul deals with some who misunderstood this and felt that they must withdraw from all the sinners of this world. He says, "I have written you in my letter not to associate with sexually immoral people—not at all meaning the people of this world who are immoral, or the greedy and swindlers, or idolators. In that case you would have to leave this world. . . . What business is it of mine to judge those outside the church? . . . God will judge those outside" (1 Cor. 5:9–13). It is not by judging but by living as the light of the world that the conviction of sin comes. It is not by judging but by living out Jesus' love for the lost in spite of what they may be that the reality of forgiveness and hope are communicated.

It is striking to realize that far more purposes of God are revealed in Scripture as His vision for the church than we have traditionally assumed. We have seen that God has a vision of:

- a restored humanity
- a people who live good lives
- a people who live His Word
- a people who are holy
- a people concerned with justice
- a people who meet the material needs of others
- a people free from materialism
- a loving community
- a praying people
- a people who live in hope
- a people who live under authority
- a people involved in spiritual warfare
- a people who do not judge others
- a worshiping people
- a witnessing, missionary people
- a ministering people
- a servant leadership
- a people who are the light of the world
- a people who associate with sinners

And we could continue! For God's vision includes a people who are hospitable, who love their enemies, who are united, who rejoice in suffering, who are disciples, etc. The point that we

175

want to make is simply this: *The people of God are to experience individually and together the call of God to give themselves to fulfill one or more of the divine visions.* Each believer can expect to be given a personal vision that calls him to participate in the fulfillment of one of the revealed purposes God has for the church.

The personal ministries of believers are thus to be perceived in the extremely broad framework provided by a biblical understanding of the purposes (or vision) of God to be accomplished through Christ's body. To help believers in a local congregation discover their own calling, it is vital that they be taught the wide-ranging purposes of the Lord. It is vital that they be guided to see how *every* ability an individual may have is in fact part of his giftedness. But it takes more than simply "telling" to communicate vision.

HOW LEADERS CAN COMMUNICATE VISION

There are a number of principles that leaders can follow to help members of a congregation discover God's vision for their lives.

Teach the concept of vision

Leadership involves teaching what the Bible says about the many objectives God wants to accomplish through the church. But it also involves many kinds of nonverbal communication.

Often in a congregation the only visible "ministries" are those institutionalized by the church. To "serve" means to take part in one of the programs or to staff one of the agencies run by the church. A Sunday school teacher or a youth sponsor has a defined and recognized role in the church program and thus a "ministry."

At one time I served as the minister of education of a large Illinois church. There were vacancies on various agency staffs, so I phoned all the members of the congregation to find out if they were willing to serve. What amazed me then was the discovery that many of the members of our congregation had personal ministries to which God had called them that were *not* associated with the programs of our church! One couple spent two Sundays each month conducting services and visiting in one of our local hospitals. They were apologetic they could not teach but were unwilling to surrender their hospital visitation. This couple, without being aware of it, had been given a vision. They were called to a ministry that in a clear and beautiful way fit into the vision of God for a *laos* con-

176

cerned for the sick, the lonely, and the forgotten.

There were others as well. One couple hosted Young Life meetings in their home and often had teens drop in for Cokes and spend the evening. They were sorry but they would not have time to serve.

What impressed me then was that here were people who had their own ministries and that if I involved them in the programs of the church I would have to take them from a probably far more significant service to God and others.

I expressed my appreciation for the ministry they had and released them from any sense of obligation to work in our church programs. Also I began a "God at Work" column in the church newsletter, designed to let the congregation know of some of the personal ministries to which their fellow believers were called. Without knowing it, what I was also doing was communicating to the congregation that "ministry" is not necessarily the same thing as holding a position in a church organization.

By *honoring the ministries of our members*, we can communicate to the people of God the concept of vision and the possibility of each believer experiencing God's call.

There are many ways in which we can distort the concept of vision by our practices—and just as many ways we can communicate it correctly. For instance, people in a local church will often identify themselves by an organizational role: "I am a Sunday school teacher." Because the quiet, personal ministry has no title it is often unrecognized and may even be hard to identify. It may help to spend time with individuals and lead them to define or even name the ministry in which they are involved.

Churches foster wrong perception of vision when they hold banquets to honor Sunday school teachers or have a "commissioning service" for them on a Sunday morning. This might be changed by ordaining *all* members of the body who are aware that they minister. We can also include the personal ministries of members on a regular basis in the prayers we offer on Sunday mornings or in prayer meetings. It is particularly important that whatever recognition is given in a congregation to those involved in the formal ministries of the church, it also be extended to those in personal ministries, so that the reality of a personal vision and call can be affirmed.

Recognize the sovereignty of God in personal callings

We need to recognize God's sovereign action in a calling to a personal ministry. Each of us has relationships and experiences that others know nothing about. Local congregations will find the community in which they live differs from that of others. Out of these differences will come unique emphases in ministry. This means that we cannot validly appeal to tradition or to the practices of others in defining our own calling. We need to be sensitive, individually and congregationally, to God's placement.

We also need to be aware of the skills and talents the Lord has given each of us.

God, in other words, will give visions to meet the needs of the people in the neighborhood of the congregation. One congregation may minister actively to the poor, be involved in structuring low-cost housing, tutoring, and maintaining a strong evangelical witness. The leaders and members of that congregation have recognized God's sovereign placement in their community, and ministries have grown up as individuals have responded to the existing needs.

When Lou and Paul retired, for example, they purchased a travel home and began to spend much of their time on the road. They discovered that many families stayed in camper villages on weekends, so they quietly began to hold Sunday services for others in their camper. Out of their unique situation a personal ministry developed that has not only helped the couple discover themselves as believer-priests but has also had a positive influence on many others.

Recognition of God's sovereignty should lead each believer to look at his situation and ask God for a vision of what to do. When we recognize God's sovereignty, we learn to look for fresh ways in which God's overall vision can find expression in our lives, rather than simply to find opportunities to serve in the existing programs of the institutional church.

A modeling process is vital

It takes more than preaching and teaching to bring to reality God's vision of a ministering people. To enflesh the concept of personal ministries, church leaders will need to be examples.

This is a basic principle, repeated over and over in the Scriptures. Leaders are called to be examples to God's flock (1 Peter 5:3). Paul encourages the Corinthians to imitate him as he imitates Christ (1 Cor. 4:16). Paul tells young Timothy who knows "all about [his] way of life" to "set an example for the believers in speech, in life, in love, in faith and in purity" (2 Tim. 3:10; 1 Tim. 4:12).

It becomes critical, then, that those who are spiritual leaders set an example by seeking and following their own vision for personal ministries! An elder in a congregation may serve on the church board—but his *ministry* may well be counseling or leading evangelistic Bible studies.

When Gib Martin got a vision of caring for outcasts in Seattle through what became the Grapevine Shelter, not everyone in the congregation shared it. He moved ahead without the total support of the church. Through many months and years of difficulty and revision, the Grapevine became a reality—a halfway house where drug addicts, prostitutes, and young people in trouble were cared for and their physical and spiritual needs met. Through Gib's example, many in the congregation became involved as his vision became theirs.

When the apostles in Acts 6 rejected the demand that they supervise the distribution of food to the widows and instead set up a team of spirit-filled men to do the job, they gave a significant explanation: "It would not be right for us to neglect the ministry of the word of God in order to wait on tables" (Acts 6:2). They did not discount the importance of waiting on tables; it is part of the total vision of God for the church. But they had their own vision and calling, their own personal ministry to which they had to be faithful. One of the tragedies of the contemporary church is that it forces pastors and others on a church staff to surrender their calling to a personal ministry in order to do the modern equivalent of waiting on tables—to administer and run the organizations and agencies of the church. To administer organizations and agencies is not unimportant. But there are gifted individuals in a congregation who can undertake such tasks. The staff of a church should be sure to seek a personal vision and calling *aside from maintenance of an institution* and be as faithful as the apostles were in giving priority to that calling. Such faithfulness will demonstrate to the members of the congregation that the calling of the Christian is to personal, and not just institutional, ministries. The example provided by the leaders will motivate members to be faithful to their own callings.

There are other associated principles, such as those relating to the definition and clarification of personal ministries, that will be developed in later chapters. At this point, however, we have seen that it is important for leaders to:

1) educate the body about the many objectives of God in the church that constitutes His vision for it;
2) teach the concept of vision both verbally and nonverbally;

3) recognize the sovereignty of God in seeking a personal vision;

4) provide a model for the congregation by personal commitment to personal ministries.

THE PLACE OF TRADITION

At this point it is necessary to comment on the impact of tradition on the church's openness to vision. Put bluntly, tradition is usually the enemy of vision. This is as true today as it was in New Testament times, when Christ deliberately condemned the Pharisees and lawyers. The import of that condemnation, stated clearly in Matthew 23, is that the leaders had put human traditions in place of the voice of God. They could not hear or respond to Him because their whole approach to religion was patterned on the codified experience of past generations.

No wonder Jesus said to them, "Why do you break the command of God for the sake of your tradition? . . . Thus you nullify the word of God for the sake of your tradition" (Matt. 15:3, 6).

It is the distinctive responsibility of each believer to live *in the present day*, in personal relationship with God and be personally responsive to His voice. Like the Pharisees we all too often close our minds and hearts to His voice because what we hear does not fit the patterns with which we have grown up. For all too many, "We've never done it that way" is a compelling and sufficient reason to reject the vision of others and the call of God.

Jesus also spoke of new wine requiring new wineskins. Of course, people prefer the old wine. But the new wine of each new generation of believer-priests must be allowed to mature in the new wineskins designed for it. If new wine is placed in the old wineskins, Jesus taught, the old skins will burst and the wine be spilled on the ground.

How important, then, that each generation of believers approach its own day with full commitment to the Word of God—and total freedom from bondage to the last generation's traditions. Within new wineskins, shaped by the Spirit, a new and heady wine *will* mature. Without the freedom provided by a recognition of the dangers of tradition, some of the new wine will be spoiled as the old wineskins burst from the inner pressure and dynamic thrust of the new life. And the potential of what might have been will be lost.

To communicate a vision is to accept the fact that there *will* be changes in the shape and experience of a local congregation. The comfortable traditions of the past will be set aside. But the process of renewal, generation by generation, is God's process. Wine maturing in new skins will be intoxicating and bring joy.

PROBE

▶ case *histories*
▶ discussion *questions*
▶ thought *provokers*
▶ resources

1. What is your personal vision? That is, what sense of call do you have to your own place within the broader vision for the body?
   Write out your own personal vision in two or three pages. If you are not aware of a personal vision, reread the brief description of God's vision in this chapter. Do you feel that any of these ideas expresses a concern of your own heart? Or do you feel you have any particular opportunities in your local church to respond to one of these visions?

2. Look at the following list of sixty reasons for being closed to the new. How many of these are related in one way or another to tradition? Put a check mark beside those you feel are related to tradition. Underline the five you feel are most often the reason why Christians may be closed to following a personal or congregational vision.

SIXTY EXCUSES FOR A CLOSED MIND

_____ We tried that before.
_____ Our place is different.
_____ It costs too much.
_____ That is beyond our responsibility.
_____ We are all too busy to do that.
_____ That is not my job.
_____ It is too radical a change.
_____ We do not have the time.
_____ We don't have enough help.
_____ That will make other equipment obsolete.
_____ Let's make a market research test of it first.
_____ Our plant is too small for it.
_____ It is not practical for operating people.
_____ The men will never buy it.
_____ The union will scream.
_____ We have never done it before.
_____ It's against company policy.
_____ It will run up our overhead.

PRACTICAL IMPLICATION

_____ We do not have the authority.
_____ That is too "ivory tower."
_____ Let's get back to reality.
_____ That is our problem.
_____ Why change it; it is still working O.K.
_____ I don't like the idea.
_____ You're right, but. . . .
_____ You're two years ahead of your time.
_____ We're not ready for that.
_____ We don't have the money, equipment, room, personnel.
_____ It is not in the budget.
_____ You can't teach an old dog new tricks.
_____ It's a good thought but impractical.
_____ Let's hold it in abeyance.
_____ Let's give it more thought.
_____ Top management would never go for it.
_____ Let's put it in writing.
_____ We'll be the laughing stock.
_____ Not that again.
_____ We would lose money in the long run.
_____ Where did you dig that one up?
_____ We've done all right without it.
_____ That's what we can expect from the staff.
_____ It's never been tried before.
_____ Let's table it for the time being.
_____ Let's form a committee.
_____ Has anyone else ever tried it?
_____ I don't see the connection.
_____ Customers won't like it.
_____ It won't work in our plant.
_____ What you are really saying is . . .
_____ Maybe that will work in your department, but not in mine.
_____ The executive committee will never go for it.
_____ Do you think we should look into it further before we act?
_____ What do they do in our competitor's plant?
_____ Let's all sleep on it.
_____ It can't be done.
_____ It's too much trouble to change.
_____ It won't pay for itself.
_____ I know a fellow who tried it.
_____ It's impossible.
_____ We've always done it this way.[1]

---

[1]Adapted from a list developed by the New York Chapter of the American Society of Training Directors, and used by permission.

3. Phone members of your congregation and see if you can find out how many of them are now involved in personal ministries. Include both institutional and noninstitutional ministries. What does your survey reveal? Summarize your findings and insights in a short essay.

4. In speaking out against *tradition,* the authors are not speaking against *history.* Which of the following statements do you believe draw valid distinctions between tradition and history or express an acceptable relationship between them?

   - Tradition is history wrapped around the church and set in cement.
   - Tradition is normally *recent history.*
   - Only a people who have no knowledge of the history of the church will be trapped by tradition.
   - History is a record of what God has done among His people across many generations, with all the complexity and adaptability of the Spirit displayed. Tradition is what God did in the last generation or two, treated as a mold into which His people and Spirit must fit today.
   - Commitment to history frees the mind to see many possibilities in the ways faith is experienced and expressed. Commitment to tradition chains the mind to see only one valid way in which people must live.

   How many additional statements (true or false) can you add to this list?

5. *Case History*

   All our life can shape us—personality and giftedness—for God's gift of a vision. Laura Billingsley Ward, an attractive Atlanta thirty-year-old, has a unique personal vision that combines many of the elements in the New Testament's portrait of God's vision for His church.

LAURA BILLINGSLEY WARD

I was working as a social caseworker with families when God started working on my heart. He made me sympathize deeply with the problems they were experiencing and the depth of their need. I could have said, "Well, Jesus has the answer," but I didn't want to come in from my home in suburbia to their inner-city homes once every six months. So God called me to live *with* the people.

About a year before coming to Brookvalley Church, I had been promoted to supervisor with the State Department, without my degree, just because of my experience. I lacked one year toward my degree, so I decided to go back to school. After graduating I began to ask God where He wanted me to go and what He wanted me to do. Jim Bevis, our minister, came to me and asked if I would be interested in working for the Christian Council of Metropolitan Atlanta. At the same time Brookvalley was interested in starting a coffee house ministry. Both of these are in the same building. I was put in charge of the coffee house for Brookvalley as a coordinator.

We saw prostitutes on the street and were concerned about their situation, but we had no clue about how to reach them with the gospel, or even what you would say to them. So we invited a couple, Jimmy and Judy Mamou, to come and tell us. Judy had been a prostitute, but through Jimmy's prayer and love she had come to the Lord. Now they have a ministry to prostitutes and help church people like me minister in the inner city. After the initial preparations, we went out on the streets to talk to a few prostitutes.

Before I came to know the Lord, I had gotten into drugs. I am very conscious of the fact that if God had not given me a new life and I had continued in the direction I was going, I could easily have been on the streets supporting the habit. I can "feel" where these girls are, maybe, in a way that someone who hasn't had this kind of experience wouldn't feel.

We shared a book, *The Other Woman,* with our contacts, and they were really interested in it. As I talked I began to see that they were just ordinary people. I became excited about the possibility of telling them what Jesus meant to me.

I met Kara, the man who is now my husband, when I rented from him the parking lot that we had selected for street work. We became good friends. He had a burden for the girls and was concerned about getting them off the street. He was very positive about what we were doing and gladly let us use his parking lot. The girls would come into the booth to get warm and take their coffee breaks. We would talk to them at that time and got to know them.

Right after Jimmy and Judy left I met Burlene in the booth. One of the churches had held some street meetings and Burlene had listened to them. She said to me, "They say they love me so much, I wonder what they'd say if I told them I had no place to stay tonight?" What she was saying was they say they care, but what would they do if you really needed them? I said, "If you really need a place to stay, Burlene, you can come home with me." That took her completely by surprise. She stayed at my place a couple of months. She had a nine-year-old daughter, who was growing up in her mother's footsteps. Her mother had already taught her how to beg for money. I tried to get close to them and share my faith with them.

On the streets they knew we were Christians. We didn't have

to say too much. Sometimes they would ask us questions. One night we had a prayer meeting right in the booth, and the girls asked us to pray for them. One night one of the girls was sick, so I took her home with me. I offered to do the same for others but often they didn't take me up on my offer. Basically we were just developing relationships, and I can't say really how much came out of it. One girl that came home with me several times is now off the streets. Another one that I helped get probation for went back to her family. Another girl, who didn't even remember me when she was on the street because she was always so high on dope, got my name from a probation officer. She wrote me an incredible letter about how she wanted to get her life right with the Lord, but didn't know how and she didn't even know who to ask. Could I help her? I went to the jail and talked with her, and she came to know the Lord. While she was in jail, she witnessed to everyone. But now she's out of jail and back working the streets! My guess is that she felt her pimp was the only person who really loved her and she didn't want to give him up.

The work is frustrating in many ways, at least in terms of the number of people who come to know the Lord. But just one would mean a lot to me.

We have a very supportive church. I don't think it would matter what I got involved with if it were the Lord's work. They would support it. I have brought prostitutes to church, and they were just as thrilled as I was that they were there. The church paid to get another girl off the street, and onto a plane so she could go home. The only thing the members haven't offered is to take the girls into their homes. I have been pushing that, but people find it very difficult to open up their homes to a prostitute. You have to have a special burden to do that.

Kara, my husband, is black. The interracial relationship exists a lot on the street, especially between white girls and black pimps. Because of my relationship to Kara, girls would say they felt like I was what they called "a down person"; in other words, I didn't think I was better than they were, or too good for them.

I think being married to Kara has helped my relationship with the girls of the street. He is able to talk with them, too, in many ways even better than I can. He is the kind of person whom people feel they can share with, and they will share their problems with him even more readily than with me.

His mother was probably one of the most godly women that has ever been—from what he tells me about her. I never met her because she died about fifteen years ago. But she was a beautiful Christian woman and really raised him in the right way. But he had never had a specific conversion experience. Deep down in his heart he always knew that he had to accept Jesus as his Savior. But he just could not make that decision. I think God set him up for it by bringing us down to the parking lot. He also has a Christian secretary who was always on his back about her faith. God started working on him. Kara knew Christianity was true and right; he just hadn't come to that born-again experience. Gradually he began to seek it, and one Sunday he went forward in our church.

Looking ahead, we both feel called to keep working with the girls on the street. I think I may turn some of our church people off, and I have in the past if they aren't burdened for what God has called me to. I have to realize that God calls people to other ministries, including ministries to the rich. God loves all people. But my concern is for the down-and-out, the rejects of society. And I think God has a special concern for these people because He says a lot about them in the Word. I just remind people, "Whatever you did for one of the least of these brothers of mine, you did for me."

PRACTICAL IMPLICATION

Identity Implications
Communicating Vision
Building Relationships and Community
Making Disciples
Equipping
Extending Freedom
Understanding Leadership

BUILDING RELATIONSHIPS AND COMMUNITY

When the gospel burst so dynamically on the first-century world, part of its power came from the stunning content of its message. The New Testament world knew nothing of a created universe or personal, supreme God. Fate ruled even the gods, and the gods were hardly concerned with individual human beings. Even the mystery religions, which sought to fill the void with various superstitions, could not provide hope. Individuals knew nothing of finding meaning for their lives through a relationship with either a purposive universe or a personal God.

The message of the gospel was startling. There *is* a personal, supreme God. He is both Creator and Judge. This God loves individuals enough to enter history in the person of His Son and promises everlasting life and personal resurrection to all who accept Him by faith.

This was a powerful message. But it would be a mistake to imagine that the sweeping victory of the Christian faith in the first century was simply the result of a "better philosophy." The core truth of the gospel was, of course, important in evangelism and in the growth of the church. But with truth came another aspect of the Christian message that was as uniquely compelling. The gospel tells of a God whose love can be experienced. It promises a transformation of the relationships between human beings who accept Jesus. Through love, the reality of the gospel message can be experienced now. The underlying core truths (who God is, resurrection, judgment to come, the dissolution of this universe, etc.) are not open to empirical verification. They will be known by experience one day, but for now they must be accepted by faith. But love! Ah, *the transformation of relationships promised in the gospel can be experienced, and demonstrated, now!*

John, the "apostle of love," put it this way in his First Epistle:

> Dear friends, let us love one another, for love comes from God. Everyone who loves has been born of God and knows God. Whoever does not love does not know God, because God is love. This is how God showed his love among us: He sent his one and only Son into the world that we might live through him. This is love: not that we loved God, but that he loved us and sent his Son as an atoning sacrifice for our sins. Dear friends, since God so loved us, we also ought to love one another. No one has ever seen God; but if we love each other, God lives in us and his love is made complete in us (1 John 4:7–12).

God, living now in His people, communicates His presence among them through the love relationships that develop. The

Christian community's acceptance, forgiveness, and commitment to one another in the sharing of material resources and in the sharing of joys and sorrows give God's love living and visible expression.

The relationship emphasis in the gospel has always been present in God's dealings with men. God's dynamic love for men has always been intended to flow out to others from those in relationship with the Lord. Look, for instance, at these words from Deuteronomy:

> To the LORD your God belong the heavens, even the highest heavens, the earth and everything in it. Yet the LORD set his affection on your forefathers and loved them, and he chose you, their descendants, above all the nations, as it is today. Circumcise your hearts, therefore, and do not be stiff-necked any longer. For the LORD your God is God of gods and Lord of lords, the great God, mighty and awesome, who shows no partiality and accepts no bribes. He defends the cause of the fatherless and the widow, and loves the alien, giving him food and clothing. And you are to love those who are aliens, for you yourselves were aliens in Egypt. Fear the LORD your God and serve him. Hold fast to him and take your oaths in his name (Deut. 10:14–20).

Brothers and strangers are to be loved, for the people of God have experienced the love of God. Thus, their own relationships are to be transformed. Law itself, according to this passage and many others, must be understood as God's guidance into a life of love. The anger that flashed out from God through the prophets against those who break the Law is not the outraged shout of a petty tyrant, but the deep concern of a God so committed to love that he cannot abide a people without compassion:

> You hate the one who reproves in court
> and despise him who tells the truth.
> You trample on the poor
> and force him to give you grain.
> Therefore, though you have built stone mansions,
> you will not live in them;
> though you have planted lush vineyards,
> you will not drink their wine.
> For I know how many are your offenses
> and how great your sins.
> You oppress the righteous and take bribes
> and you deprive the poor of justice in the courts.
> Therefore, the prudent man keeps quiet in such times,
> for the times are evil (Amos 5:10–13).

In rejecting the pathway of law, the people of Israel turned their backs on the way of love.

Paul sums up the relational nature of law in Romans 13:

Let no debt remain outstanding, except the continuing debt to love one another, for he who loves his fellow man has fulfilled the law. The commandments, "Do not commit adultery," "Do not murder," "Do not steal," "Do not covet," and whatever other commandments there may be, are summed up in this one rule: "Love your neighbor as yourself." Love does no harm to its neighbor. Therefore love is the fulfillment of the law (Rom. 13:8–10).

Little wonder that in the Gospels Jesus' "new commandment" focuses on the same old issue—but with new dimensions. "Love one another," Jesus said, adding the new standard, "just as I have loved you." He also added a promise: "All men will know that you are my disciples if you love one another" (John 13:34–35).

When we deal with the impact of relationships on personal ministries, we need to remember that *God has always been concerned about the development of loving personal relationships.* Love between believers is central to the nature of God and thus to the nature of the Christian community. Love for those outside the community of faith is also part of the essential nature of God. He loved even while we were still enemies (Rom. 5:8, 10). *It is impossible to imagine a vital Christian community without visualizing a loving people who express that love in practical and meaningful ways.*

It should be no surprise, then, when we insist that loving personal relationships provide the context in which God intends personal ministries to take place.

THE RELATIONAL DIMENSIONS OF MINISTRY

In reaching out

There is much evidence in the New Testament that what we think of as an "evangelistic" ministry is essentially personal and relational in nature. This is not to suggest that the content of the gospel message should be slighted or is in any way irrelevant. It is, however, to affirm that the gospel is best heard, and most likely responded to, when loving relationships exist between the communicator and the hearer.

In his first letter to them Paul recalls his visit to the Thessalonians to establish a church in their city. He explores both the content and the relational context of his evangelism. In the first chapter he focuses on the gospel message. The Word came "with power, with the Holy Spirit and with deep conviction" (1 Thess. 1:5). As the apostle and his co-workers lived with the people of the city ("you know how we lived among you for your sake"), many were drawn to the evangelistic team and, "in spite of severe suffering, [they] welcomed the mes-

191

sage . . ." (1 Thess. 1:6). Finally, Paul says this same message "rang out from [them]" (1 Thess. 1:8). The significance of the communication of gospel content—of core truth—is established.

In chapter 2 Paul goes into detail about the relationships he developed with the Thessalonians. The team members lived among those to whom they ministered (1 Thess. 1:5). Their deepest motives were well known (1 Thess. 2:3–5). What is even more significant, there was no question about the love of the apostle for the people among whom he had come to live. He speaks in intimate family terms of a mother's love for a tiny infant (1 Thess. 2:7). He speaks of growing to know them better, and says, "We loved you so much that we were delighted to share with you not only the gospel of God but our lives as well, because you had become so dear to us" (1 Thess. 2:8). Again, speaking in family terms, Paul reminds the new believers of his love for each individual and the time he spent with each, "encouraging, comforting and urging [them] to live lives worthy of God" (1 Thess. 2:12). The whole tone of this section of the letter is a reminder of something the Thessalonians could never forget, that the brothers and sisters who came to them with the gospel message came with love, and loved them in deeply practical and personal ways.

This theme of loving relationships established as a context for ministry is often repeated in Scripture. According to Jesus, believers are to love even their enemies! "Love your enemies and pray for those who persecute you, that you may be sons of your Father in heaven. He causes his sun to rise on the evil and the good, and sends rain on the righteous and the unrighteous. . . . Be perfect, therefore, as your heavenly Father is perfect" (Matt. 5:44–45, 48). The relationships Christians develop in their communities and in society are to mirror the love of God for a lost humanity.

This concept underlies Paul's correction of the Corinthians in chapter 5 of his first letter. Paul had told them they were not to associate with immoral members of the church. Some extended this to mean isolation from non-Christians. "I have written you in my letter," Paul explains, "not to associate with sexually immoral people—not at all meaning the people of this world who are immoral, or the greedy and swindlers, or idolators. In that case you would have to leave the world" (1 Cor. 5:9–10). Indeed Christians are not to *leave* the world. We have been sent *into* the world, as Jesus was sent into it (John 17:18). Like Jesus, who was known as the friend of sinners, and with whom prostitutes and publi-

See p. 175

cans felt comfortable, we are to build relationships with sinners in which they know we love them. Through our love they are to learn the love of God.

One thing Christians often misunderstand about building relationships with non-Christians is that such relationships are to be *nonjudgmental*. Paul says to the Corinthians, "What business is it of mine to judge those outside the church? . . . God will judge those outside" (1 Cor. 5:12–13). Jesus said of His own mission, "God did not send his Son into the world to condemn the world, but to save the world through him" (John 3:17). Confronted by the Pharisees, Jesus said "You judge by human standards; I pass judgment on no one. But if I do judge, my decisions are right . . ." (John 8:15f.). While Jesus penetrated every facade and was fully aware of the sins of those among whom He lived, He held back from passing judgment. Rather than focus on sin, He focused on forgiveness and the love of God. He knew that men are usually aware of their failures, whether or not they admit them. Men are unable to face sin because there seems to be no solution for it. The love of God and the forgiveness offered in Christ presents a solution that not only frees *from* sin, but also frees individuals to *admit* sin. There is release from the terrible frustration of our accusing or excusing conscience! It is available to human beings in the message of God's forgiveness. Through forgiveness God is able to come to us with love *in spite of* what we are and because of what Jesus has already accomplished.

It is clear, then, that the kind of relationships that Christians develop with the unsaved are to be based on acceptance and forgiveness. We are freed from any obligation to judge or condemn the non-Christians among whom we live. There is only one debt we owe, "the continuing debt to love one another, for he who loves his fellow man has fulfilled the law" (Rom. 13:8).

The portrait of the *laos* of God is a picture of a people who live lovingly among the people of the world, close enough to be observed and known as a loving people. Peter speaks of doing good and suffering for it, while yet retaining a living hope. Hope observed will bring questions, and we are to "always be prepared to give an answer to everyone who asks [us] to give the reason for the hope that [we] have" (1 Peter 3:15). We are not to participate in the evil deeds and ways of the lost world, but we are to live love in our society, drawing close enough to others that as living letters from God we may be "known and read by everybody" (2 Cor. 3:2).

193

PRACTICAL IMPLICATION

In body ministry

Ministry within the body of Christ is to be even more relational. Wherever body gifts are mentioned, as we have already seen, there is an emphasis on the quality of the relationships to be developed within the fellowship of believers.

When ministries within the body of Christ are discussed in Romans, Paul insists that love "must be sincere" and goes on to describe it.

> Be devoted to one another in brotherly love. Honor one another above yourselves. Never be lacking in zeal, but keep your spiritual fervor, serving the Lord. Be joyful in hope, patient in affliction, faithful in prayer. Share with God's people who are in need. Practice hospitality. . . . Rejoice with those who rejoice; mourn with those who mourn. Live in harmony with one another. Do not be proud, but be willing to associate with people of low position . . . (Rom. 12:9–13, 15–16).

When Romans discusses ministries within the body, Paul urges a "more excellent way," reminding us that love is utterly essential in ministry:

> And now I will show you the most excellent way.
> If I speak in the tongues of men and of angels, but have not love, I am only a resounding gong or a clanging cymbal. If I have the gift of prophecy and can fathom all mysteries and all knowledge, and if I have a faith that can move mountains, but have not love, I am nothing. If I give all I possess to the poor and surrender my body to the flames, but have not love, I gain nothing.
> Love is patient, love is kind. It does not envy, it does not boast, it is not proud. It is not rude, it is not self-seeking, it is not easily angered, it keeps no record of wrongs. Love does not delight in evil but rejoices with the truth. It always protects, always trusts, always hopes, always perseveres (1 Cor. 12:28–13:6).

In Ephesians Paul's prayer for a knitting together of the family, rooted and established in love (Eph. 3:14–19), introduces gifts and body ministry. That body ministry focuses on maturing believers, to attain "the whole measure of the fullness of Christ" (Eph. 4:13). This comes as each believer contributes his or her share and thus the whole body "builds itself up in love" (Eph. 4:16). As a renewed people of God we are His dearly loved children and are to "live a life of love, just as Christ loved us and gave himself up for us as a fragrant offering and sacrifice to God" (Eph. 5:2).

At times 1 Peter 4, which speaks of serving with all the strength God provides (v. 11), is considered with the other biblical references as a gift chapter. In the immediate context we again find love relationships stressed as the context for ministry. "Above all," Peter says, we must "love each other deeply, because love covers over a multitude of sins. Offer hospitality to one another without grumbling. Each one should use whatever spiritual gift he has received to serve others, faithfully administering God's grace in its various forms" (1 Peter 4:8–10).

The conclusion that we draw is simple and yet compelling. *The Scripture does not conceive of gifts or giftedness functioning in an impersonal setting.* The incarnation of Jesus in the *laos* of God is to be an incarnation of God's love in personal relationships. Truth *can* be spoken in an impersonal setting. But love can only be communicated where relationships are close enough for the reality of love to be experienced. When we deal with the gospel, we are dealing with *the truth about God's love.* This truth, because it is the truth about love, must be communicated in *both* words (concepts, propositions, information) and experience (the recipient of the message must *be loved* and thus experience the reality of God's love through members of the body of Christ).

The rationale for relational ministries

In a sense the rationale for the development of personal relationships as the context for personal ministries has already been established. We have seen God's consistent concern for loving relationships as an outcome and expression of His love. This remains constant through Old and New Testaments. We have seen Jesus Himself respond to the sinners of His day. And we might have documented again the already well-known depth of relationship He chose to develop with His disciples. We've seen in the New Testament that missionary outreach was conducted in a relational setting, that Christians are called on to love the men and women of the world. While we do not participate in sin, we are not to judge, but are to model the reality of God's forgiving love.

We have also seen that wherever spiritual gifts are spoken of in the New Testament there is an emphasis on a deep loving relationship between believers. When we use the gifts the Spirit has given to build up the body, our ministry is to take place in a climate defined by an overwhelming awareness of love.

These are the biblical facts. These are the biblical realities. To live Christ and to share Christ we are to be a loving people.

Actually, it's not too hard to understand why both love of God and love for others are vital for sharing Christ with one another and in the world.

In God's kind of love, there is no question of whether we should accept or value people. When God's kind of love is experienced, no individual feels threatened. God's love affirms the worth and value of each individual in spite of what he or she may have done. It is "not because of righteous things we had done" that God evaluates our worth. It was "because of his mercy" that "he saved us" (Titus 3:5). Since God's love does not place on us a demand to perform, we are free in our relationship with Him to be ourselves—and free from the frightening obligation to defend or hide ourselves.The assurance of being loved frees us to open ourselves up to self-judgment—and to change.

This is why God's kind of love must find expression through His people. When we communicate the full message of the gospel, truths about sin and judgment will, of course, be involved. But if the non-Christian knows that he is loved and valued by us *anyway,* the overwhelming reality of God's forgiveness will be sensed. Our relationships with non-Christians must *act out* the gospel so the reality of its words are experienced as well as heard.

This is also why God's kind of love must find expression *within* the community of faith. When we communicate to others in the body the identity we have in the Lord and the importance of a life worthy of our calling, aspects of sin and failure and judgment will be involved. But if the believer knows that his brothers and sisters love and value him *anyway,* he will sense the overwhelming reality of God's forgiveness and love. Our relationships with fellow believers must also *act out* the gospel so the reality of the life-transforming truths we share may be experienced as well as heard.

Ministry within the body of Christ and to those outside are both to take place in a climate shaped by loving personal relationships.

IMPLICATIONS OF MINISTRY
AS AN INTERPERSONAL TRANSACTION

In the first part of this chapter we made what we believe to be an extremely significant statement. *Ministry is essentially an interpersonal transaction.* It takes place as a love relationship between persons grows. It is in this relational context that gifts and giftedness find their most significant expression.

Let's explore this idea further to see the impact it can have on a local congregation.

Build a loving community

The church of Christ is by nature a family. It is in the reality of the family relationship that love is expressed and that the way of love is learned.

196

It's important to see the church as a fellowship within which people learn how to be loved and to love. Peter suggests that a genuine capacity to love comes from our relationship with God. "Now that you have purified yourselves by obeying the truth so that you have sincere love for your brothers," he says, "love one another deeply, from the heart" (1 Peter 1:22). *Our potential for loving is to be developed, by a conscious effort, to a deep love and care for each other.*

One of the first questions that needs to be asked in a congregation where leaders seek to develop the *laos* as a ministering people is this: Do the gatherings of the body provide opportunities for coming to know one another in loving ways?

It's possible to analyze gatherings of the body by the type of interaction that takes place in them. Such an analysis will give us some insight into the kinds of relationships we need to encourage. Let's look at three interaction types to see what we mean.

TYPE I

The first type of interaction can be symbolized by a single arrow. In this kind of interaction, the *communication flow* is *one way.* One person speaks, the others listen.

We see this interaction pattern in such church meetings as the Sunday morning service. At times the same pattern spills over into many other meetings and gatherings, from classes to prayer meetings to board meetings.

There are some definite strengths to this interaction pattern. If our goal is to communicate information in logical form, then this is an effective approach. If the time of a meeting is limited and the goal is to transmit concepts, then this interaction format will probably be the best choice.

But this format has weaknesses as well. Information communicated in this format typically is learned as concepts—but is less likely to be translated into action or transformed into attitudes and values. Another significant weakness is that in this setting there is no opportunity for

197

participants to come to know—or to learn to love—each other. A lack of interaction between the gathered members of the body creates an *impersonal* rather than *interpersonal/ transactional* climate.

The second type of interaction can be symbolized by two arrows passing. In this kind of interaction, the *communication flow* is *back* and *forth.* Usually one person speaks (a leader or teacher), and members of the group respond.

TYPE II

We see this interaction pattern in such settings as Sunday school classes, many board or committee meetings, and, at times, home Bible studies. At times this type of interaction also characterizes children's programs and clubs.

There are strengths to this interaction pattern, also. Typically, in such a setting the leader has provided information and then moderates a discussion. In the discussion the members of the group volunteer, or are asked, questions, or they are asked for clarifying illustrations and examples. Typically, there will be a *description* of the application of truth taught. For instance, it's easy in a class focusing on "love" for members in a Type-II process to illustrate love in action with such suggestions as: visit a sick person, bring home flowers, stop to listen, etc.

With the strengths, there are also weaknesses. In spite of broadening concepts by the description of behaviors related to them, it is unusual in this setting for communication to move to a personal level. It is unusual in this setting for persons to speak in "I" and "me" terms of their own personal experiences.

Part of the reason for this inhibition is that typically the teacher or leader is a party to each interaction. That is, the teacher says something; a group replies; the teacher reacts; a group member answers; etc. It is *un*usual in this setting for group members to address each other directly.

While members participate more actively in this type of setting and thus, have more of an opportunity to develop impressions of one another, the lack of direct, person-to-person interaction and the hesitancy to share personal matters are a distinct drawback if our goal is to build a loving community.

The third type of interaction can be symbolized by a number of arrows crossing each other. In this kind of interaction the *communication flow* is *free and spontaneous.* There will be a leader in the group, but he acts as a participant with other members of the group.

TYPE III

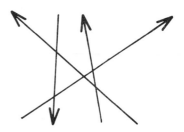

Typically, we see this interaction pattern in small Bible study groups, in some board or committee meetings —and in restaurants and living rooms. The key here is informality and the involvement of all members of the group.

The strengths of this process lie in its potential for dealing with truths and concepts—and individual needs—in a very personal way. In this kind of process it is much easier for individuals to respond to others as persons. It is also much more natural and easy to share inner personal experiences in "I" or "me" kinds of talk.

The weaknesses of this setting are also somewhat apparent. It is not a particularly good process to communicate new information or logically organized content. It is a time-consuming process and does not easily fit into a formal "one-hour" system. Of course, simply having a setting in which this interaction pattern is experienced does not guarantee that meaningful sharing will take place.

Still, there is a definite value in taking a look at the meetings of a local congregation to observe the types of interaction that take place in each. Understanding the strengths and weaknesses of each type of interaction, we can tell by observing congregational gatherings the kind of climate we are building in our church.

It's clear from a glance at the chart on page 200 that no one interaction process is "right" for the church. Surely there needs to be a combination. Type I has its place, as does the preaching ministry it represents. Type II is also significant. However, many churches fail to provide Type III interaction settings—and these are just the settings in which the community of love is most effectively built.

FIGURE 4

TYPE I	TYPE II	TYPE III
	Weaknesses	
Impersonal Difficult to transfer to attitudes/ values/action	Not good for communi- cating content/ information Unlikely to generate "I/me" sharing	Not good for communi- cating content/ information Time-consuming process
	Strengths	
Good when the time is limited Good when the goal is to communicate con- cepts logically	Good when there is a desire to illustrate actions expressing biblical principles	Good for personal sharing, coming to know others, expressing love

This is not to suggest that Christians do not get together informally and chat with each other in Type III groupings. It is to suggest that *local church leaders seldom structure or plan for such sharing that focuses on our common faith and life in Christ.* Yet it is exactly the picture of the Type III setting we receive from Scripture as the church gathers to focus on the Lord. "Let us consider how we may spur one another on toward love and good deeds," the writer to the Hebrews urges, and adds, "Let us not give up meeting together, as some are in the habit of doing, but let us encourage one another—and all the more as you see the Day approaching" (Heb. 10:24–25).

We can summarize, then, by saying that in a local congregation it is vital to have a *balance* of gathering types. If we hope to build a ministering people, a people who come to know and love one another and from whom love reaches out to meet each other's needs, then we *must* provide within our structures planned and well-designed settings for significant Type III sharing.

Visualize ministry as interpersonal

We've noted the importance of structuring opportunities for members of the body to come to know and care for each other. It is in being loved and loving in return *within the body* that most believers will be freed to reach out in loving ways to those who are yet outside God's family.

But to build a ministering people it is also important to help members of the local congregation visualize ministry as an interpersonal transaction. Coming to know and love each other must seem to be a valid element of Christian experience. Also making a contribution to others through our gift or giftedness *in that interpersonal setting* needs to be understood as a ministry.

Christians often find this difficult to grasp. So much of what has come to be known as "ministering" has been institutionalized. "Full-time Christian workers" prepare to minister by attending schools and taking degrees, and then move into well-defined roles in the local church or missions. The definition of "ministry" is found in *that role within the institution.* Preach and teach classes. Visit the sick. Perform weddings and conduct funerals. Administer the programs of the church. These and many other institutional functions have in fact given most contemporary believers their unstated but nonetheless dominant concept of what "ministry" involves.

The same institutionalized understanding has been extended to the ministry of the "part-time" worker. Training is provided (at times) and a *well-defined role* is provided *by the agency or program in which the worker participates.* Teacher's covenants and job descriptions enhance the impression that "ministry" is something that takes place at specific times and in specific places, with the task of ministering persons well defined by the institution.

None of this is to suggest that a significant ministry cannot take place in the agencies of a local congregation. However, the institutionalization of ministry has brought blindness to the *laos* of God. Most people simply do not recognize the opportunities they have to minister in the informal settings of their daily lives. The key to an effective ministry is never found in its institutional setting, but always in its relational setting. Whenever believers come to know and care for others—and reach out to share, encourage, and help—*there* is the setting for the most significant ministries that can take place.

Al Kassay, whose case history is found in the first chapter of this book, did not at first recognize as a ministry his use of two afternoons a week to help preteen-agers learn carpentry. It was only later, as this sharing of his giftedness built into the family's life, that he recognized his experience for what it was.

Paul describes a similar situation in the Book of Titus. He gives instructions about the "teaching" ministry of older women. He does not describe an institutional setting for their ministry. Instead, the setting is distinctively interpersonal. The older women are to visit the younger, to help them in their homes, and in the process to encourage them to a godly way of life. Paul calls this ministry "teaching."

But today most Christians would not think of it as teaching because their eyes have been blinded by the association in our culture of teaching with a classroom. Hear Paul's advice:

> Likewise, teach the older women to be reverent in the way they live, not to be slanderers or addicted to much wine, but to teach what is good. Then they can train the younger women to love their husbands and children, to be self-controlled and pure, to be busy at home, to be kind, and to be subject to their husbands, so that no one will malign the word of God (Titus 2:3–5).

What we need to do is *help the* laos *of God recognize every interpersonal relationship as a setting for ministry, that they might freely share their giftedness and gifts with others.*

How can this be done? We mentioned one way in an earlier chapter. We can give as much recognition to the personal ministries of members of our congregation as we give to those who minister in institutional programs. But more is required. Gib Martin has found that projects assigned in short-term "schools" or "courses" conducted frequently at Trinity have a great potential.

An assignment in one school was to bake a pie . . . and invite a neighbor over to share it. For one man the project led to the discovery of unexpected potential. And through sharing the pie, a relationship was begun with a neighbor couple that, over a period of years, led to his significant ministry to that couple at a time their marriage seemed about to break up.

An assignment was given to a discipleship group to spend the day working together on an older member's house. They cleaned, chopped wood, and cared for the yard. In the experience the group learned much about the relational context of ministry—and that this kind of caring was in itself a significant ministry.

It is also important, if members of the *laos* are to learn to visualize ministry as an interpersonal transaction, that the staff of the church *move out of its institutional roles in its own ministry.* In an earlier chapter we saw the importance of modeling by the leadership of the church. We suggested that those in positions of spiritual leadership have their own "personal ministry" or calling as well. Now we want to suggest that it is especially important for leaders to build relationships with members of the congregation in noninstitutional settings. Meet with individuals for lunch or tennis. Have people over to your home. Go on shared retreats or vacations. Build personal relationships with other church leaders so that you know each other as persons and not just as "leaders." In building relationships, share yourselves and encourage others to share. As you build bridges of love, they become structures for spontaneous personal ministries that will demonstrate your own belief in ministry as an interpersonal, rather than institutional, transaction.

Encourage the building of relationships with non-Christians

Some years ago a research project showed that the longer a person is a believer, the fewer friendships he enjoys with non-Christians.

While this is understandable and to some extent desirable (significant personal relationships must be developed within the body), it is at the same time an indictment of the *laos* whom Jesus sends into the world just as the Father sent Him (John 17:18).

The *laos* of God must maintain a consistent *outward look*. The leadership of a congregation needs to encourage such an outward look, seeking the benefit of those who have not yet come to Christ.

In the past, ministry to those outside the local congregation was also visualized primarily in an institutional framework. When I was a young Christian in New York City, our local church held annual "revival meetings." An evangelist was called to hold meetings for two weeks in our church or in a tent in the lot next door. The pastors urged all the members of the congregation to bring as many unsaved people to the meetings as possible. The same vision was held of the Sunday school. We were to bring in children and others so that, within the framework provided by the institutional program, "outsiders" might be won to Christ. Efforts were focused not so much on building relationships but on getting people into the church building. Leaders concentrated not so much on the needs of others or on coming to know others as persons, but on bringing them physically to a place where they could hear the gospel.

Without criticizing past approaches, we can say that the Christian's call to minister to those in the world goes far beyond this kind of effort. We are called to love as Jesus

loved . . . initiating contact even when others are still enemies. With that contact we build whatever relationship of love
and caring is possible. We are to love not in word only, but also
in deed.

It is often difficult for Christians who have no non-
Christian friends to build friendships with non-Christian
neighbors and coworkers. They first have to be freed from the
tendency to judge others. Too often believers feel they must
condemn what non-Christians do, and thus they communicate, not love, but nonacceptance and judgment, the antithesis of the gospel invitation! God's message to mankind in
Christ is, "I love you *anyway.*" This is the unspoken message
we are to communicate in our own personal relationships
with the non-Christian world.

How can such relationships be encouraged? In large part
by teaching and example, by helping believers learn to love
others in the context of the body, and by encouraging them to
extend the same loving concern to non-Christians. Leaders
can also focus their prayers on specific non-Christians known
to members of the local body. They can provide tools to help
members of the congregation meet and share with non-
Christians in a noninstitutional setting.* But the most important factor is to recognize that *learning to love those
within the body typically precedes reaching out in love to
those outside the body.*

Encourage team experiences and ministries

So far we have suggested that God intends personal ministries to take place in interpersonal settings. We've contrasted
this to the impersonal institutional settings many churches
have. We have also stressed the need to (1) build the congregation as a community of love, (2) visualize for the congregation the kinds of ministry that can take place as interpersonal transactions rather than institutional functions, and
(3) encourage the building of relationships with non-
Christians as a context for ministry. Now we want to suggest
one more principle related to the interpersonal nature of
ministry. We need to (4) encourage members of the body to
form supportive teams for their personal ministries.

The rationale for this is in part theological. The body of
Christ is revealed in Scripture to be an interdependent organism. Individuals have different gifts and talents enabling
them to complement each other. For instance, a group

---

*See Probe 2 at the end of this chapter.

gathering to conduct backyard Bible studies for children during their summer vacation will certainly need the help of those who are able to relate well to children and tell stories. But they will also need those who like details and are willing to handle various coordination tasks. By forming a ministering team for this personal ministry, each member is freed to function in his or her own area of strength.

There are other important benefits in association. Different experiences and perspectives provide insights that can help resolve problems one person alone might not have the resources to resolve. In a team many prayers can be linked. In a team mutual support and encouragement—or exhortation and rebuke—can be given.

It's no wonder that in the New Testament we see a strong emphasis on team ministries. While the names of Paul and Peter seem to tower over those of others, they did not move out *alone* in their ministries. Typically they moved from place to place and ministered in small groups or teams. Usually there was a stable core of mature believers (such as Silas and Barnabas) associated with a person like Paul, and also younger apprentices (like Timothy and Titus). In our society where the "one leader" concept has come to dominate, the significance of the team pattern shown in Scripture is missed. But the team pattern *is* both significant and consistently demonstrated.

Our typical approach to ministry has been to appoint one person the leader (chairman, superintendent, etc.) and then give that leader others to work *under* him. While there may be a voting system so that no single individual controls the decision-making process, usually the entire team does not participate in decisions. While this issue will be explored more fully in the last chapter of this text, it is important at this point to recognize the fact that shared responsibility, full participation, and mutual "ownership" of a ministry need to extend to each person in a ministering team.

How can a team approach to ministry be developed? In many ways. In one of the ministry schools Gib Martin conducts, he assigns participants the task of designing and building an airplane model as a team. The one requirement is that each person contribute in some way to the design. In the process they discover the importance of different viewpoints and backgrounds blending to shape the final product.

It is even more important for leaders in a congregation to function as a team. The idea of a shared ministry is thus modeled for and experienced by the congregation. In addition, training and study can focus on group learning experiences rather than on individual performance. Discipleship training (discussed in the next chapter) can be conducted by groups, with assignments and projects given to teams rather than to individuals. Those who are presently working together in ministries within the church can be helped to function as teams rather than simply as "staffs" under the direction of a superintendent or other leader.

The major concern here is that increasingly we help those God calls to personal ministries to seek and gain the support of others in the body when those ministries call for a team effort. The relational context in which believers *prepare* for their personal ministries is just as important as the relational context in which the ministries themselves are performed.

PROBE

▶ *case histories*
▶ *discussion questions*
▶ *thought provokers*
▶ *resources*

1. In this chapter we have stressed helping members of the local congregation appreciate the interpersonal nature and setting for their ministries. We have emphasized the fact that a congregation needs to be a warm and loving community. One resource designed to move toward this specific goal is a video-tape seminar developed by the authors and available to local congregations through Dynamic Church Ministries.*

2. Is it possible for traditional ministries such as teaching the Bible to build a Type III setting and also effectively communicate content? One unique system is *The Bible Alive.**

3. Can members of a local church be helped to discover for themselves that ministry is an interpersonal transaction? Here is an approach one of the authors has tested many times in seminars, conventions, and local congregations:

THE PROCESS

I. Divide the group into threes. Ask each person to think of the individual who made the greatest contribution to his or her own life. Then give him several minutes to describe that person to the others in the threesome. The description is to help the others feel they know the person described.

---

*Information is available from P.O. Box 35331, Phoenix, Arizona 85069.

II. On a chalkboard or overhead sheet draw a series of parallel lines. At the ends of each line list two contrasting traits. Ask each person to put a check mark on the line to indicate the *nature of the relationship* he had with the person he described. Here is a sample:

warm _____✓_____cold
friendly _____✓_____aloof
two-way _____✓_____one-way

Did you talk with each other, or did just one of you talk?

cared _____✓_____did not care

Did you feel this individual really cared for you as a person?

III. After you have put checks on the parallel lines, divide the lines into quarters. Then ask the group to indicate which quarter of each line their check marks fell in.

You will discover that a *very high* percentage of check marks will fall on the left quarter of the lines, illustrating compellingly that the impact of a person's ministries *is* felt in a warm, friendly, personal relationship in which there is two-way communication and a strong sense of being cared for.

4. The following article by Howard Snyder is condensed from the book *Missions, Evangelism, and Church Growth* (Herald Press), and is used with permission. Write out your reactions to it.

AN EVANGELISTIC LIFESTYLE IN THE CHURCH

"Here's Life, America" was a multimillion-dollar evangelistic effort sponsored by Campus Crusade for Christ, localized in 253 U.S. metropolitan areas. It involved over 14,500 local churches, and three-fourths of all Americans were said to have been exposed to the campaign's catchy "I Found It" slogan during the campaign.

All indications are that "Here's Life" was a great media success and a drastic evangelistic failure. Millions of Americans "heard" the message and were "influenced" by it. Those campaigns may even have produced some good in the form of preevangelism. But all empirical studies so far yield the same result: thousands of "decisions" but only the tiniest trickle of new church members. And the evidence suggests that most "converts" represent Christian rededications and transfers from one church to another.

As studies by Win Arn and others have shown, "Here's Life" has had virtually no measurable impact on church membership in the United States.[1] . . . all indications are that its impact will have been primarily on some of the individual Christians and local churches which participated, not on the mass of North American pagans "Here's Life" was supposed to have reached.

What is the church?

The major justification for such intensive evangelistic campaigns as Evangelism in Depth and "Here's Life" is, of course, that the local churches "aren't getting the job done." Churches are failing in their evangelism. Therefore a large-scale, broad-based, intensive effort sponsored by some outside or overarching entity is needed to do the job, bring in the harvest, and give churches a much needed shot of adrenalin.

But the neglected issue here is the question of the nature of the church itself. The failure of "Here's Life" and similar efforts is not, fundamentally, a technical or programming failure. The problem goes deeper than the question of methods. It is time to stop talking about programming mistakes or faulty techniques and face up to a fundamental theological error concerning the nature of the church and therefore the nature of salvation itself.

The truth is that no one can be joined to Christ the head without being joined to Christ's body, and the error is to think, first, that a person can become a Christian without being born into God's family in a visible way, and secondly, that evangelism can be authentic while ignoring this dynamic relationship of head and body.

Community of God's people

Many reasons may be cited for our failures in evangelism, and all these should be examined. But my argument here is that evangelistic effectiveness begins with proper attention to the life and integrity of the congregation. This, then, will be the focus of the following observations.

I would like to suggest six propositions which, it seems to me, are important in developing an evangelistic lifestyle for the congregation. These are based on the assumption that evangelism is a proper priority for the congregation, but that this priority fits integrally into a web of intertwined priorities to be controlled by the fundamental calling of the church to glorify God and participate in his mission.

---

[1]Win Arn, "A Church Growth Look at Here's Life America," *Church Growth: America*, 3:1 (January-February 1977), pp. 4–7, 9, 14–15, 27, 30.

The reign of God

1. The Church's first concern in evangelism is to participate in the mission of God—to do the works of Christ and work for the progressive manifestation of his reign.

Jesus came to do the work of the Father. He accomplished the work given him to do while physically present on earth. With his death and resurrection comes a new phase of his work. Before his resurrection, Jesus was limited by space and time. The body of Christ was a physical, space-time body like yours and mine. But that body was broken on the cross so that salvation could be manifested and the church could be born. Just as the bread was broken and multiplied in the feeding of the thousands, so Christ's body broken on the cross provides for his new body, the church, which by his Spirit is "multiplied" into the whole world as the community of God's people.

So Jesus tells his disciples, in effect: "It is for your good that I am going away. Now I am limited by my physical existence. But in going, I will send the Spirit. I will be with you now in a new dimension. Now you will be my physical body, spread throughout the earth, indwelt by my very Spirit. You will do the works I have done—and even greater, for through you my presence and my operation will be spread and multiplied to the whole world. You are my witnesses! You are now my body, empowered by the Holy Spirit."

An implication of the fact that we are called to participate in the mission of God is that mission covers all needs of all persons in all places. This mission of God is the kingdom of God. It is inevitably political, social, and economic, even though (and precisely because) it is fundamentally spiritual. Therefore evangelism includes witnessing to God's truth and justice in all areas of life and society.

In our evangelistic lifestyle, we need a holistic witness that gives both depth and credibility to our proclamation and evangelism.

Vitality of the congregation

2. Evangelism is sharing life, and the church cannot share what it does not possess.

A major problem with any form of evangelism that relies heavily on the mass media is that the gospel becomes largely disembodied. The truth frequently becomes removed from reality. The gospel is separated from the context of demonstrated Christian community, which is a step toward individualism, abstraction, and neglect of the horizontal dimension in the rec-

onciliation God gives. This creates the danger that becoming a Christian will be perceived as being unrelated to the whole web of relationships in one's life, that one can be joined to the head without being joined to the body. This runs counter to scriptures which say the Christian has been born into the family of God.

The more basic question is the authenticity and vitality of the local congregation itself. The fact is that many churches simply have nothing to share with unbelievers.

This is true even of doctrinally orthodox churches. We may argue that as long as it has the Bible and correct doctrine, a church has the gospel to share. But the fact is that gospel truths divorced from experience generally fail to communicate the intended message. The message may be received, but it is not comprehended as really being the gospel. Truth is not clothed in life, and therefore lacks the ring of authenticity.

The practical implications of this argument are that the authenticity and vitality of the congregation are themselves matters of evangelistic priority, and that the gospel must be presented on the basis of personal relationships. The gospel is not primarily abstract truth but primarily personal relationship with God through Jesus Christ. This will be best comprehended as we present the gospel on the basis of personal relationships and through personal relationships.

Being good news

3. Spiritual life depends upon and is deepened by a vital experience of Christian community. Genuine Christian community itself is evangelistic, and a church which is weak in community will be weak in evangelism—even though it may show "results."

Both scripture and experience teach us the importance of Christian community for personal spiritual life and growth. Much of the dynamism of the early Christian church in Jerusalem was due to the fact that believers "devoted themselves . . . to the fellowship," "were together," and "broke bread in their homes and ate together" (Acts 2:42, 44, 46). They were discovering Christian community, and in the process discovering more deeply the meaning of the reconciliation they had received from God.

This is why the New Testament need say very little about evangelism. It puts the emphasis on authentic Christian community—the reconciled life together that comes from being mutually joined to Christ and mutually growing up into him. The implication is clear: If the church is genuinely a reconciled and reconciling community, the Lord will add daily to its number those who are being saved.

The point is that the church must be good news in order to proclaim good news. . . .

Conversion and change

Whenever real community has been lost in the church, renewal movements have sprung up which have majored on the neglected area. Historically this was true in monasticism, Anabaptism, and other movements. Today the same thing is seen in literally hundreds of new intentional communities which have sprung up within the past ten years or so. Over the past three years I have come into contact with a number of such communities, and have been impressed both with the diversity and the vitality of such groups. One thing they all have in common: the excitement of discovering the freedom and joy of intimately sharing lives together in common purpose and in allegiance to Jesus Christ.

Both for its own authenticity and for its evangelistic fruitfulness, the church must learn ways to recover the dynamic of genuine Christian community.

As hinted above, I am not arguing that a church weak in community will be "unsuccessful" in evangelism. It may, in fact, show impressive numerical results evangelistically. It may see many people converted and added to the church rolls. But without genuine community there will be little discipleship. New converts will come to church and claim allegiance to Christ, but little will change in their lifestyles. Their patterns of use of time, money, and other resources will change very little. Their lives will present no real challenge to the built-in evils of oppression, prejudice, and exploitation in society.

Where community is weak, successful evangelism will do little more than hasten the church's accommodation to surrounding society.

The ecology of the church

4. Evangelism will be most effective when there is a healthy balance of worship, community, and witness in the local congregation. Therefore, worship itself is a priority for evangelistic effectiveness.

Worship, witness, and community together form the balanced ecology of a congregation. The church must first of all be oriented toward God in worship. This is the fundamental purpose and priority of the church—to live "to the praise of his glory" (Eph. 1:14). "To him be glory in the church and in Christ Jesus" (Eph. 3:21). On this basis, then, the church is joined together mutually in the community of the body of Christ, and then turned toward

211

the world in witness. Worship, community, and witness together make up the life of the balanced and growing church. (Note the use of the terms leitourgia, koinonia, marturia, and related terms in the New Testament.)

By and large, people in North America today have only the vaguest notion (if any) of who God really is. To most Americans he is either a cosmic Teddy Bear, an old-fashioned Granddaddy, or an oblong blur. To many Christians God is decidedly less than "the High and Holy One who inhabits eternity" and the "God and Father of our Lord Jesus Christ." It is our lack of real encounter with God in worship which puts the punch in the statement that if God were suddenly to vanish from the universe, in time even the church would suffer.

The church that is serious about participating in the mission of God and doing the works of Christ will take seriously the priority of worship. We can accomplish the work begun by Jesus only if we have the same consciousness of God's presence and reality that Jesus had.

The gift of evangelist

5. God gifts some people for evangelism and evangelistic leadership. Therefore effective evangelism depends on identifying, recognizing, and using these gifts.

Here the basic text is, of course, Ephesians 4:11–13—God "gave some to be apostles, some to be prophets, some to be evangelists, and some to be pastors and teachers; to prepare God's people for works of service, so that the body of Christ may be built up until we all reach unity in the faith and in the knowledge of the Son of God."

At first glance the role of evangelist here appears unclear or not directly related to bringing unbelievers to a knowledge of Jesus Christ. But note carefully what Paul is saying. First, it is in the harmonious functioning of all leadership gifts (apostle, prophet, evangelist, pastor, teacher) that God's people are prepared for ministry and the body of Christ reaches maturity. So the gift of evangelist functions in conjunction with other gifts.

Secondly, the evangelist is not merely one who wins people to Christ. He or she is one who leads the people of God in evangelism. The evangelist is that person specially, charismatically gifted by God to bring others to a knowledge of Jesus Christ and to lead others in doing the same.

As this happens, God's people are equipped for ministry and the body of Christ is built up. Thus "the whole body, joined and held together by every supporting ligament, grows and builds itself up in love, as each part does its work" (Eph. 4:16). Here is growth coming from the proper functioning of each member and each spiritual gift.

The congregation concerned to develop an evangelistic life-style will therefore give attention to the matter of spiritual gifts. It will be concerned to identify those with the gift of evangelism so that the evangelistic witness of the church can be extended. And it will be concerned with the exercise of other gifts as well, under-standing that it is the proper functioning of all the gifts together which allows the church to become the growing, functioning body described in 1 Corinthians 12–14, Romans 12:6–8, and Ephesians 4:11–16.

The fullness of Christ

6. Conversion begins a lifelong process of spiritual growth, discipleship, and sanctification toward the restoration of the image of God in the believer.

Biblically based evangelism does not focus exclusively on the death and resurrection of Jesus Christ. Rather, it sets these crucial events in the context of Jesus' earthly life and of his present reign. As Paul says in Colossians, God "has rescued us from the do-minion of darkness and brought us into the kingdom (or reign) of the Son he loves, in whom we have redemption, the forgiveness of sins . . . For God was pleased to have all his fullness dwell in him, and through him to reconcile to himself all things, whether things on earth or things in heaven, by making peace through his blood, shed on the cross" (Col. 1:13–14, 19–20).

In this passage, Paul goes on to say that God wills "to present you holy in his sight, without blemish and free from accusation" (Col. 1:22). So he says, "We proclaim him [Christ], admonishing and teaching everyone with all wisdom, so that we may present everyone perfect in Christ" (Col. 1:28). As "in Christ all the full-ness of the Deity lives in bodily form," so "you have been given fullness in Christ, who is the head over every power and author-ity" (Col. 2:9).

Focusing on Jesus' life and reign, as well as his death and resurrection, we see that God's concern is not only to rescue us from hell or redeem us for heaven. Rather, it is to recreate within us, and in the life of the congregation, "the fullness of Christ." It is to restore the image of God in our lives and in our relationships. Bringing all creation to harmony and order under the headship of Christ begins through bringing all believers to harmony and Christlikeness through the discipling and sanctifying work of the Spirit of Christ in the church.

213

PRACTICAL IMPLICATION

Evangelism is a beginning

The lifestyle implication for the congregation here is that evangelism is never an end only, but always a beginning. Or rather, it is part of a continuing cycle of life and growth in the body of Christ. Therefore the congregation must be as concerned with those processes and structures in the body which bring spiritual growth and maturity as it is with the work of evangelism itself.

We see something of a three-step process here. Individual persons must be brought to the lordship of Christ, so that the church can grow up into Christ, experience his fullness, and acknowledge his reign, so that the whole creation can be freed from its bondage to decay and be set free in joyful subservience to the God of the universe. So we keep our eyes on the larger goal, and we join evangelism to the larger work of acknowledging Christ's lordship in every area of society and culture.

5. *Case History*

We've stressed relationships as the context for personal ministry. At times relationships may be built within an institutional setting. At other times they may be completely noninstitutional. The story of Dale Morris, part of a fellowship near Denver, Colorado, illustrates God's ways of ministering through relationships in a very beautiful and simple way. His experience is well worth exploring in a case study conference.

DALE MORRIS

I came to know the Lord about six years ago. I was on a Frontier Ranch at Buena Vista watching some kids for a week. For about two years prior to that I had been going to a Bible study here in Evergreen—a couples' study led by different people. For some reason I kept going back. God made me want to, although I always prefaced everything I said in the group with, "I'm not a Christian but. . . ."

Then one night during the week at camp, it all made sense that Christ had died for me personally. Before, I figured that He had died for all and that I was more responsible than anyone else. Once I made His death personal it made sense. I stayed up that night and turned everything over to Christ—lock, stock, and barrel. I thought I would be on a boat for Africa the next day. But I already knew that whatever He called me to do He would prepare me for beforehand. With that in mind I didn't know what to expect but I was ready.

I shared my decision with my girl friend, Jacquie, the next day. Other than that I wasn't going to tell anyone, because I thought if I

214

did I would blow it and be one of those guys that "speak with a forked tongue." But a lot of things started happening—even the next day. I had a very foul tongue, but I found that the usual words just weren't coming out. For example, I caught my finger in the car door a few days later, and all I said was "Shucks" or "Gee whiz"! That sorta blew my mind. God also started to remove my desire to drink.

A chapter from the Bible that has impressed me ever since I first met the Lord is John 17—a whole chapter on the unity of the body of believers and the idea of fellowship!

I wanted to start a Bible study almost immediately at places where I was involved—like the Athletic Club. I started praying for a Bible study there, but I couldn't lead it because I was too new a Christian. So I asked God to send me a teacher. Well, within a couple of weeks somebody had given a membership in the club to Al Elliott. When I met him I asked him if he would be interested in starting a Bible study there. He said, "Yeah, I guess that's what I'm here for." So we started one. That was five years ago! It hasn't been cancelled for any reason in five years.

We started a Bible study at the Hiwan Country Club about the same time. That's on Thursday morning. When the club is closed, we meet in somebody's home. So I guess I looked for fellowship almost immediately, which is interesting because I have always been pretty much of a loner.

Looking back over the past few years, one of the experiences that has most deeply influenced me was reading a book a couple of years ago on Hebrews 13, called *Bible Men of Faith*. The thing that struck me was that these men were all men of discipline. I started praying for *self*-discipline, but nothing happened. Then I started to pray that God would discipline me, both spiritually and physically. And things started happening. He started getting me up at 4:00 and 5:00 in the morning to spend time with Him. Since then I have tried to spend two hours in prayer and Bible study before I do anything else. I don't always make it, but I usually get an hour in. That has really changed my relationship with my Lord.

I've been going to the federal prison twice a week for about two-and-a-half years now. It was strange the way that started. Paul Kramer called me one day. I had met Chuck Colson through the Prison Fellowship, and Paul Kramer was involved in prison work with him. He was coming to the Denver area to interview some men at the Englewood Federal Prison to find out about their relationship with the Lord. He said to me, "Dale, do you want to go out to the prison and sit in with me?" I said, "Sure, I've never been to prison."

So we went. After he was finished he said, "What do you

think?" And I said, "Well, they didn't seem to know the Lord, at least not according to the standards we use." He said he didn't think so either.

"How do you think we can find Christians there, Dale? We know there are some in here."

I said, "It beats me, but why don't we pray about it?"

So we prayed about it. Then we found out that the associate warden of the federal penitentiary, Ken Roets, was a believer. And a fellow who had graduated from prison had been led to come back and help with the fellows reentering society. So the two of them and I decided to meet every Thursday in the chapel to pray for the institution.

Strange things started happening. People who used to drive past the prison and had been praying for it started stopping in and saying they felt led to come in. Some of the staff who knew the Lord started coming out of the woodwork. Some of the inmates started coming. You couldn't have planned it. If you had tried to set it up, there is no way you could have done it.

After a couple of months one of the fellows asked me if we could start a Bible study. I said, "Why not? Do you have anyone else that wants to come?" And he said, "Yeah, there's another fellow." So three of us started meeting on a Tuesday night. The next Tuesday there were four, the following Tuesday there were eight, and then there were twelve. So now there are many different Bible study groups in the prison. There is a good core of believers right in the prison who are working with each other pretty well. And that is really where everything is. It isn't what we can do. It is the guys who are living in there, going through the same knot-holes. When these men see the power of God, they say, "Hey, you've got something I want."

Later, after I had resisted for a while, I started going to Canyon City. God kept opening doors and guiding things, but I still kept resisting. After about eight months I could finally tell that it was right for me to go. I had peace and joy about it. It's been an exciting time. Canyon City is the state maximum security prison. It's about two-and-a-half hours away. I usually go every couple of weeks.

Not too long ago it started to dawn on me that what I'm doing isn't really a ministry. It's just brothers getting together. They're in there and I'm out here. And I go to spend time with them. I care about them. One thing that we never fail to do is open with prayer, read the Word, and then thank the Lord for His goodness to us.

PART 2

PRACTICAL IMPLICATION

Identity Implications
Communicating Vision
Building Relationships and Community
Making Disciples
Equipping
Extending Freedom
Understanding Leadership

MAKING DISCIPLES

The *New International Dictionary of New Testament Theology* associates several Greek words with discipleship, noting that they are applied chiefly in the New Testament to Jesus and His followers. The words are:

akoloutheō (follow), which "denotes the action of a man answering the call of Jesus whose whole life is redirected in obedience."

mathētēs (a disciple), "one who has heard the call of Jesus and joins him."

mimeomai (imitate), which "emphasizes the nature of a particular kind of behaviour, modelled on someone else."[1]

Jesus summed up discipleship when He told the Twelve, "everyone who is fully trained will be like his teacher" (Luke 6:40). *Discipleship involves the redirection of the Christian's life toward obedience, so that he might become like Jesus.* In view of the truths we've seen about full participation of the whole *laos* of God in all that it means to be a Christian, we can understand why *discipleship* is for all Christians. The mission of the church is not simply to win converts, but to complete the process by making disciples. This is, in fact, the Great Commission Jesus gave after His resurrection:

CHAPTER **10**

> All authority in heaven and on earth has been given to me. Therefore go and make disciples of all nations, baptizing them in the name of the Father and of the Son and of the Holy Spirit, and teaching them to obey everything I have commanded you (Matt. 28:18–20).

Making disciples involves bringing men and women into a personal relationship with Jesus and then, under the personal authority of Jesus, to redirect their whole lives in obedience to Him.

Building a ministering *laos* must clearly involve disciple-making. So it's important for us to have at least an overview of the discipling process.

BIBLICAL AND HISTORICAL BACKGROUND

The concept of "disciple" is not well developed in the early Old Testament period. Put in postexilic Judaism it becomes common and significant. Already the idea of "follow" (*akoloutheō*) and "disciple" (*mathētēs*) were closely linked.

---

[1]Colin Brown, ed., *The New International Dictionary of the New Testament.* 3 vols. (Grand Rapids: Zondervan Publishing House, 1976–1978), 1:480.

PRACTICAL IMPLICATION

The *New International Dictionary of New Testament Theology* comments that these

> words describe the relationship of a pupil to a teacher of the Torah. The pupil who chooses to subordinate himself to a Rabbi follows him everywhere he goes, learning from him and above all serving him. . . . The goal of all his learning is a complete knowledge of the Torah, and ability to practise it in every situation.[2]

By the time of Jesus there was an emphasis on the importance of the human authority who interpreted the Torah. Developed in later rabbinic Judaism, this emphasis

> previously was entirely unknown in Israel and Judaism. Since the Rabbi's knowledge gives him direct access to the Scriptures which facilitates right hearing and right understanding, he becomes a kind of mediator between the *talmidim* [learners] and the Torah. To listen to the Scriptures without the guidance of a teacher is something to be avoided at all costs. . . . now learning is determined by the authority of the teacher and his interpretation of the Torah—not by a personal and, as far as possible, unbiased study of the Torah.[3]

In the Gospels those who linked themselves to John the Baptist were identified as his disciples (Matt. 11:2; Mark 2:18; 6:29; Luke 5:33; 11:1; John 1:35, 37). The Pharisees liked to think of themselves as Moses' disciples (John 9:28), and they had disciples of their own who followed them and their interpretations of the Torah (Matt. 22:16; Mark 2:18).

In a series of essays printed in 1968 by London's Soncino Press, Moses Aberbach describes the rabbi-disciple pattern of education. As summarized in *Pastoral Renewal,*

> The pattern is tied to a committed personal relationship between the student and the teacher. Though studying by oneself was not unknown, it was widely looked upon with disapproval, as liable to result in aberrations.
>
> The training that a disciple received from his master included much more than academic study, and went well beyond the classroom. The disciple spent as much time with the teacher as possible, often living with him in the same house. Aberbach says, "Disciples were expected not only to study the law in all its ramifications, but also to acquaint themselves with the specific way of life, which could be done only through constant attendance upon a master. . . . The rabbis taught as much from example as by precept. For this reason the disciple needed to take note of his master's daily conversation and habits, as well as his teaching."
>
> Students related to their masters with the greatest deference and respect. To "follow" a teacher meant to accept his teaching, but when accompanying their master, disciples were expected literally to walk behind him, and to one side or the other. Students also served their

---

[2]Ibid., 1:481.
[3]Ibid., 1:485.

teacher in many practical ways ranging from setting up the benches in the room used for instruction to shopping and cooking for him. Assisting one's master at the bathhouse was a service so commonly associated with discipleship that the saying, "I shall bring his clothes for him to the bathhouse" became proverbial for "I shall become his disciple."

Despite the subordination and customs of respect that characterized the master-disciple relationship, it was in no way a distant or merely formal relationship. The teacher attempted to raise his disciples as sons: he cared for them, provided for them (usually this education was at the rabbi's expense), and praised or admonished his disciples as he saw fit. Aberbach describes the relationship as an intense paternal-filial love.[4]

There are similarities and differences with the rabbinic approach to discipleship reflected in the Christian Scriptures.

First, there are several striking similarities. The Bible speaks of Jesus' choice of the Twelve and says that He chose them "to be with him" (Mark 3:14). Jesus' approach to training disciples was not academic but relational. His goal was not simply the transmission of knowledge but the communication of likeness (Luke 6:40). It is much the same in the Epistles. Paul writes to the Corinthians to follow his example, as he follows the example of Christ. He reminds Timothy of the intimate acquaintance he gained of Paul's life and teaching while they were part of a missionary team. "You know all about my teaching," Paul says, and adds "my way of life, my purpose, faith, patience, love, endurance, persecutions, sufferings" (2 Tim. 3:10–11). Timothy is to hold firm to the pattern of sound teaching he received from Paul, not neglecting faith and love in Christ Jesus (2 Tim. 1:13). Timothy is to repeat the pattern in his own ministry, entrusting what he has been taught to reliable men who will in turn teach others (2 Tim. 2:2). For this ministry Timothy will have to "watch [his] life and doctrine closely" (1 Tim. 4:16), and in his speech and by a life of love, faith, and purity set an example for the believers (1 Tim. 4:12).

The personal and informal nature of discipling is reflected and reinforced in the team relationships exhibited in the missionary ministry through which so many were equipped in the early church, and in the pattern of Jesus' own relationship with His followers. Watching, sharing, and participating with the more mature with a view to personal maturity as a follower of Jesus is a consistent aspect of discipling in the New Testament.

There are also differences between the rabbinical and bib-

---

[4]From *Pastoral Renewal*, July 1978.

lical pictures. There is no hint in either the Old Testament or the rabbinical approach of a disciple *becoming like God.* But this is just the emphasis in New Testament discipleship! In the New Testament portrait, *discipleship is not to an individual, but to Christ Himself.* Paul could say to the Corinthians, "Follow my example," but he had to put this exhortation into perspective by adding "as I follow the example of Christ" (1 Cor. 11:1). Christ is being formed in the believer. It is the Christ in the mature believer whom the disciple is to follow.

Without downplaying the importance of the believer who invests his life discipling others, we can definitely say that the New Testament knows no such thing as "Paul's disciples" or "Cephas' disciples"—or Gib Martin's disciples or Larry Richards' disciples. There is a divisiveness that develops in paying too much honor to human beings and claiming to follow one over another (cf. 1 Cor. 1:12f.). Paul identifies it with carnality. Under the new covenant, leaders, like all other believers, are merely servants. Only God makes things grow (1 Cor. 3:6).

What is even more significant, discipleship in the New Testament is a *mutual enterprise.* Rabbinic discipleship was based on the assumption that the rabbi's special knowledge gave him a direct access to God and the Torah and this was denied to others. But this is the age of the new covenant, and "they will all know me, from the least of them to the greatest" (Jer. 31:34). This reality is reflected in Paul's attitude as expressed in statements like the following: "I long to see you so that I may impart to you some spiritual gift to make you strong—that is, that you and I may be mutually encouraged by each other's faith" (Rom. 1:11–12). Paul sees himself as able to contribute to the lives of others. But he is aware that *they* are gifted, too, and that he will be ministered to as well as minister. No wonder Paul later teaches that we are "in humility" to "consider others better than [ourselves]" (Phil. 2:3).

In other words, in the body of Christ, where all the *laos* of God are believer-priests, *we are called to disciple each other!*

There is another element in the New Testament picture of discipleship that is especially significant. In the rabbinical system an individual would choose a particular leader to follow. But in the New Testament Jesus makes the choice! He is the One who calls men into a discipling relationship with Himself (Luke 5:1–11; Matt. 4:18ff.; Mark 1:16ff.; Luke 9:57–62; John 1:43). Because He is Lord, His call to commitment is decisive.

The call to discipleship involves Jesus' unique invitation to become like Him (Luke 6:40) and to be a full participant in His mission. "Come, follow me, and I will make you fishers of men" links discipleship with carrying the good news to all (Mark 1:15, 17; Luke 5:10), while the occasions on which Jesus sent the Twelve or the Seventy out by twos (Mark 6:7–13; Luke 10:1–20) show that He expects disciples to be fully involved in service to others as well.

We can understand discipleship under the new covenant by noting the following:

- Making disciples, not simply making converts, is Jesus' Great Commission to the church.
- Making disciples involves a redirection of a person's life toward obedience to Christ.
- Making disciples takes place in the context of close and loving personal relationships.
- Making disciples is not a one-on-one process, but rather a group process in which each participant contributes to the growth in commitment of the others.
- Making disciples involves helping others respond to Christ's call to service and godliness.
- The high calling of discipleship is the privilege, and the responsibility, of every believer in the body of Christ.

MAKING DISCIPLES IN OUR DAY

At this point many want a clearly outlined "discipleship program." However, it's impossible to develop a road map that will tell leaders of every congregation how to make disciples. A universalized "discipleship program" simply will not work. Thus Scripture presents not a road map but a compass. Various precepts are taught that must be worked out in the experience of each congregation. So we can provide helpful guidelines, but no step-by-step instructions.

Before we look at relevant precepts, let's note that while discipleship is the calling of all Christians, not all members of a congregation will be ready at a given time to commit themselves to a discipling process. However, some are ready now. And when readiness comes, there must be an opportunity. We need to provide believers with the opportunity to be involved in a discipling process. This may be a two-year initiating commitment, but whatever our approach it must be designed to lead to lifelong commitment.

An initiating process will have a variety of characteristics, including disciplined study, regular meetings with others, and various projects and experiences. An initiating program will need to be infused by the following four precepts.

Precept one: New wine, new wineskins

This precept has been mentioned briefly before. Jesus taught that new wine must be placed in new wineskins if it is to mature. The implications of this precept are both organizational and generational.

Organizationally, much training associated with discipling has focused on perpetuating ecclesiastical systems. This is particularly true of processes by which believers are trained for a "full-time" ministry. A person is discipled into a *role*. The focuses of the training process are the knowledge, skills, and attitudes required to fulfill the role. We often find a similar focus in the training of potential leaders within a congregation.

What I am saying is that training a person to be a Sunday school teacher, or a visitation worker, or a youth club leader should not be confused with discipleship. Such training is often totally valid, but making disciples is *not* providing the skills needed for any given role.

Instead, making disciples focuses on freeing individuals for growth in their own personal faith and uniqueness, with the expectation that while it is maturing, giftedness *may* lead into an organizational expression, but it *need not*. The discipling structure, then, needs to concentrate on building relationships and using a variety of learning settings and experiences. We must give priority to people. Structures must be designed to encourage growth and fruitfulness. We are not to try to squeeze people into the organizational mold of structures developed in the past.

The wineskins principle is also generational. It affirms that God shapes each new generation for the society and culture in which it lives. The call to discipleship is a call to follow Jesus in the reality of the world of the here-and-now. In each generation's present world and in each generation's personal relationship with the living Lord, fruit is to be born.

Fruitfulness in the Bible is always associated with a close, obedient, "abiding" relationship that each person can have with Jesus. The goal of discipleship is not to have the new generation recapitulate the experiences of Christians in the past, but to have that new generation so grow in its relationship with the Lord that it will respond to His leading and bear its own fruit. As we will see shortly, discipleship does not simply involve passing on data from generation to generation so that each can "know about" God. Discipleship involves bringing persons to a deeper, more personal "knowing" of God, so that His voice might be heard speaking to them.

The new wine of discipleship cannot be forced into the wineskins in which we have matured. Old forms and structures will break under the pressures of the new day and, as Jesus warned, the new wine will be spilled. It is the challenge of the present leadership of the church to be sensitive to the need for new wineskins, and to free disciples to mature in frameworks that are fitted to them and their times.

Precept two: Priestly, interpersonal process

We noted earlier that discipleship in the Gospels and in the early church era was a team or group process. This is necessary because the church is itself composed of persons all of whom under the new covenant are believer-priests. All are gifted; thus each is to minister to others.

This means that in designing a discipling process leaders need to shape a process in which participants teach and learn from each other, rather than learning from a single leader, as in the rabbinical system.

Two "new wineskins" patterns used at Trinity over the years illustrate how this can be done. In one case, a study center was established. This was a live-in facility to which individuals or couples came to live for a six-month period or longer. The participants made significant commitments to the community and agreed to live under the discipline of the elder of the church who guided them. Each resident at the study center committed himself to about four hours of study a day. Assignments varied from written reports on special study projects to the keeping of a journal of their daily walk with God. Study insights were shared with others in the community and with the guiding elders. In addition, residents worked on their jobs or contributed four hours of work a day serving various ministries or people in the local community. Within this tightly knit community the members worked out their relationships and ministered to one another.

In another case a group of some fifteen individuals have committed themselves to a discipling process that has extended over a two-year period. There are regular early morning meetings for guided study and sharing. In this setting, too, there are study assignments geared to the individuals, with outcomes shared with the whole group. Members share a variety of other experiences as well, including work projects.

It is important to see the shared process as a struggle

rather than a series of classroom exercises. Sharing experiences that test an individual's commitment is part of the total process. For instance, "fasting" sometimes plays a part in the discipling process Gib Martin has structured. This fasting is more than refraining from food, although that may be part of it. One discipleship group "fasted" from newspapers, TV, and general reading for seven weeks, committing itself to studying Scripture instead. Out of this shared common experience came much personal growth and ministry to each other.

The role of the leader in discipling is to be sensitive to process and to individuals. He designs various experiences that the group can share so each individual can grow personally and contribute to the growth of others.

Precept three: Indigenousness and contextualization

In discipling there is no way to escape from life while we take time out to study life. This is one of the fallacies of much "training" for Christian service. Rather than provide a classroom learning situation for an isolated three- or four-year period, learning to follow Jesus calls us to become immersed in the reality of the world in which we are called to live.

Christ called His followers to this kind of life. They knew suffering, hunger, testing, stress. They even knew the threat of death. Only in the crucible of reality could the disciples discover the joy of Jesus' presence and the power of God's Spirit available to overcome the problems.

It is in view of the fact that discipleship takes place in the context of reality that indigenous and contextual precepts are significant.

"Indigenous" is usually associated with missions. When a work has been fully taken over by nationals, growing naturally without help or direction from foreign influences, the work is considered to be "indigenous." In discipling, too, an indigenous principle is to be followed. There should be no effort to shape individuals or a group into something predetermined by someone else's experience. Discipling is a spiritual process in which a believer discovers himself and his resources in Christ. There is growth as a person and growth within the individual's own personal situation. Discipleship extends freedom to respond uniquely to God's grace and permits each individual to live by the Spirit's guidance. Increasingly, a growing disciple is able to function alone. Yet he is increasingly committed to his brothers and sisters in the community of faith.

Discipling rejects a "cookie cutter" approach to faith and

expects fresh expressions of Christ's life to grow in individuals and communities.

It is at this point that we can better understand what is meant by contextualization. In missions this is again a critical contemporary issue. How greatly is the culture to shape a people's understanding and expression of the gospel? How much of the "Christianity" imported from the Western world to the Third World reflects biblical Christianity, and how much has been distorted by centuries of association with Western thought and ways? There is no easy answer to these questions. But we must realize that our traditional approach to theology and faith tends to create a rigid, institutionalized Christianity. In discipleship there is a struggle to break away from frozen expressions of faith and under the lordship of Christ to find a Christianity that better expresses Jesus' presence in the world today.

Western theology has taken the route of building tight doctrinal systems and insisting that each new generation be bound to and bound by the thinking of the past. Systems that developed centuries ago and dealt in a vital way with the issues raised at the time come to be taught as "The System" within which all Christians must think. If the systems are unresponsive to present issues or simply do not deal with them, then contemporary thought is rejected as ungodly. Teaching tends to become less and less relevant to the realities with which we live. Along with the stress on maintaining doctrinal systems and creedal statements, there is a parallel fear of the relational. In part this is because the exchange of insights and the sharing of views raises questions about the formulations of the faith of past generations. In sharing with one another in intimate ways, there is a dynamic that leads to new expressions of truth and new ways to communicate the gospel in the contemporary world.

In general, Western theology has tended to pass on past statements of belief as a final formulation, not as something on which new generations may build. But the Reformers and other great men of the past were men just as we are. They were fallible, as we are. And they lived in a day when many of the issues that we must address did not even exist.

To speak of "contextualizing discipleship" means to build on the foundation of the past, but to expect that in the fellowship of shared study and exploration new insights and understanding of God's will will come. To protect this process of building contemporary theologies, the discipling process must stress three elements:

PRACTICAL IMPLICATION

1. a total commitment to Scripture as the trustworthy and reliable Word of God.
2. a total commitment to Jesus Christ as Lord and an openness to hearing and obeying His voice.
3. a total commitment to one another in the body of Christ, that our insights might be tested and confirmed by brothers and sisters who also walk with Jesus.

And we can add to this

4. listening to the historic voice of the church of Christ, which through the centuries has maintained a clear vision of the core truths of Christian faith.

In contextualization each growing disciple studies the Bible. Disciples share their lives, that the issues and tensions faced *now* might be explored together in the light of Scripture. There is also a major stress on the importance of *knowing God,* not just knowing about Him. At various times Gib Martin will give assignments that stimulate the process of contextualization to different discipleship groups, such as the following:

1. List three areas of stress you feel in your life today. Number them in terms of their acuteness.
2. Share these areas with your group.
3. Appoint a person to make a list of all the areas in which members of your group feel stress, and how often each area is mentioned.

FOLLOW-THROUGH

Study 2 Peter and Jude. What sources of stress do you find? What resources or approaches to handling stress are suggested? How is God speaking to you about the areas of stress in your own life?

JOURNAL

Maintain a daily journal, monitoring the areas of stress you listed. Record your feelings, thoughts, and actions or reactions. Record how God has spoken to you in these situations and how you have responded to Him.

Making disciples, then, involves believers in the process of facing *together* the realities of their own world and, under the guidance of the living and written Word, of building a vital understanding of God's present will for them.

Precept four: Discipling leads into service

Service is an important dimension of new covenant teaching, kingdom teaching, and servanthood teaching in the Scriptures. It certainly is to be expected that disciples will be like their Master and serve rather than be served.

We must be particularly careful about our wineskins in the area of service. The traditional approach of the church is *to emphasize the goals of existing programs, agencies, or structures.* Discipleship tends to be seen as leading people into roles in established ministry programs so that stated *goals* can be achieved.

In disciple-making, however, it is important to give priority to *needs.* Structures will grow out of an understanding of needs and how needs can best be met. We must never confuse a structure with a ministry or give it such priority that all our efforts unconsciously go into maintaining an organization rather than actually meeting needs. Effective discipleship training will always place the priority on identifying needs and then seek in the disciples the gifts through which needs can be met.

The process of growth that takes place in discipleship is basic to service. Being *who we are* in Christ always comes before significant *doing.* Discipleship, working out in the realities of our own situation the meaning of the written and living Word, is God's way to help us *become.* It is also a context in which we learn to exercise our spiritual gifts and giftedness and become aware of how we can serve others. As we relate Scripture to the context of our own lives we become aware of needs in our society and begin to reach out to do what we can to meet them. As we serve and come to a better understanding of the need, the structure to meet that need will gradually unfold. (We'll see more of this process in chapters 11 and 12.) What is important is to realize that in our discipling process we want to help individuals become aware of and be involved in the needs that exist in our own community.

In summary, the method used to make disciples is a distinctive process that will differ from one congregation and community to the next. Yet to be effective the process should embody several important precepts. Making disciples will avoid attempting to force new wine into old wineskins. Making disciples is a priestly, and thus interpersonal, process. Discipleship will not normally be a one-on-one process but rather a group process. Making disciples must involve indigenousness and contextualization as basic to its goal and method. Making disciples means leading disciples into active service, with a focus on meeting the needs of individuals and the community rather than on maintaining institutional structures or programs (unless these structures are "need focused"). Under the guidance of God, a distinctive disciple-making process will emerge in each local congregation.

PROBE

▶ *assignments*
▶ *resources*
▶ *case histories*
▶ *discussion questions*
▶ *thought provokers*

1. Read through one of the synoptic Gospels and make a chart showing Jesus' process of training His disciples. Read the selected Gospel once to get an idea of the elements you want to show on your chart. Then work through each chapter carefully and show the factors you have selected.

2. Do a detailed study of Matthew 10:5–39. Write down your insights. Relate this project Jesus assigned to the four precepts discussed in this chapter. Determine *when* in a discipling process such a project would be appropriate. (Hint: Examine carefully all that *preceded* this project in Jesus' ministry with the disciples.) What similar projects might this suggest for a contemporary discipleship group?

3. On the following pages are illustrations of assignments given those involved in various discipleship training groups. First is an individual assignment. Second is a group project undertaken by individuals at the Live-in Study Center. Third is a project given to a group meeting weekly for a two-year discipling experience.

INDIVIDUAL DISCIPLESHIP ASSIGNMENT

Paul wrote: "May the God who gives endurance and encouragement give you a spirit of unity among yourselves as you follow Christ Jesus, so that with one heart and mouth you may glorify the God and Father of our Lord Jesus Christ" (Rom. 15:5–6).

Summer Experiment: Life is always full of dissonant sounds, "sounds" that prevent the "one heart and mouth" from being fully expressed. Unity is not conformity, but it is in some way related to the voice of God coming to a "resolve" through the voice of the body "that with one heart and mouth you may glorify . . . God. . . ."

Making Disciples

Project: For three months you are to study and develop a "course of study" on "How to Hear the Voice of God." What is the voice of God today? Can we hear it? How will it produce harmony? How will it encourage body-life when truly heard?

I. Develop a six-to-ten-week course of study that could be used in our School of Christian Living. This study should include a complete outline of topics, suggested Scriptures, a summary of six to ten talks, a format for teaching the materials, individual and group projects (family projects), and training concepts for those who will assist you in the teaching of the materials.

II. To assist in the perfecting of your materials, you are to select one elder and his wife, two to three high-school-age persons, two to three young-adult types, and two adults over thirty-five. Meet with these persons at least four times in the next three months. They must be committed to you and the project.

III. Twenty-five copies should be ready for distribution not later than September 1. The church office will assist you in the duplication of the materials.

STUDY CENTER SEMINAR

I. This seminar is to begin on July 18 and is to be completed no later than August 29, a total of six weeks.

II. This is a discipleship seminar:

THE GOAL OF DISCIPLESHIP: Mark 12:9–31 (plus cross references)
All true discipleship must be designed to build our love for God— Father, Son, and Holy Spirit

THE GOAL OF THE DISCIPLE: (1 Corinthians 10:31)
When our love is sincere, then our lives will be lived for His glory.

III. Love is forever a personal matter. It cannot be taught, but it can be caught and it can be perfected. This is the chief goal of the Summer Seminar.

IV. The key to love is a walk with the Holy Spirit and a life focused on Jesus, the Christ. Memorize Luke 11:13 and 1 Corinthians 13.

V. GROUP ASSIGNMENT:
A. Read the entire New Testament during the seminar. There are 260 chapters, or six chapters each day (plus one nine-ten chapter day a week). This is approximately forty-three chapters per week.
B. Take approximately five minutes to pray before you begin your reading each day. This is to be "open eye" prayer, i.e. you are to jot down your needs and ask God to meet the needs of your life in some way as you approach this "voice-assignment." You are seeking to hear God's voice (Heb. 3). You must not be satisfied with less—under any circumstances. You must read until you hear.
C. Write what you hear in a journal, daily. At the end of the six weeks you are to have forty-two journal entries. Each entry must be numbered and dated.
D. Your journal entries are to be shared freely with others in the Study Center, but not until twenty-four hours after you write them.
E. Special journal entries: As you read, begin to look for significant theological themes, such as—the new covenant, priesthood, grace, salvation, sanctification, prayer, authority, Christ as mediator, gifts, hospitality, the Trinity, etc. Keep a separate sheet for each subject and seek to

231

get an overview of what the New Testament teaches about several important subject areas.

F. Be prepared to lead the entire church-body in a learning experience at September Praise. Each member of the house will share equally in this group expression.

VI. Individual assignment: For the entire six weeks seek daily to use what you are gleaning from the Word as a service to at least one other person outside the house. You create the project. Keep a record of ways you have made this study practical.

DISCIPLESHIP SEMINAR
SUBJECT: Workshop on Writing Commentaries

INTRODUCTION

When thinking about writing a commentary on the New Covenant (Testament) books, I am not supposing that this will be an exhaustive study. That is not possible. It is possible, however, to become relatively informed as to the basic message of each book and in so doing to "feel at home" in the biblical text.

What I am looking for is a studied way to grasp the intent of the New Covenant writers. A commentary is a series of interpretations and/or explanations that enable us to grasp the thoughts of God and people whom God has called to write. This is serious work. It takes serious concentration, prayer, research, and discipline, but the rewards are great if we set our minds to do our very best. This "very best" will vary due to your background, your commitment, and the time you have to give to the study.

SUGGESTIONS ON HOW TO WRITE A COMMENTARY

I. Read every book at least three to five times before you begin to make notations.
   A. Familiarize yourself with the author's thinking and insights.
   B. Use this time to draw near to God and His Word.
   C. Pray that God will create in you a deep desire to perceive and practice what you are learning from this study.
   D. Record your own findings, first.

II. Take time to study introductory materials, including:
   A. New Covenant introductions by biblical scholars.
   B. Various commentaries that seek to explain and interpret the text.
   C. Materials that help you appreciate the various authors, those to whom the letters were written, the possible time and place of the writing of the books, key doctrines that are discussed, and key words that reveal the major concerns of the writers.

III. Draft an outline of the entire book. Try to be original.
   A. Look at a variety of outlines in other writings, including those in
      1. Bibles
      2. commentaries
      3. New Covenant introductions
      4. Bible dictionaries
   B. Keep your outline simple:
      1. words
      2. short phrases
      3. simple sentences
   C. Use your outline in the context of the commentary

IV. The Body of the Commentary
   A. Work with paragraphs of thought, not just verses. Evaluate verses in the light of the paragraph and of the book as a whole.
   B. Look for connectives (what gives the author's thought a sense of coherence), conjunctions such as therefore, hence, thus, moreover, then, etc., that give the writing its unique expression of purpose.
   C. Record your thoughts in a way that is natural to you yet faithful to the biblical text.
   D. Plan to revise and rewrite as you discover deeper, more significant insights.
   E. Be humble. Do not overstate. This will only put others on guard.
   F. Seek to be clear; do not take shortcuts at the cost of clarity.
   G. State, whenever possible, what you believe to be the implications of the truths you analyze.

CONCLUSION

Our goal is to grow, not just to know! Thus there must be a creative tension between the mystical (emotional), the historical, and the cognitive (intellectual or scientific). Therefore, the disciplines discussed in Richard J. Foster's book, *Celebration of Discipline* (San Francisco: Harper and Row, 1978), need to be practiced as we seek to put together a theology that is truly biblical. God created us "spirit, soul, and body" and intended all learning to give close attention to the whole person.

4. Case History

We met Ivan Loughlen earlier and heard about his conversion through Trinity's Grapevine Ministry. Now we meet him again and hear him share about the discipling process he is involved in. Use the case study method to explore, through Ivan's sharing, the disciple-making process.

During the past year Ivan has been through a tragic divorce. About it he says, "I've been through a process in the last year that almost destroyed me. If it wasn't for my contact with people who loved and cared about me, I would never have made it. I've been torn apart emotionally. But God used that turmoil in my life to make me a deeper person. Joe Cook says that it is not in spite of our faults and failings or the adversity in our life but because of them that God transforms us. I like that."

This then is the context in which Ivan has sought to grow as a disciple.

IVAN LOUGHLEN

I was in a discipleship class that was more content oriented. It is interesting to watch a man grow as he disciples others. It blows my mind to see how much Gib Martin matured as he discipled me!

The difference is that he was not pumping me full of content. He was teaching me how to think for myself. That dimension of the discipling process helped to transform me. It helped me be the disciplined person that I was not. I had to get in there and dig and find out what God was saying to Ivan Loughlen that day. And that had a powerful effect on me.

What made the biggest impact on my life was writing a theology, introduction, and commentary on 1 and 2 Peter. The first time it was not without a lot of instruction, but it was really helpful to me. All of a sudden I was "in the middle of the ocean." I had to paddle for myself and discover what the Lord was saying to me. His Word became personal. It wasn't something that Gib Martin said that God said; it was firsthand experience. It was so much more dynamic.

I tend to be a relational person. Sometimes I think the relationships we have are too shallow. But mine are growing. In a year and a half, moving from not knowing anyone to having one or two close friendships has helped me.

It is hard to get close to guys sometimes, especially when you are in a discipleship context. Sometimes there is a competitiveness about it that keeps you from really getting to know each other. Because of the emotional problems and the divorce I've gone through in the past few years, there have been times—like a couple of months ago—when there was anger and bitterness deep inside me. I had dreams at night about my ex-wife stabbing me with a knife. I was so uneasy in the seminar. At the end Gib Martin said, "Ivan, you don't look good." Then all the guys gathered around me and laid hands on me and prayed for me. I cried, and I could feel all the anger and bitterness draining out of me.

I like being vulnerable—but not all the time. That was one of the times I didn't like being vulnerable. I remember driving down the road and saying, "Why does it always have to be me who has his dirty laundry hanging out?" And yet God uses those kinds of experiences in a group to draw us together. And I thought, *Yeah, that was really a good experience for everyone there, because they began to care about me, and I began to care about them.* I could see that here were guys who really wanted to support me.

Sometimes in this seminar I was "out of it." I sat there and that's about all, because emotionally I couldn't handle being a part of it in any other way. It was just being there with some guys who loved me. So a lot of the time I was "out in left field."

Maybe because of the Grapevine experience that I have been through myself, I have a heart for street people. And somehow I want to have an impact on their lives. I have tried to skirt the issues. I have wanted to get myself hooked up with a man of God to disciple me and do all kinds of things the easy way. But time after time God keeps telling me that I need an education to have the kind of impact on the community He wants me to have. Right now I have decided to work part-time. I need thirty credits to finish an A.A. degree. Then I want to go on and finish the last two years of college. So I have decided to be obedient for at least three quarters and go on from there.

5. Case History

Ivan is in the process of discipling, on the way to discovering himself and his giftedness. Kathy has lived through the process a little longer and has seen herself shaped by God through many of the resources explored in this and earlier chapters. A case study conference exploring Kathy's life will reveal the many influences—and the produce—of discipleship carried out, not one-on-one, but in the functioning body.

KATHY VLASCK

I was born in Indiana and at the age of three moved to a farm in Wisconsin. I was a real farm girl for ten years. That is where God began to touch my life.

My parents had a hard marriage, and I really needed God in a special way. We had neighbors who were very faithful about calling on my family for two years. They never gave up inviting us to church, and finally we went. I found the Lord as my Savior then and later went to a General Association of Regular Baptists church when we moved to Washington state. Then I went to Western Baptist College. That's when I thought that I would be a missionary nurse, but God called me into campus work in New York. I also spent two years in California working in a church youth group and then a year in New York doing the same thing.

There I met a girl who was demon possessed. That is when Gib Martin came into the picture. When I came home for Christmas, my brother said Gib could help me with her. So I came to him for advice. He offered me a job at Grapevine. I can see how God has often put me "in the way." I think that verse typifies my life: "I being in the way, God led me." So I really prayed about it and felt that God was leading me to Trinity.

I didn't know anything about the church's theology, just the man Gib Martin. From the two meetings he impressed me as a man who knew God. He described the Study Center program and the Grapevine to me, and I felt that was where I belonged. I accepted the job.

The discipling was a very positive experience. I had tried to be a disciple anyway, but perhaps not every day. One of the other girls in the group and I went down to California during that time and did our reading together in the car. We shared what God was saying. It was a very special time.

I was on the Grapevine staff for four years. For the first time I had in-depth relationships with Christians. I had had some dear brothers in the Lord before—both married and single—but not like the real family I had there. I think that would be one of the most important things that happened there; we worked together as a team. There were six or eight of us who became almost like one person; we could anticipate how the other one would feel. I tend to be mercy oriented, and another person in the group is very analytical and concerned with justice. Mark is middle-of-the-road. I learned by being close to them how to acquire some of these other qualities in my own life.

For instance, there was a resident who had violated a rule that was harmful to him. As a mercy-oriented person I tended to find out why he did it and said, "Oh, we understand, and don't let it happen again," rather than tell him the consequences and administer discipline. I'd help people avoid the consequences of their actions, thinking this was mercy, rather than help them see that the consequences were part of the learning process.

Our church had supported one missionary for four years. I heard him speak about the Christians in Eastern Europe, and I got a burden for them. Then in my third year at the Grapevine a girl who was organizing trips to Europe came by the Grapevine. We were sitting at the kitchen table having a good time, laughing about how I could build secret pockets in my long full skirts to carry Bibles, and I said, "I wish I could go. I wish I were a different kind of person and could hold up under a trip like that." She looked at me and said, "Kathy, I think you are perfect."

Something in that statement clicked with me. I knew then it was something that God wanted me to do, and I was going to have to make a few sacrifices and go. So I applied to go on a trip—and was accepted!

One of the questions on the application form was "Trace your spiritual development." So much had happened during my time at Trinity, and I thought how precious everyone was to me there. I started to cry. I thought, *What if some day God calls me away?* I had no idea that God *would* call me away, but just the thought of it made me cry.

Then in Eastern Europe we were going through a little village, and I was meeting people there, and all of a sudden it was as if God spoke to me and said, "Would you be willing to live here?" The faces of everyone on the Grapevine staff who were so dear to me went before me, just as they say happens when you are about to die. Mark's laugh, and Gib's twinkling eyes, and all the different

236

faces went before me in a second. And I thought, Yes, I could leave them all if God asked me to.

Most people who go into Communist countries feel a heavy burden, but I was bubbling inside. Then about three days before we were to come out, an inexplicable grief came over me. I would break down and cry at the thought of leaving. I didn't understand what was happening at that time, until I came back and walked into the Grapevine. Different staff members were hugging me and crying and were so glad I was back. I couldn't honestly say, "I'm glad I'm back." I couldn't talk to anyone on staff about it for the longest time. But I knew that my heart was somewhere else, that God had taken it. But I didn't yet know why.

Finally, I was just not able to do the work anymore. God took away my ability. Then I told Mark that I was resigning. Of course no one believed me. They thought that I needed some time off. But I knew in my heart that God had called me. I called Brother Andrew. The call was a miracle because he had been thinking of writing to me! Now I am a secretary for Brother Andrew. This year God has been teaching me about caring about the things on His heart. I don't know what He wants to do with me yet, but the vision that is developing in me is to go to a Third-World country and share the gospel concept of discipleship—just go into some of the little communities, perhaps attend a church group for two years, and pass on what I learned at Trinity. And then just disciple.

PART 2

PRACTICAL IMPLICATION

Identity Implications
Communicating Vision
Building Relationships and Community
Making Disciples
Equipping
Extending Freedom
Understanding Leadership

EQUIPPING

The case histories in this text have consistently demonstrated that growth toward effectiveness in personal ministry is a process of years. Giftedness is not something that bursts into sudden flower with a single exhortation, flows from a series of sermons, or bursts into being after a six-week training course. Building a ministering people involves a complex growth process tended by the Spirit of God. Growth toward an awareness of one's identity as part of God's people, toward spiritual maturity, toward sensitivity to the needs of others, toward confidence in our understanding of and response to God's voice, is gradual.

Understanding the gradual nature of this process, we see that leaders in a local congregation must equip believers for service and train them for ministry by providing a context in which the growth process will be healthy and natural.

All too often we miss the importance of providing such a context. We attempt to force individuals into ministry in ways that shortcut the process, burn them out, and turn them off as ministering persons.

CHAPTER **11**

Illustrations of this "shortcut" approach are all too familiar. A couple joins a church. Following the precept "Use them or lose them," we immediately "get them involved." The couple is invited to take a Sunday school class, or become youth sponsors, or children's church workers. Because they honestly want to serve the Lord and because they believe this means taking some role in a church agency, the couple accepts. Perhaps we provide a few weeks of training, usually not. In any case, the couple soon discovers that the "ministry" is a chore. Usually they do not develop significant relationships with those to whom they minister. They see individuals for only an hour or so a week, in a formal learning setting, lost in a group of others. Typically, after two years the couple can see no impact from their ministry in terms of changed lives. They have entered the ministry without a deep sense of call, without an awareness of how the ministry fits their giftedness, and without an awareness of the real needs they are seeking to meet. Soon they lose their motivation and drop out of the program. They have tried "ministry." And the result is only a sense of frustration and failure. They conclude that they just do not have the needed "spiritual gifts," and it will be extremely hard to get them to serve again.

Or take the young person who feels a deepening sense of commitment to serve God. He or she is pressured by the Christian community to go to seminary or to a Bible college to prepare for "full-time Christian service." The community forces the youth out of the context of a body in which he or she might grow and into a "training" experience that is often little more than a gathering of intellectual data about the faith. Then the totally unprepared twenty-four- or twenty-six-year-old is called to a position of staff "leadership" in a local church! The growing years, eighteen through thirty, in which a young person should have the freedom to grow in the Lord and serve in a variety of ways, have been stolen. The opportunity to try and fail, to back off to rethink and pray through an experience, and in the process to discover both himself and his giftedness, has also been taken away by an institutional view of "ministry." The young person is thus forced into the only path we recognize as a valid preparation for ministry. When "prepared," such a young person, without the experience of growing up within the body and without an opportunity to experience failure in a nonpressure situation, is thrust into the role of pastor or minister of education or youth minister. Every failure and mistake is deeply threatening and can be destructive.

Let's restate the key concept underlying this chapter. Training members of the body to become effective as ministering persons is neither a short- or long-term formal "training course" alone. Equipping for personal ministry involves the creation of a context within which growth into personal ministries can take place in a natural and healthy way.

THE GRAPEVINE

We can illustrate the idea of "providing a context for growth into personal ministries" by the impact, over the years, of the Grapevine Shelter in Seattle. When we have reviewed its history, we will go back and look at the principles it is based on. But even as we review, we can see the two most important aspects: (1) The Grapevine became a focus through which members of the body became aware of and involved with the needs of others; and (2) involvement in needs led to a high motivation for training. These themes are central as we review the history of the Grapevine Shelter.

The Grapevine was begun in the sixties as Gib Martin and the Trinity eldership became more and more aware of the impact of drugs on young people in Seattle. Originally the Grapevine was a coffee house, begun to establish contact with the youth of the community. It was a place to come, rap, drink coffee, and hear music provided by the staff and the street kids themselves.

Not everyone in the church was open to the Grapevine. Some adults were suspicious of kids with long hair, didn't want their own children contaminated, and tended to view any interaction with social problems as a "social gospel," a watering down of the gospel. But Gib Martin and others were deeply concerned. As he had become aware of the ravages of drugs on Seattle youth, at first Gib had been angry with the churches of the community for their failure to do anything. Then he realized that God was calling Trinity to do something.

But he didn't know what to do or how to do it. So the coffee house was begun. It was a place to meet the kids of the community and, by spending time with them, to identify their needs as well as minister the gospel. It was, as Gib now says, "training for me."

The coffee house operated outside the structure of Trinity and had its own council and funding. As the ministry developed, several other churches (often the "liberal" ones) grouped around to help financially and in other ways.

The coffee house experience *was* a learning experience for all involved. The kids who came did not respond to preaching or talks. The ones who came to know Christ and who were helped in other ways were invariably kids the staff met one-on-one and gradually built relationships with over a period of time.

In time the coffee house was forced to close because the kids who came and drug pushers misused it. But Gib and the staff had learned much in the process about youth and their needs. Soon the coffee house came back to life in a new form: as the Grapevine, a residence and live-in facility for drug-oriented youth, prostitutes, and others in need of help.

During these years of the development of the ministry, Gib Martin was the leader. But increasingly other members of the local body gathered around him. An auxiliary was formed to raise money for the ministry. One of its projects became the Country Store, a thrift shop staffed by the women of Trinity and one or two other churches. Since the Country Store was next door to the Grapevine, the older women who worked at the store increasingly spent time with the Grapevine residents. Other members of the Trinity body, such as Arvilla, donated time to serve as unpaid secretaries and counselors. Each week a supper and prayer meeting was held at the Shelter so members of the Trinity family could come to know and care for Grapevine residents. More and more members of the body came to know the young people and began to sense the needs of others in the community. More and more began to be involved in a variety of helping ways.

243

One of the ministries to the community that developed out of the Grapevine was a drug clinic the staff organized. A team visited colleges and other organizations and shared facts on drugs and drug abuse, personal stories, and the gospel. Some of the women of the church began a research team, took courses at Seattle universities and then one morning a week taught Gib Martin and the staff what they were being taught. In a very natural and gradual way, those who wanted to help were built into the ministry in one way or another. It was through involvement in the Grapevine ministry that individuals became sensitive to the needs of those around them and began to become aware of areas of personal giftedness.

In time the Grapevine became a counseling and crisis aid service that receives as many as four hundred referrals a month from other churches in the community, courts or social agencies, or people on the streets. Some fifteen to twenty members of the Trinity family serve as counselors, each with his or her own "case load." These believers, who lack degrees in social work or psychiatry but who have been trained by Gib and Mark (the Grapevine director), deal successfully with marital problems, attempted suicide, drug addiction, homosexuality, wife beating, child abuse, and every other problem the community contains. They work in close cooperation with government and social agencies and have high credibility for their compassion and effectiveness.

Another outgrowth is several smaller "communities" that have grown up within the body. These are formed by two or more families or several singles who are led to live together and share a ministering vision. The week I wrote this chapter members of these groups helped two attempted suicides. Three young women took one, a young social worker, into their home and surrounded her with love and support. Two young men in the Trinity family who have themselves been through almost identical circumstances gave the same kind of support to a young man just divorced from his wife and separated from his young daughter.

By sharing in a ministry of compassion and growing with it, many individuals in the body at Trinity have over the years discovered their giftedness. They have heard the voice of God and been led into significant personal ministries of their own.

PRINCIPLES

We can see in this brief outline of Grapevine history several principles related to equipping.

The need for mature examples

Earlier in the text we discussed the importance of spiritual leaders seeking their own personal vision rather than seeing their total call as a ministry within a fellowship or institution. This stress was based on the vital place Scripture gives to modeling by leaders. Leaders lead by example as well as by teaching. In fact, teaching and example must give a harmonious witness if the Word taught is to have any life-changing impact.

In the situation described at Trinity, it was Gib Martin's initiating action and concern that helped give others the confidence to step out. It is easier to learn *with* a trusted leader than simply to act on the exhortation of a leader to "go" and do what he himself is not doing.

It is also important to note the multiplying impact of examples. While Gib Martin was the one with the initial vision and drive, others in the body gathered around, became involved, and soon became examples themselves. The effectiveness of one of the women in counseling, for instance, soon gives other "lay persons" added confidence. This is important to understand. The principle speaks of *mature* examples, *not of professional* examples! As the Grapevine ministry developed over the years, an increasing number of mature examples emerged in the congregation. As the number of mature examples increased, their impact within the local body was multiplied.

It's appropriate to add a word of warning here. There will always be a tendency for elders (or deacons, or board members) in any congregation to see their "decision-making" function on the church board as their ministry. This parallels the tendency for staff members of a congregation to see their position on the staff as their ministry. This is extremely dangerous and must always be guarded against. All spiritual leaders, staff and nonstaff, are called on primarily to guard the life processes of the local body and to provide an example of a maturing faith that will bring the congregation closer to Christ. We have seen in the first part of this text that our very identity as the *laos* of God is intrinsically linked with ministry and service. Thus, if we are to avoid an ingrown, self-centered, and self-occupied congregation, it is vital that the leaders seek a personal ministry and call *beyond* their role within the fellowship. Only if they maintain a deep commitment to servanthood within the leadership will the church of Christ be the healthy, serving body that incarnates the reality of Christ's love.

The need for access

One of the difficulties in simply urging believers to "go and minister" is that few of the members of most churches have any significant access to those in need. We may be aware of needs in society without having any contact with those we could respond to.

There are several precepts concerning access that the Grapevine illustrates. On the one hand, those ministered to through the Grapevine originally—and in many cases today—would not feel comfortable in a "church." Thus the traditional place of worship is not a good point of contact because it is not a location where those ministered to feel at ease.

This is a very vital concept. Each of us feels more secure in a setting that is familiar or in which we feel at home. A child is frightened in a hospital because it is so different from his home, so strange that he feels powerless. An adult will often feel the same way if called into the IRS office for an audit. Simply being on the other person's turf signals "danger" and causes us to close up, act defensively, and resist open relationships. Because the Grapevine was originally a coffee house and then a separate residence that looked like (and was) simply a house, the people who came there were in a place in which they felt secure enough to enter into dialogue.

We see the same thing in the ministry Laura Billingsley Ward was called to in Atlanta. To meet and begin to care for prostitutes, Laura found herself forced to walk on the streets the girls worked. She could not stay comfortably in her respectable world and minister to them.

Laura's boldness points out the reverse precept of access. It is also important for the believer to feel at ease if he or she is going to build significant ministering relationships. Few in Laura's church have her freedom or boldness. Thus, our initiating approach will normally seek to provide a setting in which believers can become involved with some degree of comfort. The Grapevine was not the church. But the Grapevine was not the street corner, either. While not all at Trinity (or in any other congregation) would feel at ease even in the Grapevine setting, there was enough sense of "safe ground" there to draw an increasing number of believers into the building, and thus into contact with the young people to whom the ministry was directed.

This was one of the advantages of the weekly prayer dinner, "EPIC" (Everyone Praying in Concert). Members of Trinity could come with others to the Grapevine to meet and eat with the residents. In the process they began to respond to their needs. Whether that response was one of increased prayer, a support ministry such as the research team or Country Store, or a direct daily involvement by becoming part of the Grapevine operating staff, the result of becoming personally involved in a secure setting was important in guiding the people of Trinity into ministry. Out of that initial contact and concern have come many who are increasingly bold and competent in ministering to others in response to the voice of God.

Whenever we seek God's leading for ways to help a congregation become sensitive to the needs of others, we need to be aware of the importance of this dynamic. We need to be sensitive to providing a place of relative security for those we seek to serve and the servants to meet and come to know, trust, and respond to one another.

Openness to various supportive relationships

The Grapevine originally began with a council (responsible for funding the ministry) and a small staff that would meet and talk with the kids who came to the coffee house. As the ministry took a new shape and evolved ultimately into a residential halfway house, many different support teams developed.

A number of them were mentioned in the historical section of this chapter. Some of the women developed an auxiliary and undertook projects to raise funds. Out of that auxiliary grew the Country Store, a resale shop that not only raises funds but also helps and evangelizes. Others who spent time with residents at the Grapevine and responded to the many calls for help that came into that facility discovered they had counseling gifts. Out of this grew the present Grapevine counseling staff. Out of the drug research teams grew the seminars conducted for colleges and churches. Two years of such seminars not only communicated needed information about drugs but also softened the hearts of those in many congregations to society's outcasts. And through the gospel presentation that was a part of each seminar, a significant number came to know Christ.

None of these adjunct ministries was foreseen when the Grapevine ministry began. Each grew out of the giftedness and interests of individuals who came and said, "I want to help." Thus an initiating ministry can provide a focus around which multiple additional ministries grow.

It is very important, then, to keep an attitude of openness

and to provide freedom. The tendency of most individuals or governing councils would be to plan rigidly what others can do and to tell them how they must fit in. More wisdom was demonstrated at the Grapevine. There there was a process of exploring with individuals their interests and concerns, of giving suggestions, but with the suggestions giving freedom to go in unique ways. The atmosphere of freedom said to all, "You are important in your own way and for your own special giftedness," rather than, "You are important in how you fit into our preplanned program." In this climate God could speak and be heard. The creativity of the Holy Spirit was evidenced in the way *He* guided those drawn by a desire to help into personal ministries that no one could have foreseen.

This, then, is a principle to be aware of. You can expect others to want to help, drawn by an initial ministry. When they do come, treat them with integrity as believer-priests. Resist the temptation to make them fit into preconceived plans or programs. Explore with them their own desires, abilities, and leadings. Share needs that exist, and be open to what evolves.

Progression to structures

It would be easy, because of the stress in this book on "personal ministries" and our obvious concern with the impact of the current tendency to institutionalize ministry in the church, to misunderstand our discussion. We do *not* favor completely unstructured or nonorganized ministry. This is *not* what we are saying. Any ministry has *order, process,* and *structure.* What we are concerned about is that the structure that develops not be a control structure designed to force others into patterns predetermined by the leaders. Instead, we insist that the kind of order and structure that is appropriate to the body of Christ is an order and structure that provide freedom and make the people of God responsible to live in response to Jesus' guidance.

Structure and order are always important in any group ministry. There must always be safeguards to guard the *laos* against any misunderstanding of God's voice and against immature responses. The difficulty, of course, is providing a balance. On the one hand we must avoid controls that muffle the voice of God and rob the priesthood of its responsibility to the Lord. On the other hand we must guard against immature hastiness, undisciplined rush, and unthinking reason.

It is significant to notice in the description of the Grapevine that in each supportive ministry a process developed that moved from an individual who said, "How can I help?" to a team that together worked out the helping system.

This is the basis for understanding the structure that is to exist in the church itself and in its organized missions. The team must provide balance and integrity and share responsibility for organizing and conducting the ministry. The development of a team, we will see in chapter 12, is one vital aspect of the confirmation of God's voice. The team shares the responsibility of guarding and disciplining its members as well as stimulating, encouraging, and instructing them. It is responsible for confirming God's leading by seeking consensus —that unified testimony of each member that, yes, this direction *is* the will of God.

This, then, is the significance of the phenomenon we noted not only in the history of the Grapevine but also in the case-history experience of so many who have shared with us. One person may express an initial vision or desire to help. But soon others group around him or her to make the venture the mission of a team. The team, those who mutually share responsibility for the vision and for each other, *is* the structure and guards order and process in the body of Christ.

At this point we might pause to note that Gib Martin, while operating in his own giftedness at Trinity and perceived by most as "the pastor," does not operate except out of the team context. In each ministry involvement there is a team gathered around to support, guard, and guide the process together. In one way we might even say that Gib's most significant ministry over the years has been to form, or stimulate the formation of, teams that share in the many different ministries initiated through Trinity—or that have grown their own ministries out of their experience at Trinity.

It is important to watch for and to be sensitive to the formation of teams in training and guiding others into ministry. Encourage the development of teams to share the ministries to which God calls. Help each member of the team become responsible together with others for each other member and for following the voice of God in fulfilling their calling.

Recognize needs for training

In a list of six significant benefits to believers who grow as believer-priests, Gib Martin has suggested a number of the themes developed so far in this text. And he has suggested an emphasis we need to explore here. In notes developed in 1977 he suggested the following benefits to the *laos* when they recognize themselves as believer-priests:

1. They all discover their significance.
2. They all discover that they are gifted and needed.
3. They all discover that they are called to be God's servants.
4. They all discern that they need training.
5. They all discern that they need discipline and love.
6. They all discern that they need to grow to deeper commitment and sacrifice.

The terminology here is significant. At first there is *discovery* in the process of wanting to help, moving on to help, and thus exercising priesthood. But as the priestly ministry is entered into, several things are *discerned.* There is growing awareness of a need for training, and discipline, and love (being discipled). There is a growing awareness that the course launched on will lead to deeper commitments and sacrifices.

It is important in guiding the *laos* into ministry to become sensitive to the appropriate time for training. All too often the approach the church has taken is to provide training too soon—before the individual feels he needs it. Or it has provided no training at all, and thus has left people with a growing sense of inadequacy.

One of the kinds of training that became necessary as the Grapevine ministry took shape in Seattle was training for counseling. Many in the body had come beside others in supportive relationships. But they constantly ran into situations for which they knew no guiding principles. As a result the members of the body who were involved discerned a need for training! At that point training was introduced.

When we think of training, particularly in an area like counseling, we need to be very clear about one thing. *Our approach to any and every aspect of life in the church of Christ is to be theological.* That is, we are to explore the need and develop our response to the need in the light of the biblical revelation. Over the years Gib Martin has conducted a number of counseling seminars. His introduction to one seminar series begun in October of 1976 helps to show the approach. (Several lesson outlines included in the Probe section at the end of this chapter will give insight into some of the topics covered.)

A THEOLOGY OF CHRISTIAN COUNSELING

INTRODUCTION: The need for a theology of Christian counseling is profoundly evident in the light of the Word of God to the prophet Isaiah: "To the law (teaching) and to the testimony! If they do not speak according to this Word, they have no light of dawn" (Isa. 8:20). Today, we have many voices in the field of counseling that "do not speak according to this Word." It is both distressing and alarming that the science of psychology and the discipline of theology have drifted so far apart. God has raised up men and women in both disciplines to seek to discover and integrate the insights of both. This is a difficult process because of the absence of mutual respect, the scientific mindset that negates the place and importance of biblical revelation, and the theological mentality that rejects any form of empiricism with distaste or suspicion or that embraces scientific research without reserve and careful examination.

In 1959, a book titled *Psychoanalysis and Psychotherapy, 36 Systems* was written. If a sequel were to be written today, Dr. L. J. Crabb, Jr., a psychologist, said, "at least double that number of counseling approaches could be identified."[1]

Think of it, sixty to eighty different schools of thought on the subject of "counsel." Yet, we do *not* have a serious theology on the subject. We have many who have entered the field and who are making an important contribution to a Christian perspective in counseling, but a "contribution" is not a full theological statement. Somewhat tongue-in-cheek I am calling this seminar, "A Theology of Christian Counseling."

For such a work actually to be written, a person needs to be a trained theologian and a trained psychologist. Well, I confess, I am neither. But I have spent eighteen years in Scripture and theology and thirteen years in counseling. I have sought to read as widely as possible in psychology and theology. So in one sense this is "a theology." It is the way that I approach a ministry in counseling. I have tested my precepts and principles against the insights of scientific study and I have sought to discern what the Word of God teaches about this important area of ministry. It has been my desire to keep this study simple, clear, and useable. It is designed to encourage the priesthood, nonprofessional people, to undertake a serious ministry of sharing their lives and understanding through a ministry of counsel.

What does it mean to counsel? How do you view a ministry of counseling? What qualifies a person to be able to give counsel?

We know that the Word of God states: "For lack of guidance a nation falls, but many advisors make victory sure" (Prov. 11:14). The preacher in Proverbs wrote "Plans fail for lack of counsel, but with many advisors they succeed" (Prov. 15:22).

It has been the pattern for ages for teachers to record their insights, ideas, and theories for the benefit of those they teach. To the believers in Rome, Paul penned, "For everything that was written in the past was written to teach us, so that through endurance and the encouragement of the Scriptures we might have hope" (Rom. 15:4).

The insights I share with you through these "notes" are designed to be tested in the greater light of God's Word and under the guidance of the Holy Spirit. The precepts and principles taught here are found in the pages of His Word. Thus, my only purpose, ultimately, in providing these notes, is to encourage you to search the Word of God, for therein is your joy and hope. Jesus in His high priestly prayer asked the Father to, "Sanctify them by the truth; your word is truth" (John 17:17). It is my desire that these notes will serve to encourage the ministry of sanctification in your minds and hearts.

---

[1]Lawrence J. Crabb, Jr., *Basic Principles of Biblical Counseling* (Grand Rapids: Zondervan Publishing House, 1975), p. 21.

PRACTICAL IMPLICATION

It's critical, then, for church leaders to be sensitive to the time when members of the body discern their need for training. It is not necessary that the training process always be developed by the pastor or other leaders of the local congregation. Often other resource persons in the community or larger body can be called on. But it is vital that the training provided always be theological in essence, and that guidelines for responses in ministry be firmly rooted in the Word rather than in fluctuating human theories.

Carry-over into personal life

We've noted the tendency of ministries quite naturally to take on a team structure and we suggested that this should be encouraged. Understanding the team as the way in which any organism structures its elements, we want to give teams that are formed any support and help we can, so that they might function effectively.

Now we want to note what will happen in the body as people are drawn into such ministries. The maturity and giftedness nurtured by the shared experience in the ministry team setting will increasingly shape the rest of the life of the believer. What has been developed in the "safe" setting will find freer and freer expression in the daily life and contacts of the individual. The participants will become increasingly competent to function in every setting of their lives.

For more than one person the Grapevine experiences made a difference in their family life. Parents whose own children were involved with drugs developed new compassion and understanding. They opened their homes to take in people in need. Today, one outgrowth of that style of ministry is a growing vision for international students to live with them during the school year. This very special aspect of the missionary vision of Trinity is an outgrowth of the confidence in ministry many gained by being part of ministry teams.

No believer will ever come to the place where he or she can live completely *alone.* That simply is not the way God has designed His body. We are bound together in a web of relationships because we are family and need each other for personal spiritual growth. But at the same time we are to become increasingly confident in the Holy Spirit and our giftedness, and we are to be freed increasingly to minister without dependence on others.

This, too, is one of the outgrowths of the kind of initiation and training process we've seen in reviewing the growth of the Grapevine ministry.

In brief, then, we have suggested that if we are to guide the members of a congregation into ministry and equip them for their calling, there are several principles we need to follow, and several processes of which we need to be aware. These include the following:

- Recognize the need for mature examples of individuals with personal ministries, probably to be cultivated by the leadership of the congregation.
- Recognize the importance of access to those being ministered to and a setting that they and those ministering see as nonthreatening.
- Remain open to various unexpected and unplanned supportive ministries that will be stimulated as more and more individuals want to help with the initial ministry.
- Expect to see the emergence of helping ministries and encourage the formation of teams that share this responsibility.
- Expect those engaged in ministries to discern a need for training and provide a training that is basically biblical and theological.
- Expect what has been learned to carry over into the personal lives of individuals.
- Expect maturing and competent believers to encourage more members of the body to go into new ministries.

There is no truly effective way to guide a body of believers into its shared identity as a ministering *laos* without the initiating stimulus of mature examples. The leaders of the congregation may initially provide the example. In time many mature examples of ministry will develop in the local body. They will multiply the impact of ministry throughout the congregation.

If we are to reach the world for Christ in our generation, the process will not be through raising millions upon millions of dollars for highly organized, media-intensive campaigns. The process will instead be the gradual and natural growth of the *laos* of God into a full experience of their identity. Out of that discovery of identity will come a servant church, which God will lead into all the world to communicate the gospel of Christ not in word only, but in power, in the Spirit, and in the one script that is to be read by all men. That script is the living Word, written on the hearts of those who live out the love and servanthood of Jesus Christ.

PRACTICAL IMPLICATION

PROBE

▶ *case histories*
▶ *discussion questions*
▶ *thought provokers*
▶ *resources*

1. Following are outlines of two of the training seminars on counseling Gib Martin led in 1978. They are included so that you can gain a sense of the kind of training, and the precepts involved in training at Trinity.

THE NATURE OF CHRISTIAN COUNSELING
A Seminar on Counseling from a Biblical-Theistic Perspective

Lesson 5

INTRODUCTION. Thus far in our seminar on counseling from a biblical-theistic perspective we have:

I. Discussed the role of the counselor.
   A. The Wonderful Counselor is our example.
   B. A life well-lived is our primary thesis. It is here we gain our credentials.
   C. We have suggested a definition of what counseling should entail (cf. pp. 250–252).
   D. We have looked at specific qualifications of a counselor from a biblical perspective (cf. pp. 250–252).

II. Discussed the nature of man from both a scientific and a biblical perspective, thus seeking to better understand the nature of the counselee (as well as our own nature).

In the latter part of the thirteenth century, Thomistic theology introduced a sharp cleavage between faith and reason. St. Thomas Aquinas (1225–1274) was the father of a new dualism in his battle to preserve the faith. He broke with earlier theologians, especially Augustine, by insisting that there are basically two types of knowledge. One he called "natural knowledge" such as we find in the writings of Aristotle and Plato, the other he called "supernatural knowledge" or knowledge revealed by God and discussed by Christian theologians. Ultimately, this left the mind undaunted by the Fall of man. It began to be taught that in the Fall only the "will" of man was fallen, not the intellect.

This is a clear break with biblical revelation. It was like opening Pandora's Box to the natural unregenerate mind. In this view, man's intellect became autonomous. Man no longer needed the mind of Christ to interpret the natural creation; it was only for "spiritual things." This dualism is still a sick part of both the Catholic and the Protestant churches.

Eventually, Thomistic dualism led to the birth of the humanistic Renaissance that ultimately led to the need for the Reformation under Luther and Calvin.

This is why we must return to the Bible if we ever hope to learn how to counsel in a godly way. We must not allow a dualism in our counseling or teaching. This causes the pollution of intellectual thought.

The Fall of man was total. God made the whole man as spirit, body, and soul, and the whole man has fallen from God. Only God is truly autonomous. Thus the Reformation fathers established once again that ultimate knowledge about man and nature must be based on the authority of the Bible, and the Bible alone. "Scripture alone" was the battle cry of the Reformation fathers; it must be our cry today if we are going to have any significant effect on the deadness that fills the human heart. Paul the apostle wrote, "For God has bound all men over to disobedience so that he may have mercy on them all" (Rom. 11:32). This simple statement of revelation summarizes God's point of view on this entire subject!

With this review and this brief addendum on Thomistic dualism we are ready to examine the principles of counseling that will help both the counselee and the counselor. The first principle is one I call the participation principle.

I. The Principle of Participation: In all of life, there is too much talk and too little participation. In counseling this is very destructive. We must learn to participate. The word "participate" means to possess something of the nature of a person, a thing, or a quality.

This is more than listening (yet it is listening). This is genuinely seeking to discern the other person's needs, desires, and mind-set while at the very same moment maintaining your own heart and mind under the control of the Holy Spirit. When you participate in another person's life, you suggest to him that you are willing to be involved in real ways, healing ways, personal ways.

The Creator Himself initiated the participation principle when He visited with the first human parents daily in the Garden of Eden. He taught them the principle of participation by participating with them in life.

God not only walked with man in the Garden, but when the God-man, Jesus, came as the Messiah to this planet, the key to the training of His disciples was that He participated with them in the ministry. He shared His life, not just the thoughts of His mind. And He shared His love, not just His counsel.

In sharing His life with His disciples, He of necessity had to share His mind, His sorrows, His rebukes, His joys, and even His secrets. Jesus participated with those men, and many women, in deep and meaningful ways. If He felt this to be necessary if His work with them was to be complete, how much more ought we to feel the necessity of participation. This is a very important principle in creative, competent counseling.

Each of the passages suggested below highlights in various ways the principle of participation. Take time to consider each passage from the point of view of participation. In addition, make a list of biblical passages that you feel support or question the idea of participation.

Illustration:

A. Man and God: Acts 17:28; 1 John 1
B. Mind and Spirit: Romans 12; 1 Corinthians 2; 12
C. Faith: Hebrews 11:1–6; 12
D. Persons: Romans 12:3ff. (counselor); Galatians 2 (counselee); 1 Corinthians 11; Hebrews 12
E. Fruit of a godly life: Galatians 5; Matthew 5; 2 Corinthians 12

The apostle Paul said to the Corinthians; "Be imitators of me, as I am of Christ" (cf. 1 Cor. 10:31–11:1; etc.). In 2 Corinthians 3:2 Paul states, "You yourselves are our letter, written on our hearts, known and read by everybody." People will often "plug in" to us until they can find the needed grace to "plug in" to the God of all grace.

Time is an important factor in the participation principle. But I have

found that real participation does not have to be lengthy, nor even re-
petitive; it must simply be real, both to the counselee and the counselor.

We are really talking about the quality and not so much the quantity
of time. At first, it might require more hours of time, but if the time you
have together is real, then it can usually be brief because it is significant.

Quality participation includes the following:

I. Meet from time to time, so that the person will know you are genuinely
interested in him.

II. Take time to share in meaningful prayer.

III. Be responsive to key moments.

IV. Be aware of those you are with on all occasions: in a store, at a worship
service, etc.

• • •

Lesson 8

INTRODUCTION: Our subject is *The Work of Collecting Data* Principles
to Guide Our Thinking.

I. Observe "Tender Spots." I constantly look for the "tender spots" in
a person's life. Frequently, when a person is hurting, we carelessly
"jump" all over him. A hurting person is already a bruised person. And a
bruise is a "tender spot" that needs protection until it receives divine
healing. Correct we must, but in the light of God's healing balm: "Be
kind and compassionate to one another, forgiving each other, just as in
Christ God forgave you," is the admonition of the apostle Paul (Eph.
4:32).

Paul wrote to the Galatians, "Brothers, if someone is caught in a sin,
you who are spiritual [have been given counsel] should restore him
gently" (Gal. 6:1).

You can often find a tender area if you listen thoughtfully to the
hurting person. By the time he has the courage to come to a counselor,
his defenses are beginning to be lowered. He is more vulnerable, sometimes unknowingly more open and transparent. He will use expressions
and demonstrate certain behavior traits that others who are struggling in
these areas also use. A good counselor will begin to discern these signs.

For example, a person suffering from:

A. *alcoholism* will often blame others for his behavior or express verbal or
nonverbal feelings of loneliness, helplessness, or sorrow;

B. *bitterness* will often mask his true feelings, express anger, be
judgmental, sense guilt, threaten, condemn, etc.;

C. *personal inadequacies* will often find it hard to read, study, or
socialize, and will express his feelings through tears, tenseness, nail
biting, and twisting of the hair.

This list could be augmented. The counselor needs to develop a sense
of discernment by carefully observing and by seeking the Holy Spirit's
guidance to make the right decisions.

Tender spots can be talked about—if you are considerate, compassionate, wise, understanding. Build a fence around the tender area—just
as you do new grass. Learn to build a special rapport with every person;
every person is different. The "fence" helps us remember not to trample
where the person is hurting. Let them point out the areas that hurt! They
will if you are patient.

Illustration: A young woman came to me recently and told me she had

256

a friend who was a homosexual and a Christian. She came with a very defensive spirit. How should Christians treat a brother or sister with this kind of perspective on life (you could not say sin)? Discuss how you would approach such a person.

To honor a tender area does not imply that you avoid sharing God's viewpoint, that is *if* you are certain of His viewpoint. The Spirit heals via the oil of truth, but He knows when to apply the oil (John 16:7–15)! It is our holy responsibility to be guided by the Holy Spirit.

II. Observe the Lying Tongue: I am more and more convinced that a "lie" is at the root of most of our anxiety, bitterness, loneliness, and fears. People camouflage the truth with untruth. If it is not the personal "lie" of the counselee, it is the "lie" of another person in their life. Paul often pointed to the fact of falsehood in the flock: "Therefore each of you must put off falsehood and speak truthfully to his neighbor, for we are all members of one body. . . . Get rid of all bitterness, rage and anger, brawling and slander . . ." (Eph. 4:25, 31).

One of the seven things that God hates is a lying tongue. If God hates it, we must hate it if we are to serve God fully (cf. Prov. 6:16–19).

Lying is a habit, a sign of mistrust in the spirit of the person. It is a form of personal protection, and a cover for feelings of inferiority.

Love will cover a multitude of sins, but it will eventually expose a lie. It must, lest it kill love. I believe that love is the only real cure for lying (1 Cor. 13:7; Rom. 5:6).

III. Look for Practical Ways to Meet a Need of the Counselee Today. While you are in the data-collecting stage of a relationship, you should be discovering pragmatic ways to encourage, love, and assist the counselee. Consider some of the following:

A. A Kleenex to dry tears!
B. A warm coat to keep out the cold.
C. A warm meal to encourage and set free (James 2:14), hospitality (1 Peter 4).
D. A shelter from life.
E. A word of care.
F. Money.

Always keep in mind: You are dealing with a person . . . not a patient. Christian counseling is always person-oriented and never patient-oriented. Help, of the caring kind, will act as a catalyst to bring healing. It is a bridge-builder and it is in perfect accord with the will of God, God's good intentions (Matt. 25:31–46).

IV. Look for Scriptural Illustrations, Principles, and Passages That Help to Understand Certain Problems:

- Death: Philippians 2:19–26, etc.
- Marriage: Ephesians 5; 1 Peter 3; 1 Corinthians 7; Proverbs 31
- Salvation: John 1; Ephesians 2; John 3; 1 John 5

READ: 2 Timothy 3:16–17, Romans 15:1–6, and Acts 20:26ff.

THUS: Confidentiality . . . Responsible reactions . . . The art of sorting data . . . Observe tender spots . . . Observe the lying tongue . . . Meet practical needs today . . . Look for scriptural principles to guide your counsel. This, and much more are guidelines to assist you in the work of collecting data, data that assists you in being a servant to a brother or a sister. Let us be our brother's brother.

PRACTICAL IMPLICATION

2. One basic concern all of us share is the missionary calling of the church. It's helpful to trace the impact of the teaching and lifestyle encouraged at Trinity on those who have been called from the body into various aspects of the missionary task. This is a brief description of the mission emphasis and impact of Trinity:

The "mission" concept at Trinity is shaped and encouraged in a variety of ways:

I.   Ministry is understood as helping people see themselves as unique, significant, and responsible (concepts such as priesthood, giftedness, servanthood, etc.).

II.   The idea that "the world is the field" has been part of the foundational understanding; therefore our understanding of ministry has been broad.

III.   Our sense of responsibility is tied to a sense of accountability (e.g., the need for training and the exercising of gifts). We urge people to be discipled (i.e., to participate in one of the many training opportunities that are provided).

IV.   We have stressed the idea that ministry teams need a clear sense of *local* mission (e.g., the Grapevine Ministries, Campus Life).

V.   "Home-grown" missionaries, people with special ministries in our congregation, have helped us identify more clearly with missions in other countries.

VI.   Mission prayer-support teams that have formed around some of our missionaries meet monthly and exercise a ministry of intercession, communication, helps, teaching, and hospitality. Any need of the missionary while on the field or on furlough is the concern of this team.

VII.   Letters from missionaries are duplicated; a missions-education resource center is being built; other prayer groups meet; the Wineskin Tape Ministry sends Trinity tapes to missionaries.

VIII.   Some members of Trinity have become short-term missionaries.

IX.   Some serve locally through missions organizations that have a world-wide impact.

The "priesthood" concept frees people to view themselves as responsible servants of God, ministers with authority. For example:

I.   *Mel and Lucy and family:*

Mel is an elder at Trinity, employed in the Air Cargo business. They serve in a variety of ways, especially in the

Grapevine Shelter. Mel helps train young men in vocational skills through factory-type projects he supervises.

Mel always wanted to be a missionary. Eventually he and his family went to Irian Jaya with the Missionary Aviation Fellowship. He became a business manager of operations there. Lucy's ministry of encouragement at Trinity was needed in Irian Jaya. She greeted all new arrivals from the plane, cooked meals, and opened her home to people who needed to stay overnight.

II.   *Kathy:*

Kathy came to Trinity from New York where she had served on a church staff. She came to Seattle to be part of the Study Center, a residential discipleship center for women. She also served as a part-time staff member at the Grapevine Shelter, Trinity's mercy center. Kathy exercised her gift of mercy through hours of intense counseling, crisis intervention, home decorating, and meal serving. Her vision for the hurting and oppressed world-wide increased, and when an opportunity opened for her to become a part of the Open Doors ministry, she joined Brother Andrew and his team in Holland.

III.   *Marc and Penny and family:*

Marc, a special-education teacher, and Penny, a nurse, exercised their spiritual gifts through music, evangelism, service, and hospitality. Marc was part of a two-year discipleship program in which he and other men met weekly. Penny was active in the women's fellowship. Increasingly their concern was for an overseas ministry, so they joined Operation Mobilization and now serve in Austria.

IV.   *Al and Nancy:*

Al, a graduate of Dallas Theological Seminary and a speech therapist, came to Trinity in order to develop more fully as part of a ministering team. Both Al and Nancy were active in our teaching ministry. Nancy's gift of leadership and administration found an outlet in her work on the women's fellowship council. Both were gifted in putting people at ease and their home soon became a gathering place for many people, especially the lonely, discouraged, or seeking. Together they exercised a ministry of mercy, encouragement, and evangelism that gave them practical experience for the discipleship ministry they now have through Operation Mobilization.

V.   *Roberta:*

Roberta, an elementary school teacher gifted in the area of administration ministered at Trinity in a variety of ways.

She traveled to the Sudan one summer to assist a missionary family and her organizational abilities were most helpful there. Following her return to Trinity, she continued to teach, but again decided to assist a missionary family in Kenya, and committed herself to a two-year assignment as an office manager.

3. Case History

Today another area of ministry is beginning to emerge at Trinity. Many of the principles shared in this chapter are already beginning to find expression as several young people have become involved in a distinctive ministry of music. See how many of these principles and practices you discern in the following story of one person on the music team.

TERRI BRUCE

My spiritual gifts seem to center around music. Well, they have since I've come to know the Lord. I've always wanted to be involved with music. I have never been comfortable in front of people, so I never sought to be a leader. But I was the only one who played the guitar in my youth group, so I always ended up being the song leader. I was in our small youth choir and sang in duets, quartets, or other groups. I loved singing, but I never wanted to be a soloist.

The more involved I got in music, the more confident I became. Then God took it away for a few years. I lost all my confidence and did a lot of soul searching. Who am I? Where do I fit in God's plan? Is He really that personal type of God I've been told He is? Does He really have a plan for me? Or is this all really a hoax and am I just following the crowd?

During this period of frustration and skepticism about the Lord, I didn't do any singing at all. But God planted in me the knowledge that He was who He said He was. He was God. And He was intimately concerned with all of my fears. Over a two-year period they magnified and gained a grip on me I couldn't understand. God became very personal during that time, and I began to have more and more of a desire to sing once again.

But there was no one to sing with anymore. All my old friends were either not walking with God at the time or had gone off somewhere else. I knew I needed someone to sing with. I play the guitar but not well enough to hack it by myself. So I began praying. I was still confused, but I wanted to use my musical ability as part of Christ's body.

A year after I began praying, I met John. He had been around Trinity a while, but I didn't know him. I found out that he had some of the same musical goals I had. We started practicing together. Then his wife, Kenni, joined us. She wanted to be involved in the same ministry John was in, and she was musically gifted. So the three of us became a team.

We began seeking God's will. Okay, God, why are we together as a team? Sure, John sings and plays, Terri sings and plays, Kenni sings and plays. Big deal!

God began *very* slowly to carve out a path for us. I wanted to see the body at Trinity sing more informal songs and Scripture choruses. I didn't feel any freedom in the worship there, and I knew there were other people who felt the same way. I also wanted to see more formal singing that would cause the total body to focus on Jesus Christ in a unified manner.

It was about a year before the church began teaching music and having a regular time of singing together. Then the elders went through a very difficult period. We knew they were experiencing a lot of difficulty, and we wanted to be a part of their agony. I read in 1 Samuel about the effect of David's playing for Saul and wondered if the same thing could happen today. Why don't people visit more in one another's homes and minister to each other in song there instead of always having to sing at the corporate level? We put together a package of about seven songs. We then went around to about six of the elder's homes and sang to them and their families.

Seeing the way our music ministered to people, I wanted to see music become more a part of our Christian lives together. I wanted to see people go to one another's homes and encourage each other through song.

We sent a tape of our music to missionaries we knew in Egypt because we hoped to communicate some of the same things to them in music. We also decided that as long as we were making a tape, and everybody at Trinity knew it, we might as well make enough for everyone to have. Right now they are being duplicated.

God has been revealing to me the importance of having a soft heart toward Him. I have begun to see that I am very hard in some ways, especially toward the suffering in the world around me. I realize that I am wrapped up in my own little world, hoarding my blessings for myself. God made it clear that I was saved so I could be salt and light for other people in a newer and deeper way than I had ever thought about before. All of us in the trio are deeply concerned about that idea. John is writing some music about having compassion for hurting people.

I also want to encourage others to develop their musical gifts. I would like to see more small groups and more individuals actively developing their musical gifts. I hope other people will get involved because of the way we are developing a musical ministry.

PART 2

PRACTICAL IMPLICATION

Identity Implications
Communicating Vision
Building Relationships and Community
Making Disciples
Equipping
Extending Freedom
Understanding Leadership

EXTENDING FREEDOM

In one of His discourses Jesus said something that divided His listeners and led some to call Him "raving mad" (John 10:20). He talked about a shepherd and his flock and clearly identified them with Himself and His followers.

In the discourse Jesus emphasized the sheep's recognition of the shepherd's voice. "The sheep listen to his voice," Jesus said. "He calls his own sheep by name and leads them out. When he has brought out all his own, he goes on ahead of them, and his sheep follow him because they know his voice. But they will never follow a stranger; in fact, they will run away from him because they do not recognize a stranger's voice" (John 10:3-5).

Jesus was describing a very familiar Palestinian scene. We see a common fold where the sheep of many shepherds are kept at night, guarded by a watchman. When the shepherds come in the morning, each one calls out. The sheep of that shepherd recognize his voice and respond. The sheep of another will not come, for they are tuned to respond only to the voice of their own shepherd. If a sheep fails to respond at first, the shepherd calls it by name, giving it the individual attention needed to bring a response. The sheep follow the shepherd out of the fold where they are mixed with the sheep of other shepherds. Through all that day the shepherd goes before his sheep. He leads them, and they continue to follow him because "they know his voice." It's clear from the context that Jesus is illustrating first of all the response of human beings to the call to faith. Some hear the invitation, recognize the voice of God in the Good News, and in faith respond by choosing to follow Him. But it's also clear that, after the initial response "when he has brought them all out," the Good Shepherd continues to lead His flock. Those to whom Jesus has given eternal life (John 10:27-28) continue to be responsive to the voice of the One who has redeemed them.

It is because of this fact that the writer to the Hebrews can place so much emphasis on responding to the voice of God. "Today," he warns, "if you hear his voice, do not harden your hearts as you did in the rebellion" (Heb. 3:15). There is a notable assumption here. The assumption is that the Christian's problem in his relationship with God will not be one of *recognizing* the voice of God but one of *responding* to it.

In the "time of rebellion" the writer refers to, God had told the Israelites to enter and take the land promised to them. They *knew it was God commanding them to move boldly into the land.* But they turned back because of a sinful, unbelieving heart (Heb. 3:12). According to the author, believers under the new covenant face the same issue. Because of the distinctive relationship of the *laos* of God to the Spirit and the Son, *the voice of God will be heard and recognized!* The danger is that we, like Israel, will disobey because of lack of faith in the God who spoke to us. So the writer says, "Encourage one another daily, as long as it is called Today, so that none of you may be hardened by sin's deceitfulness" (Heb. 3:13). We are to encourage each other to be open and responsive to the voice of God, which, as followers of Jesus, the *laos* of God will hear.

The whole idea of an intimate, personal, and to a great extent *subjective and individual* responsibility to hear and respond to God's voice troubles many. They feel much more comfortable in a structure in which a human leader or leadership group controls the lives and ministries of brothers and sisters. But the Bible's teaching on the identity of the people of God opposes this institutional approach to life and ministry. The confident expectation of Jesus and the Epistles is that God's own will hear His voice personally.

Earlier we noted the statement in 1 Corinthians that "we have the mind of Christ." While "the spiritual man makes judgments about all things, . . . he himself is not subject to any man's judgment" (1 Cor. 2:15–16). In Romans we've seen a similar emphasis; an insistence that believers have no right to pass judgment on each other (in areas in which God has not already revealed His judgment of certain acts as sin). We are free *not* to judge and *not* to attempt to control the lives and convictions of our brothers because we realize that "Christ died and returned to life so that he might be the Lord of both the dead and the living" (Rom. 14:9). In view of this we can neither judge nor look down on our brothers. Nor dare we put any obstacles in our brother's way (Rom. 14:13). We extend to our brothers and sisters the freedom to listen for God's voice and to respond, and we try to remove any obstacles that might hinder a response to Jesus as Lord. In fact, we want to build into the lifestyle of the local congregation a freedom that is in fact responsibility—the freedom and responsibility of each brother and sister to listen for the voice of the Lord and respond to Him as He leads them into that personal ministry for which they have been gifted and called.

The issues we want to deal with in this chapter, then, are: How can we encourage the congregation to hear and respond to God's voice? How can we remove obstacles to the functional lordship of Jesus? And how can we guard against the misuse of freedom that results in a following of the passions rather than of the voice of God? To answer, we want to suggest and illustrate a number of very important principles.

TRAIN A PEOPLE WHO LISTEN FOR GOD'S VOICE

The Old Testament is often misunderstood when it presents God as "jealous." What we seem to hear is that distortion that all too often finds expression in our fellowmen. They experience jealousy as a burning desire for something that should not be theirs. In the Scriptures jealousy, when applied to God, is a completely holy and healthy thing. It speaks of God's burning desire that He and He alone be the focus of the believer's life, that He be, indeed, God for us. This is a holy desire because it is right. He *is* God. It is also completely healthy, for it is only in our relationship to God as God that we find our destiny of wholeness. God is jealous *for* us and not *of* us. He does not want any thing or any person to take His place in our hearts.

No wonder, then, that learning to hear God's voice, to discern it in the babble of competing voices around us, is so vital. Each Christian, gifted with the Spirit and with a direct access to God, is to give allegiance to his brothers and sisters, but in obedience only to God. No Christian leader, no matter how well trained in the interpretation of Scripture, no matter how certain of his own convictions, dare take the place of the Lord in the lives of members of the congregation. Instead, leaders must reject manipulation and the pressuring of others into patterns of life just because those patterns fit the leader's conscience or leading. Instead, leaders need to give the people of God freedom—and train them to be responsive to the voice of God.

Provide a scriptural anchor

Most Christians draw back intuitively from a call to listen for God's voice and be directly responsible to Him. It somehow seems safer—and even more biblical—to let a spiritual leader who is trained and "special" be responsible for directing our lives. Some leaders may even reject this concept of God's voice and call it "existential" and "subjective." They may insist that God's revelation is completed when we have a systematic, objective exposition of the propositional teachings of Scripture. But in fact the doctrine of God's voice is itself part of this systematic, objective revelation. Because it is taught in Scripture, it must be given a place in the experience of the people of God.

Also, because people are not normally open to the teaching

or the experience, it is important that our own communication of this reality be firmly anchored in Scripture. Hebrews 3 is a central passage. It needs to be taught, and referred to, and built into the worship experience of the congregation. "Today, if you hear his voice . . . ," the writer begins. He goes on to show that in every generation, under both old covenant and new, there is to be a "today" experience of God's leading. Under the old covenant the prophet heard and spoke—and the people listened to the voice of God through the prophet. Under the old covenant a leader like Nehemiah heard and then directed the rebuilding of Jerusalem—and the people listened to the voice of God through Nehemiah. But today "you shall all know him," for God speaks out in that direct personal relationship He maintains with each one of us.

A people sensitive to the living voice of God who speaks to each person individually and to groups corporately *is* the teaching of Scripture. To build a people who are sensitive and open to the voice of God we must be sure they understand this experience as it is taught in Scripture. Knowing the biblical teaching on the voice of God provides a confidence that will grow as the congregational members increasingly experience hearing that voice.

Encourage a contemplative process

One of the critical steps in developing a sensitivity to the voice of God involves guiding the *laos* into a thinking relationship with God. What we mean by this is that we need to help each individual learn to orient his or her thoughts and life to God.

The best way this can be done is through a distinctive use of Scripture. This use involves an extremely simple exercise but one that introduces the contemplative process. At Trinity for many years Gib Martin featured a simple, short expression from Scripture in the bulletin each week. The people were to meditate on that key thought daily. "What are the implications of this statement?" "How can this find expression in my life?" This kind of personalized thinking or meditation focused the awareness of the congregation on God and encouraged the realization that each believer could make personal discoveries and hear God speaking to him or her in the Word.

Such a simple practice, with its affirmation of the Bible's teaching about the voice of God, is a significant step toward building a people who are sensitive and open to that voice. Here is a list of some of the phrases, taken from Scripture, used at Trinity over the years in this process:

"If I speak in . . . tongues . . . if I have the gift of prophecy . . . if I have a faith . . . if I give all I possess . . . if I . . . surrender my body to the flames, but have not love, I gain nothing" (1 Cor. 13:1-3).

The apostle Paul asked the Roman Christians, "Who shall separate us from the love of Christ?" This great man of God saw love as the "glue" that holds God's people to God and together. God's love is the "fruit of the Holy Spirit." Therefore Paul wrote, ". . . God has poured his love into our hearts by the Holy Spirit, whom he has given us" (Rom. 5:5). Thus, love, from God's perspective, is not first a release of human emotion, but a reflection of God's presence through His committed servants.

• • •

". . . I will follow you wherever you go" (Luke 9:57b).

These were the words of a man who had failed to count the cost of discipleship, so Jesus warned him that a commitment to Him would cost him much, if not everything. Let us not fear to commit our all to the Lord Jesus. Reservation with Him amounts to rejection!

• • •

"You believe that there is one God. Good! Even the demons believe that—and shudder" (James 2:19).

James, the half brother of our Lord, points up a very significant truth in this terse statement. Too frequently, even among the redeemed, "believe" has a superficial, anomalous meaning. To say you "believe in God" and that you believe there "is one God" is foundational and fundamental to spiritual reality, but at the same time it is ludicrous if it does not result in wholehearted dedication to Jesus Christ and personal transformation.

• • •

"There will be signs. . . . When these things begin to take place, stand up and lift up your heads, because your redemption is drawing near" (Luke 21:25a, 28).

The Christian who walks in the power of the Holy Spirit cannot walk with his eyes cast down and his head drooping. This is in contradiction to the Word of truth. Yet this is not to suggest that the "hurt" of circumstances is not real. It is, but so is God's comfort and counsel in those moments.

• • •

"Don't let anyone look down upon you because you are young, but set an example for the believers in speech, in life, in love, in faith and in purity" (1 Tim. 4:12).

Paul, God's apostle, wrote this to young Timothy. He is suggesting that you do not have to be old and wrinkled to be obedient and wise. God is looking for young men and young women who are ready for a change of heart toward Him, that He might change the world through them.

• • •

". . . you must love one another. . . . All men will know that you are my disciples if you love one another" (John 13:34-35).

Jesus chose twelve men to disciple. For approximately three years He ministered to their needs . . . He coached them in God's truth . . . He prayed for them that, when sifted by Satan and his "system," their "faith would not fail them." But this was not enough to keep them faithful to God. We read in John's Gospel that He loved them. This is the

269

PRACTICAL IMPLICATION

true badge of genuine Christian experience—to be loved by God and to love God and the world He came to save. "Love one another."

● ● ●

". . . Jesus said to Simon Peter, "Simon son of John, do you truly love me . . . ?" (John 21:15).

After His resurrection from the grave, Jesus asked Peter, "Do you love me?" Jesus Christ is still asking this question of each of us. A faith that fails to comprehend God's love at a personal level—the "me" level—will prove to be a fruitless, empty faith.

● ● ●

". . . we also rejoice in our sufferings, because we know that suffering produces perseverance; perseverance, character; and character, hope" (Rom. 5:3–4).

Here we see that perseverance means patience, steadfastness, and endurance, and these produce tested character. The impatience, the lack of character, or the hopelessness expressed by people today are the litmus that reveals the acidity of the age. This is the moment in history in which we are called to serve—to serve patiently, with hope, supported by a character that is being transformed into the image of Jesus Christ through the ministry of God's Holy Spirit.

● ● ●

"Commit your way to the Lord; trust in him and he will do this" (Ps. 37:5).

Commitment is difficult for all of us because it is always costly. Commitment does not begin with us, it begins with the Lord. He committed Himself to us. His commitment to us cost Him His life! Costly? To be sure! Our commitment will cost us no less. By definition, commitment involves all that I am—body, soul, and spirit; time, talent, and money; possessions, property, and earning power. They cannot ultimately be separated. All are gifts from God. The second step in commitment is our will. We must choose to trust in Him.

● ● ●

". . . Love the Lord your God with all your heart . . . soul . . . strength . . . mind. . . ." (Luke 10:27).

Commitment is a costly concept. Whatever you are committed to is literally costing you your very life. Jesus knew this when He said, "You cannot serve God and Mammon." To try to walk with God and embrace the diverse philosophies of man at the same time leads to total confusion, not total commitment. A man once asked Jesus, "Teacher, what must I do to inherit eternal life?" Jesus replied, "What is written in the Law? How do you read it?" The man answered, "Love the Lord your God with all your heart, with all your soul and with all your strength and with all your mind"; and, "Love your neighbor as yourself." Commitment is a costly concept.

● ● ●

"Now faith is being sure of what we hope for and certain of what we do not see." (Heb. 11:1).

Do you feel unsure? Do you feel a lack of certainty? Then you have allowed something or someone to come between you and your God! If you remain in this attitude you will give Satan a "handle" on which to grab, and he will begin to control you. A true faith is accompanied by a positive assurance and a deep sense of conviction.

• • •

"Therefore, the promise comes by faith, so that it may be by grace and may be guaranteed to all Abraham's offspring— not only to those who are of the law but also to those who are of the faith of Abraham. He is the father of us all" (Rom. 4:16).

The apostle Paul, in a sentence, summarizes the theological basis for new covenant living. In this brief statement he tells the world how the Triune God has made provision for all men through the covenant He made with the patriarch Abraham.

• • •

"Do not be anxious about anything, but in everything, by prayer and petition, with thanksgiving, present your requests to God" (Phil. 4:6).

Anxiety has helped to shape a cavorting humanity. Running from this to that, from here to there, failing to discern the meaning of life, ungrateful people! Yet God in the richness of His grace has offered an appropriate solution to man's foolishness. He has exhorted: Choose against anxiety. Trust Me. I will lead you. I will bless you. Come to Me in prayer. I hear you. I will answer you. I love you. Be thankful, lest you fall into the pit of the godless.

• • •

Jesus said, "Do not judge, and you will not be judged. Do not condemn, and you will not be condemned. Forgive, and you will be forgiven. Give, and it will be given to you. A good measure, pressed down, shaken together and running over, will be poured into your lap. For with the measure you use, it will be measured to you" (Luke 6:37–38).

This statement by Jesus is the foundation of our faith at Trinity Church. With this message inscribed on the spirit of our hearts, there is no assignment from the Lord too difficult to tackle. We can never out-give the Giver!

• • •

"For God's gifts and his call are irrevocable" (Rom. 11:29).

Those of us who have been gifted and called to teach have badly garbled biblical teaching on "gifts" and "call." What a paradox! It must grieve the heart of our gracious Father. Thus, it is necessary for each of us to reexamine what the Word of God teaches on this vital aspect of truth. Since our gifts and our call are irrevocable, then it behooves us, no matter how old (or young) we are, to begin again to think through this matter of *our* gifts and how they relate to our "going" and to our "giving."

• • •

"You do not lack any spiritual gift. . ." (1 Cor. 1:7a).

Paul spent sufficient time in Corinth (Acts 18) to instruct this young body of believers in a new covenant theology on spiritual gifts. When he left for Antioch, he had seen the full array of gifts manifested in this one church body. What a credit to Paul's submission to the ministry of the Holy Spirit! Yet after such a blessing, the church of Corinth became carnal and divided. A true walk with God must be a daily walk, lest we, too, become carnal and open to division and strife.

• • •

PRACTICAL IMPLICATION

"Let the word of Christ dwell in you richly as you teach and admonish one another in all wisdom, and as you sing psalms, hymns and spiritual songs with gratitude in your hearts to God" (Col. 3:16).

God is glorified by those who love Him and are able to lift their hearts in praise and song. Music is one of the great tools of communication that God has given man. Let us learn to use it to His glory.

• • •

"Salvation is found in no one else . . ." (Acts 4:12).

Educators have sought to save the human family through mass education. Science has tried to save the human race through the pragmatic development of accumulated knowledge. The arts have sought for truth and light and meaning through various physical media. But what have education, science, and art done to save the human race from the pending ecological and moral catastrophe? The truth "salvation is found in no one else . . ." has even more significance in that light.

• • •

"Consequently, you are no longer foreigners . . . but . . . members of God's household, built on the foundation of the apostles and prophets, with Christ Jesus himself as the chief cornerstone" (Eph. 2:19–20).

Stop! Are you still hungup trying to build spiritual foundations? God has not called us to build foundations, but rather to discover the foundations that He has laid. We are to build "superstructures," that is, a life that is resting on that sure cornerstone—a life that is creatively exercising its God-given gifts and talents. This is living!

• • •

"We have different gifts, according to the grace given us. If a [person's] gift is . . . , let him use it . . ." (Rom. 12:6).

What do you understand about the "gifts" that Jesus Christ has given to His body, the church? What gift has He given you? Do you know? Or are you like Peter Drucker who once said, "Here I am fifty-eight and I still don't know what I'm going to do when I grow up." God has given gifts to every member of Christ's body, gifts that are designed to enable us to find fulfillment and blessing in God's service. Paul says we are to use them. To do this, we must first unwrap them.

• • •

"New wine must be poured into new wineskins" (Luke 5:38).

Every generation, including ours, has ignored this simple truth, ever since the founder of our faith spoke it. It is peculiar how we can hold so tenaciously to some of our Lord's teachings and so completely ignore others. We wonder why the young struggle to discover a faith. It's no wonder—rather, it's a miracle!—that any bother with it. The church has always stood against change. Why? Jesus was for it. Note: new wine must (not "may," not "can," but "must") be poured into new wineskins. Herein is one of the keys to continued revival.

• • •

Specific training processes

It is also possible to use specific training experiences to develop sensitivity to God's voice.

One experience shared by the residents of the Study

Center in Seattle illustrates the principle and the process. The residents were given this assignment. For forty days they were to use only Scripture (no other resource books or commentaries). Each day everyone was to read and then meditate for at least fifteen minutes on an assigned passage, which in this case took them progressively through one of the Gospels. Afterward they were to paraphrase what God had said to them in the reading. The participants were to live for the next twenty-four hours in the light of the discovered truths. Then they were to record their responses in the journals in which the paraphrase had been recorded. Only after the full twenty-four-hour process could they share their insights with the other residents.

The significant elements of this assignment involved structuring "thinking relationships with God," as mentioned above, and a totally nonmanipulative process. It was nonmanipulative in that no person could be directly influenced by another's interpretation but everyone had to listen closely to and rely totally on God to speak to him or her.

At the end of the forty days, the residents shared the whole experience. They read their journals and gave reports on their responses to God's voice. That generated a tremendous excitement. They each shared the realities they had experienced through this disciplined relationship with God.

Today, some six years after this experience, many of the participants tell of the impact of discovering God's voice in their daily lives. Many have built on the confidence gained through that experience and today live with a deepened awareness of God's presence and personal guidance.

EXPECT THE CONFIRMATION OF GOD'S VOICE

There is a distinctly subjective aspect to the doctrine of God's voice. And there is the possibility of mistakes. In the words of James, an individual may be "dragged away and enticed" by "his own evil desires" (James 1:14). When Paul speaks of our possession of the mind of Christ, he qualifies this concept. In the same context he speaks of the "spiritual man" (one who is living in the Spirit) in contrast to the believers who are living "like mere men" (1 Cor. 3:3). While the individual who hears God's voice and thus has "the mind of Christ" makes judgments for which he is himself "not subject to any man's judgment" (1 Cor. 2:15), not every Christian is immediately ready for this experience. An immature outlook, or a lifestyle that matches that of non-Christians rather than that of the *laos* of God, will never mark believers who are willing to distinguish God's voice from the other calls that have so much attraction.

The distinction that we need to help the people of God make at this point is the distinction between *judging* and *confirming*. None of us is able to judge a brother or to say confidently "this is" or "this is not" God's will for him. However, because within the body we function in a context of intimate relationships, it is possible for others to confirm a call as our character and gifts become known. It is important to help individuals learn to seek confirmation as a part of the process of hearing and responding to God's voice.

When Harvey announced to the elders that God had called him to teach neighborhood Bible classes and asked them to announce the dates and encourage people to attend, the elders were stunned. Harvey had shown no gift for teaching. Without telling him that he could not conduct classes, they gave him some honest feedback. They told him that they could not affirm his view of himself as one called to teach. He refused to listen to them and insisted that he hold the classes. He asked them again to announce the times and dates for his home study classes. Reluctantly the elders agreed and announced to the congregation his invitation. And they listed times and dates in the bulletin.

But the classes didn't prosper. They started well, with a good attendance. But each week attendance dropped. Finally attendance dwindled to nothing. Unwilling to believe he had acted out of his own strong personal needs and desires rather than in response to the voice of God, Harvey bitterly blamed the elders. The failure was their fault, because they did not give him the support he needed; they did not insist that members of the congregation come! He angrily left the church and joined another congregation in the area.

The problem here was not with the elders, who acted correctly. They did not try to control Harvey—or anyone else in the congregation. Instead they gave him the freedom to follow what he insisted was his leading from God. At the same time they gave him an honest evaluation and told him they could not confirm his leading. They asked him to reconsider, to pray more about his plans.

The problem was with Harvey, who was unwilling to listen to the guidance of the church elders or to seek their confirmation of his calling. It is, in fact, just this ministry of guidance and confirmation that the writer to the Hebrews speaks of when he writes (in words that our *translators often misunderstand*), "Obey your leaders and submit to their authority"

(Heb. 13:17). The original gives this stress: "Never harden your hearts to those whom God has given you as guides along your way, but be responsive to their instruction." The writer is not extending to human leaders the controlling role that belongs to Jesus alone. But he is warning us to seek a confirmation of our understanding of God's voice from those who are the mature in the local body.

With this important concept of confirmation stated, let's look at several principles that we need to teach and build into congregational life.

Focus on being, not doing

This has been stated before, but needs to be amplified. There is always a tendency for persons to seek to define themselves and give themselves a sense of worth and identity by their actions. The gospel message is that God values us, first as human beings made in God's image, and, when redeemed by Christ, as God's dear children. There is no higher identity than this: we are God's children, He loves us, and we are heirs with Jesus of the kingdom.

The tendency to seek other kinds of identity has historically led to status and role differentiation in the church. Some, the "clergy," were lifted up over the "laity." There are also status differences within the typical local congregation based on an individual's participation in various programs or activities. A board member, a Sunday school teacher, a committee chairman, or the leader of a children's ministry tends to be identified by what he *does* rather than who he *is*.

Paul specifically guards against such a differentiation. In 1 Corinthians he affirms differences in gifts but insists that, as each is essential to the body, no one is greater or less than another because he or she possesses a particular gift or plays a particular role in the body.

This is a vital word of warning for us today. If we remove the status ascriptions institutionalized ministries now give, congregations will tend to construct status hierarchies that reflect the member's involvement or noninvolvement in a personal ministry. But as persons are valued in the body for what they do, unusual pressure is placed on the less mature. The new Christian and the believer who has just begun to grow after a long period of being on a plateau senses without ever being told which ministries and persons the congregation honors. They will seek out similar ministries or similar gifts. They will be likely to confuse the voice of God with the implicit distinctions the congregation makes.

PRACTICAL IMPLICATION

We need to remember that God is primarily concerned with our personal growth toward Christlikeness. What we are is something He gives higher priority to than what we *do*. In a congregation in which status is ascribed on the basis of personal ministries and the possession of certain gifts, young believers will feel a tremendous pressure to perform. They may miss the fact that God's voice will call them to their ministry when they are ready and feel instead that they must experience His call now. Rather than being released to grow to maturity, they will feel bound to work and serve, and mistake their sense of bondage for the compelling call of God's voice.

To maintain this delicate tension is a distinct challenge to the spiritual leadership of the church. On the one hand, the church must try to create a loving, accepting climate in which people are accepted and valued for themselves. It is this supportive family relationship in which spiritual growth takes place. Believers must be freed in the community to be themselves, without any pressure to "perform."

At the same time, there needs to be in this accepting climate a continuing expectation that believers will grow, recognize their gifts, and be called to that ministry of service for which God has shaped and suited them. There must be a confident expectation that believers will hear the voice of God, but without any expectation as to when the call will come.

There are no rules for maintaining this kind of tension. Leaders need to be aware of the pressures that will grow and sensitive to the misunderstandings that can so easily develop.

Write out your vision

Spiritual leaders play an important role in helping members of the body hear, evaluate, and respond to the voice of God. This ranges from sensitivity to the climate of the congregation (making sure that acceptance and love are at the heart of community relationships) to specific expressions of confirmation and even words of warning. The important distinction is to make sure that individuals who believe they have heard the voice of God are clear about what has been heard.

One of the most significant things that can be done to help a Christian understand visions is to have them write detailed descriptions of them. Once the description has been written out, the elders and those who have received the visions need to take time to discuss and pray about them together.

When reviewing a vision, elders need to ask some of the following questions:

1. Is there a clearly defined need to be met?
2. Is there evidence of a gift or giftedness?
3. Is there a realistic appraisal of the first steps to be taken in response to the vision?
4. Is there a local way to respond to the vision?
5. Does the individual seem to sense any personal responsibility?

The purpose of exploring such issues is *not* to pass judgment on a Christian's perception of God's voice. The purpose is to affirm, to support, and to help. Each issue above is explored in order to help individuals clarify their vision, and obey God. Each area is important. As we've seen, personal ministries flow out of the existence and recognition of a need or needs. To plan a "ministry" without a burden or any awareness of needs raises immediate questions that should be placed before the individual. In the same way, an awareness of what the individual has to contribute to meet a need is important. The goal of such mutual exploring is not to discourage but to help individuals act responsibly. It is in this light that questions 3 and 4 above are important. If there is no *local* focus to the call, there should be significant questions raised. For instance, an individual who wants to develop a program that will "help all the churches in the United States . . ." to accomplish a certain goal may not understand the principles of contextualization and indigenousness we described in chapter 10. It may be that a ministry developed on a local level will eventually be adopted beyond a single congregation. But in general, unless the calling of the individual is apostolic (and thus to serve the whole church), a local and immediate focus for the calling is important.

The final question, relating to personal responsibility, is also significant. Is the vision for me or for others? Am I stating in my vision what I sense God has called me to do, or am I saying that God has told me what others are to do? If there isn't a sense of personal responsibility for the vision, counseling is definitely required.

Writing out the vision, then, and presenting it to mature brothers and sisters for their counsel and affirmation is an important part of the process of distinguishing God's voice in our congregations today.

However, we would like to add a word of caution. The elders give counsel. They do not pass on the validity of the vision. Proverbs points out that "for lack of guidance a nation falls, but many advisers [counselors] make victory sure" (Prov. 11:14). The precept is not that the group of elders, even though mature in the Lord, make the decisions for others. The precept is that, as a group of mature believers explore the vision with the individual to whom it has come, the understanding of the individual is clarified and God's guidance recognized. No individual or group is to take the place of God in the life of another. But individuals and groups may counsel with others as part of the process of distinguishing and clarifying what God has said.

A case in point is Paul's call to go to Jerusalem, which he testified he undertook because he was "compelled by the Spirit." Yet he admitted that he did not know what would happen to him there (Acts 20:22). As Paul journeyed, the believers in every city warned him of the dangers he would face. In one place a prophet named Agabus warned that the Spirit had revealed that the Jews would bind Paul and "hand him over to the Gentiles" (Acts 21:10ff.). Some have taken these warnings as evidence that God did not want Paul to go and have thought Paul was being disobedient to God in continuing his journey. This is not the point at all. What was happening was that through the body the Spirit was revealing to Paul more and more of what his call to Jerusalem involved and the difficulties he would have to face. In spite of the clarification, which showed the price following the voice of God would cost, Paul was committed to obedience. He did experience all the difficulties—but brought the gospel to the very court of Caesar in Rome!

We must always, even when counsel reveals difficulties, give our brothers and sisters the freedom to live in obedience to the voice of God as they hear Him speak. We must never mistake our counseling role for one of judgment on whether or not God has spoken.

Seek a supportive team

There are very few lonely callings in personal ministry. God has purposefully given us body relationships with others. The purposes are intimately related to our growth toward maturity —and to our service. Because gifts differ, most ministries that we will undertake require a blend of gifts for maximum effectiveness. Even if one's gift is singing solos, many kinds of support are needed. Someone has to play an accompaniment, or make arrangements for a piano to be tuned. If the singing is beyond the local congregation, someone has to plan, organize and promote; this requires an administrative gift. If the ministry is to have any impact, there is always a need for others to pray. So even the most "individual" of personal ministries will benefit from supportive team relationships.

This fact leads us to recognize a very important aspect of confirmation. If God has spoken to us, He may well be speaking to others in our fellowship as well, calling them to a team relationship with us to meet a need. So it is very appropriate, as individuals clarify the visions they have been given, that the vision be shared with the body, shared with a request that others pray about the possibility of banding together to form a mission team.

There may be times, of course, when an individual must take the first steps of faith alone, until others see the vision confirmed and then respond. But the growth of a team to support the vision is one of the most significant confirmations of the voice of God that can occur. And in general a team will develop to support the personal ministry if steps are taken to share the vision and encourage prayer.

The growth of a team is often God's indication of right timing. To hear the voice of God does not mean that the vision will be immediately translated into reality. Often months and even years will pass before God's timing is right. We should actively seek to respond to God's voice, but at the same time we must be aware that He is responsible for the timing.

In general, then, we can say the following things about the process through which members of a congregation should go as they seek to define and confirm the voice of God calling them to specific personal ministries. Given, of course, that the calling is in full harmony with Scripture, those who believe they have heard God's voice should be encouraged to:

1. write out the vision so that it can be clarified and tested;
2. present the vision to the elders or other mature believers in the church for counsel and affirmation;
3. expect the confirmation of the vision as a team of others emerge to support the development of the ministry.

If, as may well happen in the process, the individual discovers a need for training to fulfill the vision, the training may be available within the context of the body or it may be that training outside the congregation will be required. If so, this too can be encouraged.

THE STRUCTURE REQUIRED TO PROVIDE FREEDOM AND ENCOURAGE RESPONSIBILITY

One of the most serious features of contemporary congregational structures is "organization for the purpose of control."[1] In most churches leaders are conceived of as the chief operating officers of an organization. Boards of elders or deacons function as the decision-making (i.e., controlling) body of the local church.

Under this structure, which when diagramed shows the same form as that of a military or business organization, the local church "owns" its ministries. That is, something like a Sunday school or a children's club or a choir is perceived as a program of the church, and hence the responsibility of the leaders of the church.

This kind of structure and the perceptions of ministry that it encourages place many obstacles in the way of the development of personal ministries. The structure tends to (1) substitute human control for the lordship of Christ; (2) force the leaders of the congregation into unscriptural "control" roles; and (3) remove personal responsibility from most of those whom God has called to special ministries. In the process of time the structure becomes a substitute for the living voice of God. There is less readiness to change in response to God's leading as the old wineskins of "this is how we've always done it" squeeze persons into roles which too soon grow stagnant and dead.

We need to remove such obstacles to the development of a ministering people. We are to reject any approach that robs the *laos* of God of the opportunity, freedom, and responsibility to respond directly to Christ and to God's voice. Following are several principles we need to follow if we are to develop freedom-affirming structures.

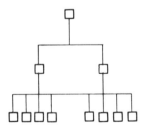

1. *Avoid hierarchy*

A look at the organizational chart of most congregations shows us immediately that our organization, like that of military and business organizations, is hierarchical in nature. In this system, which is designed for the effective func-

---

[1]The issue of organization is treated extensively in Larry Richards, *A Theology of Church Leadership* (Grand Rapids: Zondervan Publishing House, 1980).

tioning of an organization, authority (i.e., direction) flows down the organizational chart and responsibility flows up. This simply means that those at the top are viewed as the final decision-makers and thus are in control of those below them. And each person at a lower level is responsible to the person or persons above him in the structure.

But the *laos* of God all have immediate, direct access to God. The Spirit lives in each as the present voice through which Jesus Himself exercises lordship. The kind of organizational structures that we develop in the church, following secular models, simply does not "fit" the Bible's picture of the church as the body of Christ. We are a living organism with each member in direct communication with and directly responsible to the head. God has given no one in the body of Christ the right to "play God" in the lives of his brothers and sisters.

There is an alternative to the hierarchical approach to structuring ministries. This is a radical concept, developed in detail in Larry Richards's *A Theology of Church Leadership.* Simply put, the alternative is to treat the ministering activities of the people of God and the structures that develop consistently as wineskins for the ministries, as though they are owned by those called to the ministry, not by "the church."

When the families in a small Colorado church first sensed a need for a youth ministry, the first approach of many was typical and traditional. They went to the leaders of the congregation and said, "We need a youth program for our teens." The leaders were wise; they did not respond to the pressure. They did not immediately go about hiring a church "youth minister" and setting up a church program. Instead, the congregation discussed, prayed over, talked, and complained about the problem for some months. In the process all who shared the concern got together to explore the need. It was clear that the congregation needed to reach into the community as well as minister to the teens within the church family. The members also realized that they needed help in ministering to teens, not someone to "do it for us." The result was that some members set up a not-for-profit corporation. They committed themselves to define the needs, to give financially and in other ways, and to search for a couple who could come to teach as well as do the work of ministering to the young people of the community.

The resulting corporation is not a program of that church. It is not under the control of the church elders. Instead, those who felt the call of God to be active in meeting the needs of the young people are themselves responsible for everything associated with their calling—including the call of the couple to serve "full time" in helping them with their mission.

It is, of course, not necessary to set up a corporate structure in which every vision can be carried out. In some cases, however, this is exactly what is required to develop a sense of personal responsibility and to avoid falling into a hierarchical pattern the spiritual leaders of the congregation are expected to control and direct.

When there is no separate structure, there still needs to be the conscious development of a sense of responsibility in those called to a ministry for its conduct. Rather than pushing decisions up the "chain of command," wise leaders will make sure that those responsible for a ministry's conduct make the key decisions. Rather than becoming lords over the people of God, wise leaders guide and instruct ministry teams as to how to seek God's leading in the decisions they must make. Increasingly the awareness will grow within the local congregation that ministering individuals or ministering teams are responsible to Christ and are to seek His leading. Rather than looking to superintendents or elders or boards or pastors to make decisions, they will accept the responsibility to seek God's will together and to carry it out.

Where possible, the ministries of members of a local congregation should be organizationally separated from the church. Where this is not possible, church leaders should refuse to control and make decisions for others but should instead guide them to seek God's leading and will.

2. Seek the counsel of leaders

The spiritual leaders of a congregation have been, in Scripture's pattern, selected for their Christlike character and maturity. Their ministry is one of providing an example, teaching, and counsel. As we've seen, leaders are not tyrants nor are they the vicars of Christ. They are, however, called and gifted to a ministry of oversight within the body. They should keep in close touch with the members of the congregation and their needs.

Those involved in an individual or team ministry that they "own" are personally responsible for that ministry. Yet they should not try to "go it alone." Again we remember that God has placed us in a body and that He has placed those with leadership gifts and insights among us. It is our responsibility to submit ourselves to the Lord as He speaks to us through the body and to constantly test what we are doing by the insights of other believers, and especially our spiritual leaders. Where maturity has developed in a body, such a testing and probing approach will operate constantly.

3. *View structures as temporary*

In our recent history we have come to view "success" as something that can be measured by numbers or monuments. Numbers are self-explanatory. By monuments, I mean by the establishment of self-perpetuating structures. We are successful, in this view, if the structure we have developed to meet some need continues to exist, whether or not it currently meets the original need.

We can protect against confusing a structure with ministry by keeping open to changes in structures. Recently a nationwide youth evangelistic organization printed studies that had been developed over several years of experience with teens. The problem was that the materials were designed to function in a particular kind of meeting structure. Those meetings were effective as recently as two years ago. But in the meantime the youth culture has changed enough so that that particular meeting structure no longer functions well. Yet the materials were printed and a strong effort made to perpetuate the structure that had worked so well just a few years ago.

There is no value in the perpetuation of a program or agency if the conditions that made it successful in meeting needs have changed, or if God is calling the body to develop a better approach.

Because of the dangers of institutionalization, we'll want to help individuals set and maintain short-range goals—and help them evaluate regularly to see if the need being addressed is actually being met. We will encourage a constant openness to God's leading and be willing to accept and value purposive change.

There are many objections that can (and should) be raised to the proposals in this part of the chapter. There is the danger of chaos. There is the danger that the wrong persons will become responsible for ministries. There is the danger that ministries will be uncoordinated. There is the danger that less spiritual people will make the decisions. People may make mistakes that could have been avoided. We could go on and on.

But note one thing: Each of the criticisms assumes a false understanding of the *laos* of God! Each assumes that there are two levels or classes of Christians—the adequate (the few, the leaders in the hierarchy) and the inadequate (the laity, who are unable to make correct decisions or discover God's will for themselves).

This is the critical issue this text is raising. Are there second-class Christians? Or are we all a new covenant people? Are we *all* believer priests? Are we all citizens in the kingdom? Are we all indwelt by the Spirit? Are we all to hear and respond to God's voice? The answer that we have discovered in Scripture is a resounding "YES!" And the obligation these truths about the people of God place on us is a simple one: *We are actively to pursue the building of a local body in which the people of God enter their full heritage and grow to ministering maturity.*

There are risks in redesigning organizational structures in the local congregation to give the *laos* freedom and responsibility. But the risks are far fewer than those involved in relying on control structures that in fact deny the *laos* their right to be responsible to the voice of God and the leading of the Spirit.

But the risks are less than we fear, for God has built into the body His own checks and balances. In a functioning people, ministries are conducted in a team setting with all members of the team responsible to God and each other. Decisions are made by consensus and all are to sense a particular direction as God's will. Leaders are available for counsel, and with each viewing "others better than themselves" there should be an open and mature consideration of actions to be taken.

Of course there will be immature actions and reactions. But the mistakes will not be fatal, and through the process all grow. God's approach to life in the church is never to insulate us from struggle or challenge, or to so isolate us that we can never make mistakes. His approach to life in the church is to redeem even our mistakes, so that "in all things God works for the good of those who love him" (Rom. 8:28). Through this process He moves us individually and corporately toward likeness to Jesus (Rom. 8:29).

And this must be our approach as well. We must become a risking community rather than a fearful one. No, not a foolishly risking people. But a people who risk wisely by opening themselves up with a childlike trust to obey God's Word and follow His ways, no matter how foolish they may seem to the reasoning of the natural mind.

Extending Freedom

PROBE

▶ *case histories*
▶ *discussion questions*
▶ *thought provokers*
▶ *resources*

1. It should be clear from this chapter that the local church's approach to personal ministries must reject the idea that leaders control others. This is not an affirmation of chaos or disorder in the body. There is a definite role for leaders and for the body itself to play in encouraging and confirming the experience and giftedness and gifts in personal ministries.

   Take time now to review, without looking back over the chapter, ways in which "order" operates in the body as personal ministries are encouraged. How is balance maintained between freedom and license? How is Christ affirmed as Lord and yet human leaders of the body are affirmed as leaders? List the procedures and safeguards outlined in the chapter that provide a framework for freedom and order.

   Then after you have made your list, explain each item in a sentence or two.

   Finally, reread the chapter to see if you have missed any significant factors.

2. It is hard to suggest the kind of organizational structure discussed in the last part of this chapter without being able to go into the details of how such a system works. Refer to *A Theology of Church Leadership,* and summarize the extensive analysis of this kind of structure and its function you find there.

3. Case History

   The experience of Fr. Jim Ferry, administrator of St. Antoninus Roman Catholic Church in Newark, New Jersey, illustrates the process that is often involved when believers open themselves up to new approaches in response to the voice of God. It is helpful to explore this case history, shared with the readers of *Pastoral Renewal* (June 1979), to see some of the concepts suggested in this chapter in operation.

FR. JIM FERRY

Several times in the past ten years the Lord has called me to make a new beginning. Each time, He has dared me to risk changing completely—to give up something good in order to receive something better.

In 1969 I was baptized in the Spirit and, with a few other people, began a prayer meeting in the parish I served in Northvale, in northeastern New Jersey. It was the first charismatic Catholic prayer meeting in the area. It grew large very fast.

I saw, though, that while the prayer group was *in* the parish it was not at the *heart* of the parish. It was connected to the parish, but it couldn't directly change the parish. I realized that I should try to work in a pastoral structure where I could fully use everything we were learning in the renewal: the centrality of conversion, the primacy of the lordship of Jesus, the importance of openness to the Holy Spirit. I saw the need to work with people who were of a like mind and heart.

This was provided for me when I asked our bishop if I could leave the parish, and the thriving prayer group, and begin what was called a "house of prayer experience" (H.O.P.E.), in Stanfordville, New York. The idea was that I and a handful of others would live a life of prayer together, open to others who could come for a while and find renewal in their relationship with Christ. The bishop said yes, so we left the parish prayer group that looked so good and moved to a farmhouse where we had to build from scratch.

This quickly grew also. After a couple of years we moved into a 150-room building in Convent Station, New Jersey. Many people thought we would finally settle there and simply have a big retreat center. But, while we stayed there, we kept seeing other needs, and branched out in other directions.

For one thing, we added a Christian school in New Brunswick. For another, we thought the Lord wanted us to work in nearby Newark. We went to the bishop and asked for a parish that was almost dead so that we could begin rebuilding at the foundation. In 1975 a group of us began working and living here in St. Antoninus parish, a hundred-year-old church in the heart of Newark.

So by 1977 we had three separate things going—the retreat house, the school, and the parish—with altogether about forty full-time people. Things were working very well.

A new direction

Our group was made up of single people, mostly priests and nuns. But a number of couples had become associated with us, and many of them were ready to make some kind of commitment to us. Some of them were ready to share in leadership.

We saw that God was doing something that we could not accommodate. We believed the Lord was pleased with our work, but we realized that we might not yet have the structure the Lord wanted us to have.

We faced the decision whether to become a community with families, in which family life would be a kind of foundation. We

286

had been a group devoted primarily to service, especially evangelism. Would we now become a community that gave equal attention to building a supportive life together?

With these questions in mind, some of the leaders and I visited a large interdenominational covenant community in the Midwest in 1977.

When we returned home, we looked to see if we had the potential to become a full community, and we saw that we had people with the necessary maturity and gifts.

In the past I had sometimes made the mistake of experiencing something in another place and trying to import it wholesale at home. This time, I made sure that the leaders came to a common vision first. We talked about what it would mean to be a covenant community and decided to do it.

Then we told everyone else, including the married people who were associated with us, that we were going to present to them teaching about Christian community. We didn't ask them to make any decision but simply to come to the eight teaching sessions. More than one hundred people did so. After this, we had a weekend retreat at which we tried to give everyone a taste of what community life would be like.

Only after that did we invite whoever was able to and wanted to, to enter a commitment to the community. We told people who didn't feel ready to wait before making a decision. Some of them joined the community a few months later. It was all gradual and voluntary.

What has happened is that by daring to make this kind of change, we have been able to have the best of both worlds—the old and the new. As the celibate people have bound themselves to married brothers and sisters, we have become a stronger community. We are able to carry on the kind of outreach we did before, with a greater base of support within the community.

My reason for sharing this is not to encourage people to form covenant communities. Rather, the lesson we have learned is to listen carefully for the call of the Lord and to be willing to risk what we have in order to receive the good things that He will make possible.

4. Case History

The basic equipping for any ministry is our identity in Christ, with all it means to be one of the *laos* of God. But there is much that wise leaders can do to aid growth and encourage believer-priests in their calling.

Dave Eby's sensitivity and wisdom in dealing with a young Christian, Rick Baldacci, illustrate leadership at its best.

PRACTICAL IMPLICATION

RICK BALDACCI

Neither Ellen or I were Christians when we got married. We really had a lot of trouble in our marriage, and I can remember the night Ellen told me that she didn't love me anymore. But she also said to me, "I have no other place to go, because I can't afford to raise the kids, and you are my only support. So I'm willing to stay with you for economic reasons." So I said, "Okay."

That summer—I think it was the summer of 1974—she told me that she would be willing to go with me to a Marriage Enrichment course that Bill McKenzie led. He had stopped by the church we were attending in Evergreen to offer this course. I don't think we went to save our marriage. We went because it couldn't hurt. I can remember telling Ellen, "Boy, Bill and Sue McKenzie have something in their marriage that sure stands out."

I told Bill it would be great to get together sometime and get to know each other better. Bill called me about two months later and said that he was going to have a group! It would be a small group of couples who would get together for thirteen weeks every other Friday to study a book called *The Edge of Adventure*, by Keith Miller and Bruce Larson. He asked Ellen and me if we would like to participate. We said we would. I told Ellen not to tell anyone that we weren't Christians because I thoroughly enjoyed everyone's company, and it would just be neat to be with those people.

She agreed. But I can remember the first night that someone held my hand in the group as we were going to pray, and someone else said "Jesus Christ." I remember vividly how I cringed and said, "I just can't believe it."

As we read chapter by chapter and began participating, I began to realize that Christianity in these people's hearts was not the Christianity that I had grown up with. It was a different kind. I began getting closer and closer to the Lord, and little did I know that Ellen was getting closer, too. Our marriage seemed to be changing for some reason. Suddenly Ellen was saying, "I'm not sure that I don't love you. Maybe I do love you." As time went on I can remember sitting in Bill and Sue's house one night during the meeting, and it just came to me in the middle of the meeting. I can remember saying, "You know something. I honestly believe that Jesus is who He says He is!" And I remember Sue bowing her head and saying, "Thank You, Lord."

Ellen's conversion came very shortly after. She was in the driveway shoveling snow, and one verse kept coming to her! "No one comes to the Father except by me." She kept on saying, "I don't understand, I don't understand." Finally she said, "I think I *do* understand!" And she became a Christian. She must have said that verse a thousand times while she was shoveling the snow, until finally she began to realize that it was truer than she could ever imagine. So we both became Christians, and we grew together as a couple.

We started ministering to the kids in our church. The group grew to about fifteen to twenty kids. One night Bill asked me to come over to his house and see a fellow named Dave Eby. Dave was talking to me, and I was sharing with him. "Dave, I'm running out of things to do with the group. I can't keep them entertained." And he said, "Why don't you tell them a gospel story each night —just make it real short, about fifteen minutes. Make it interesting and simple and give it your best shot." And he gave me a couple of examples of how to do that. So I tried it and it worked. We would go into the sanctuary and I would tell the story for about fifteen minutes, and it seemed to be one of their more special moments. I began to realize that the telling of the gospel was a big part of what the ministry was about.

But that church was not founded on the Word and was doing things that were hard for me to deal with. So Bill asked me over again to his house, and he really touched my heart with the thought that "It's neat that you're ministering to those kids, Rick, but who is ministering to you?" That struck me deeply. I realized that I needed to be fed so that I could feed those kids, and I wasn't getting it anywhere. So I told Ellen, "Let's go and visit a couple of other churches."

We visited the Fellowship, and immediately fell in love with the way the worship service went and the things that we got out of it, and we began to grow. It was a real struggle for us to leave the other church. The minister had put a real heavy thing on us by saying, "Well, if you're going to go to the Fellowship, you can't minister to our children." Ellen and I found another couple in that church whom we loved dearly. They agreed to take over the kids and teach them the Word of God. At that point we felt as if God had opened the door for us to leave and go to the Fellowship.

I began talking to Dave Eby, who is an elder at the Fellowship, and told him how excited I was and what a good time I had had with the kids. He said there was an outreach group he was trying to start with junior high school kids. Would I be interested in working with him? I told him that I thoroughly enjoyed the junior high age because they were still open to the Word of God. And he said, "Great, come on over. Dar and I are leading a group." We went and thoroughly enjoyed it. But quite honestly, being in the background and not being able to give that message depressed me. I kept telling Dave, "Dave, I really want to do this or that." He said, "Rick, I don't think you are ready yet. I don't think you are founded. Your foundation isn't laid so that you can minister to children the way God would have you minister."

That was a shock to me. Dave and I talked about it at length. We had four or five sessions together over lunch. I kept telling Dave I was ready, and he kept telling me I wasn't. Finally he said, "I'll tell you what I'll do. Let's lay out a program and get you ready. I would like you to read these books of the Bible, and I would like you to read *Basic Christianity* and a few other books." I did, and we talked about each of the books and each of the books of the Bible.

Finally one day over lunch he said, "Rick, what do you really want?" And I said, "Dave, I know how much you love the kids. But I really want you to give it to me, because I feel the Lord is leading me to minister to those kids."

And he said, "In many ways I think you have a long way to grow. But I believe God really wants you to do that, and I am willing to give them up." He did. Ellen and I began ministering to the kids, not as a Fellowship group, but as an outreach to the junior high school.

Dave and I had met to study numerous times, and he and I were participating in a Bible study at the Burger Chef every Tuesday morning. Every Tuesday morning I would say, "Are you free for lunch this week? When are you free, and when can we get together? I have finished these books and I want to sit down and talk to you about them."

I can say now that by the grace of God Dave let me do that junior high group. As I look back I wasn't as knowledgeable as I think a Christian should have been. I'm just thankful that the Lord was with Dave at that point to say, "Hey, Dave, I know he doesn't look ready, but I'll be with him to guide him the rest of the way." And it worked out great.

One of the most touching things for me is the story of a girl in the old church Ellen and I were ministering to. We were very concerned about her as she was from a broken home. When we left the old church she cried very hard. I thought I would never see her again, and I felt very guilty about not being able to minister to her. About six weeks after we took over the junior high group from Dave, she came and joined. And we developed a very good relationship with her, all the way through her eighth and ninth grades. It was amazing to see that when we started the junior high group there were ten kids. It grew that first year to about sixty-seven kids. We took forty-eight of them to Estes Park for a retreat.

All during this time Ellen and I were in a small group studying the Bible, enjoying the fellowship of the other couples, and falling in love with each other as we had never done before. I was going to a Tuesday morning Bible study at the Burger Chef, going to the Fellowship every Sunday, and still reading. Now I had gotten my feet on the ground. I began a conscientious effort to study certain sections of the Bible so I could understand what God's message was.

The process took about five years. God repaired my marriage, and after that He got me founded in His Word. And He gave us a ministry with the junior high group. Ever since that day it's been amazing. My marriage has been saved, I'm being fed by the Fellowship, Ellen and I are in a good Christian couples' group together, and I read the Word daily in my own special quiet times with the Lord. My life has been completely changed. Absolutely changed! The change from the night Ellen told me she didn't love me anymore to the point we are at now is a miracle. "His works are mighty! The steadfastness of the Lord never ceases."

PART 2

PRACTICAL IMPLICATION

Identity Implications
Communicating Vision
Building Relationships and Community
Making Disciples
Equipping
Extending Freedom
Understanding Leadership

UNDERSTANDING LEADERSHIP

In this text we have purposely and consciously rejected the clergy/laity distinctions that have grown up in the church over the centuries. We have suggested that the whole *laos* is called to minister, that each believer is personally responsible to the Lord for developing his or her ministry. This teaching clearly challenges the understanding of authority and leadership in the congregation—at least as they have been traditionally perceived.

The concepts and practices suggested here do threaten "pastoral authority." They also threaten the traditional role of congregational leaders as "decision makers." What needs to be understood, however, is that the affirmation of the *laos* as a believer-priesthood does not threaten the *biblical* view of leadership. God has given to the body of Christ those whose gifts are leadership gifts and whose maturity fits them to exercise those gifts. To affirm the whole people of God as ministers directly responsible to the leading of God does not threaten human leaders *unless we have a distorted concept of what Christian leadership actually is!*

CHAPTER **13**

In this last chapter we simply want to outline something of what the Bible teaches about leadership in the church.

CHRIST IS THE HEAD OF HIS CHURCH

The Bible uses a number of word pictures to help us understand the nature of the church. One such picture is that of a family (cf. Eph. 3:14f., etc.). This picture stresses the *relational identity* of the church. Another picture speaks of the church as a spiritual house (cf. 1 Peter 2:4f.). This picture represents the *spiritual identity* of the church. Yet perhaps the dominant picture is that of the church as a living body. This picture stresses our *functional identity.* We operate in the world as a body operates—not as an organization made up of many individuals of independent will.

None of the scriptural pictures is meant as a simile or metaphor. Each is to be taken seriously as representing a reality. When the Bible speaks of the church as a body, we are bound to take very seriously its character as a living organism. Any attempt to function as an organization rather than as an organism will move us toward a lifestyle that creates obstacles to the development of the *laos* as a ministering people.

While secular management theorists have attempted to treat the organization and administration of institutions using the analogy of an organism, these attempts have failed for a very simple reason. An organism is by its nature an entity with a single will. That single will is transmitted from the head to the various parts of the body so that a coordinated response to the environment can be made. However, a business or military or any other kind of human organization is made up of individuals with independent wills. The purpose of organizing hierarchies, structures, procedures, etc., is that the independent will might be subordinated in some degree to the will of those who lead the organization. Good management today stresses the involvement of all the members of the organization in decision-making—as much as is possible. Nonetheless, the organizational structure itself is still designed to give some—the leaders—control over others who are lower on the organizational scale.

We would have to conceive the church of Christ in the same way, with leaders having an analogous control responsibility—if it were not for one thing. The church *is* an organism. It is not natural but supernatural. *The church has a single, living head who is in direct relationship with every part of the body!* Everything that is done in the church, and especially those things designed to facilitate the development of the whole *laos* as a ministering people, must affirm this organismic reality.

It is because of the reality of Christ's personal headship of the church and over every individual believer that we must deny the traditional "leader" role to those who are leaders in the church. Spiritual leaders do not control God's people directly or indirectly. They do not "run" the church, which is Jesus' body. Instead, the role of leaders in the church is unique. It has no analogy to human institutions, which are by nature organizations.

LEADERS SERVE, THEY DO NOT CONTROL

There is one particular passage in Scripture that makes the servant principle of leadership unmistakably clear. The mother of James and John has just asked Jesus to give her sons positions of power when the kingdom comes. Jesus tells the two sons that they don't know what they are asking. Later, when the others hear about the attempt of James and John to gain "higher" positions for themselves, Jesus uses the occasion to teach about spiritual leadership. He contrasts secular and spiritual leadership in this way—and once and for all rules out for the church any use of a secular leadership approach.

You know that the rulers of the Gentiles lord it over them, and their high officials exercise authority over them. Not so with you. Instead, whoever wants to become great among you must be your servant, and whoever wants to be first must be your slave—just as the Son of Man did not come to be served, but to serve, and to give his life a ransom for many (Matt. 20:25–27).

We note immediately that there are aspects of the secular style that are not appropriate for the church and are thus to be rejected. Specifically:

- *Rulers in the secular context are over others.* The hierarchical organizational chart accurately pictures relationships that exist between the leaders and the led. But in the church of Christ there is nothing higher than to be one of God's *laos.* When Jesus said, "Call no man master," He was not suggesting a lack of respect for authorities. Instead He was warning against placing anyone in the place of God, who alone is Lord. There is no one "over" the people of God but Jesus, the head of the body.

- *Rulers in the secular context "exercise authority over" the ruled.* Implied in this phrase is the right and power to control the behavior of others. In the secular context this power is based partly on custom but ultimately on coercive power. That is, the ones ruled recognize that the leader does have a certain right to command obedience. But also the ruler has at his command various sanctions by which he can *enforce* his will.

  Christ completely rules out the whole pattern of giving to others a right to rule and the possession of the one in authority of a power to force obedience as a valid pattern for the church.

- *Rulers in the church find their model in servanthood.* Servanthood is the antithesis of power. Rather than having the right to control others, a servant lives his life under another's control. Rather than being over, a servant spends his life ministering among. Rather than being able to tell others what to do, a servant's role is to be obedient. While a servant may by his active ministry provide an example for others, he has no power or authority by which to coerce them to follow him.

  That the servant rather than the ruler is the model for Christian leadership is again possible only because of the supernatural nature of the church. As leaders give their obedience to Christ, He works in the lives of the *laos* to motivate them to follow.

297

As we explore this issue more deeply, we can see the necessity for what some might call a "powerless" or even "weak" leadership.

The goal of secular leadership is to control behavior. What a person does is the important issue. An individual may rage inside, but all that is important is that his behavior conform to the leader's demand.

In the church God seeks to transform personalities. His goal is that we become more and more like Christ in our attitudes, values, emotions, and commitment, as well as in our behavior. The goal of Christian leadership, then, is not to produce conformity but to bring believers to the place of personal commitment. What they do must flow spontaneously out of who they are.

We cannot expect an approach to leadership designed to produce conformity to produce commitment. If we truly value commitment, we will refrain from suing a coercive or manipulative style of leadership. That style may produce conformity, but in the long run it will do so at the expense of personal commitment and growth.

In the church of Christ, leaders are purposely to reject power over others. They are to reject the temptation to tell others what to do. In the church leaders are supposed to provide freedom so that individuals may grow to be responsible. They see their role as serving others to bring them to maturity and effectiveness.

We can chart some of the contrasts in these two approaches to structure as in the chart on the following page.

As we have often pointed out, to function in the biblical pattern is *not* chaotic or laissez-faire. Leaders have definite responsibilities to carry out. But the leader's role is different from the role of the leader in the secular model. Strong leadership is provided, but in very different modes. Servant leadership means working with a brother or sister to pray through his or her vision. Servant leadership means spending time to train or to show how a ministry may be carried out. All the leader surrenders in the biblical approach is any claim of a right to control or make decisions for others. Christ is the head of the church, and His will is discovered by the *laos* as the Spirit acts as God's voice to them.

AUTHORITY IS SELF-AUTHENTICATING

The authority of the leader in the church is different in kind from that of the secular leader. Secular authority claims a right to control that the Christian leader rejects. Secular

FIGURE 5

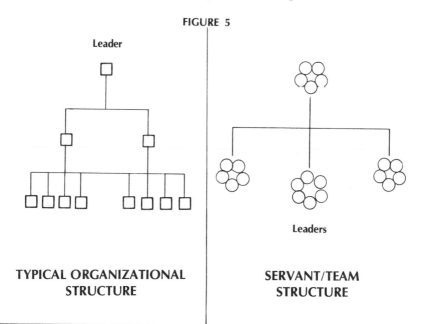

TYPICAL ORGANIZATIONAL STRUCTURE

SERVANT/TEAM STRUCTURE

In the typical organization the leader is perceived as being at the top of the pyramid.

In the typical structure there are several strata of persons in leadership roles between operating personnel and "the" leader(s) at the top.

In the typical structure decision-making is pushed *upward* through the structure, with decisions made further and further away from the actual operating situation. (At times this is essential, as only the "man at the top" can coordinate, in virtue of information that may not be available on lower levels.)

In the typical structure goals are set at the top and directives pass downward through the structure. Ultimately those at the top are the real "owners" of the activities at every level.

In the church, leaders are perceived as being in a lower, supportive position.

In the church, decision-making is "owned" by those performing them. As they function in teams, hierarchical separation between persons is ruled out.

In the church decision-making is *also* pushed *upward* in the structure. But the structure is "upside down" so that decisions are made by the actual teams operating the ministry. (Coordination is possible here because as an *organism,* a single head leads and directs all members of the body.)

In the church, goals are set by the head, Jesus Christ, and His will is sought, discovered, and worked through by the ministering individuals or teams. Thus each person actually "owns" and is responsible for his own ministry.

299

authority rests on a coercive power to command behavior. This the Christian leader also rejects. In their place the Christian leader seeks to help believers mature to the place of personal commitment and responsiveness to the voice of God. Thus the Christian leader lays claim to a God-given right to influence.

This exercise of leadership is self-authenticating in several ways. Scripture gives clear instructions about the persons who are to be recognized as leaders in the Christian community. These instructions in 1 and 2 Timothy and Titus, emphasize a life that *demonstrates maturing Christlikeness.* The Christian leader is followed not because of his degrees or training, or even because of his particular gifts. The leader is followed because his or her character bears the visible stamp of the work of God. The quality of life and character of the Christian is the first self-authenticating mark. The community recognizes the individual as to some extent the kind of person all Christians are called in Christ to become.

The exercise of spiritual leadership is also self-authenticating. The leader operates in the realm of the kingdom, in which Jesus Himself is present. Thus Jesus, who operates in the leader, also operates in the rest of the *laos* to bring the people into a respectful and self-chosen submission to leaders. This is what Paul means in 2 Corinthians when he writes about unresponsive believers. "On my return," he says, "I will not spare those who sinned earlier or any of the others, since you are demanding proof that Christ is speaking through me" (2 Cor. 13:2-3). The authority of the leader rests on the fact that God has chosen him to be a leader in the body, and does in fact speak through him to guide, teach, and care for the church.

But what of the threat, "I will not spare you"? Doesn't this reflect a use of coercive power? Not at all! For Paul goes on to explain that "He [Christ] is not weak in dealing with you, but is powerful among you" (2 Cor. 13:3). The apostle Paul will not use coercive power. He does not have to. Jesus, the head of the church, "is not weak in dealing with you." Christ Himself, powerful among His people, will act to discipline and correct and bring the people of God into an appropriate relationship of responsiveness to their leaders.

Thus leaders will be recognized and honored by the body as the congregation grows and matures and learns how to function as God's *laos.* This will not happen overnight. In the initial stages of the process it is possible, and even likely, that the servant approach to leadership will be misunderstood.

Those who are immature or who seek someone else to make decisions for them, and to be responsible for the church, may react angrily. But over the years as the congregation's members learn to live together as God's ministering people, the biblical approach to leadership *will* build a strong and healthy body. Through that kind of body Jesus will express Himself and His love for our world.

MATURITY, NOT GIFTEDNESS, MEASURES LEADERS

It is important to remember that Scripture does not associate any particular body-gift or giftedness with leadership in the body of Christ. Leaders are to be "apt to teach." But in the biblical context, "teaching" is not at all the formal activity we think of, nor is it limited to the preaching role. Teaching is the ability to communicate the meaning of the Word of God for life. A person with the gift of teaching will help others move toward a life that is in full harmony with the Word of God. See Titus 2, in which a variety of words for teaching gives us a picture of that gift and ministry.

Why is maturity so significant? Because as servants the leaders of the congregation are to minister among the people of God and by their service be an example. The importance of modeling is developed more fully in *A Theology of Christian Education*, by Larry Richards. However, our chapters on servanthood and discipling in this book have given some evidence of the central importance of this concept in the Scriptures. Christians need to have leaders among them whose lives provide enfleshed examples of what all God's people are called to become. Thus the writer to Hebrews says, "Remember your leaders," and instructs his readers to "consider the outcome of their way of life and imitate their faith" (Heb. 13:7).

The presence of leaders in the body does not necessarily mean that there needs to be an organizational entity such as a "board." It simply means that there will be recognized, mature believers who know God has called them to care for His church. They will care for the church by living in close relationship with its members so they can minister in a family context, so significant to all ministry. They will care for the church by watching the various processes taking place in the congregation as a whole and seeing that in the activities of the gathered body there is a healthy balance between instruction, worship, and coming to know and love one another. They will care for the church by advising, affirming, correcting, training, and in every way possible helping the *laos* to be successful in fulfilling individual and team calls to ministry. All these things they will do without exercising a coercive authority, without demanding or accepting control over the lives or ministries of others. Through the ministry of such a leadership, we will become what we are: the world-shaking *laos* of God.

PROBE

▶ *case histories*
▶ *discussion questions*
▶ *thought provokers*
▶ *resources*

1. Review this entire textbook and make a list of all the elements of leadership described or recommended in it. From that list and from the concepts presented in this chapter, (1) create an organizational chart for the "ideal church"; (2) write a job description for an elder in your own local congregation.

2. What in this text do you believe is true to the Word of God? How do you see these truths affecting your own life and ministry?

3. From your answer to 2 above, write out your own "personal commitment" statement. What are you going to do to be obedient to what you believe is God's pathway for you?

INDEXES

Index of Persons

305

Index of Persons

Matthew, 91. *See also* Scripture Index
Melchizedek, 12, 33-34, 36
Miller, Keith, 288
Million, Mark, 65-67
Morris, Dale, 214-16
Moses, 16, 18, 27, 33, 37, 75, 220
Moss, Sharon, 154-56
Muller, George, 65, 128
Munger, Robert B., 13

Nehemiah, 268. *See also* Scripture Index
Newell, William R., 161
Nixon, Richard, 125
Noah, 28n

O'Connor, Elizabeth, 126, 128
Othniel, 112

Packer, J. I., 155
Paul (apostle): call of, 277; journeys of, 96, 191, 277; ministry of, 18, 37, 40, 96, 102, 173, 192, 205, 222, 271; prayers of, 170, 194; relationships of, 192; teaching of, 12, 17, 28, 35, 37-38, 51, 57, 64, 73, 79, 97-102 *passim*, 113-19, 126, 129, 130, 143, 145, 158, 166-75 *passim*, 178, 190-93, 194, 202, 212-13, 221-22, 230, 251, 255, 256, 257, 269, 271-72, 273, 275, 300.
Peter, Simon: disciple of Jesus, 55, 79-80, 270; ministry of, 60, 96, 205; teaching of, 12-13, 39, 100, 103, 126, 166, 169, 170, 171, 193, 194, 197.
Pfeiffer, Charles F., 161
Philip, 59, 93, 96
Pierson, A. T., 65, 128
Plato, 254
Pollock, J. C., 128

Pontius Pilate, 60
Potiphar, 112

Richards, Larry, 48, 104-7, 136, 222, 281, 301
Roets, Ken, 216

Samson, 112
Sanford, Agnes, 128
Saul (king of Israel), 261
Saul (of Tarsus). *See* Paul
Schaeffer, Francis, 127
Schniewind, J., 56
Silas, 205
Simon Peter. *See* Peter, Simon
Smith, William, 161
Snyder, Howard, 207
Solomon, 57, 125
Stedman, Ray, 128
Stifler, James M., 161
Stott, John R. W., 13

Taylor, Kenneth N., 160
Tenney, Merrill C., 161
Thiessen, Henry C., 161
Timothy, 64, 174, 178, 205, 221, 269. *See also* Scripture Index
Titus, 64, 171, 205. *See also* Scripture Index
Trueblood, Elton, 19
Turner, Steve, 153

Unger, Merrill F., 161

Vine, W. E., 161
Vlasck, Kathy, 235-37

Wald, Oletta, 158-59
Ward, Kara, 184-86
Ward, Laura Billingsley, 183-86, 246
Wood, Jack, 45-48, 134-36
Wood, Mary Lou, 134, 136-37

Zwingli, Ulrich, 12-13

Index of Subjects

Abilities: from God, 112, 114, 117, 121, 148, 149, 176, 248. *See also* Gifts; Talents

Abrahamic covenant. *See* Covenant, Abrahamic

Abundant life, 133

Acceptance: God's, 172; in body of Christ, 43, 190, 276; in ministering to non-Christians, 193; of Christ by faith, 185, 189

Access: direct to God, 40, 165, 222, 267, 281; to ministry, 246, 253

Accountability, 258

Administration: gift of, 132, 259, 278; of church organizations, 179, 201; of God's grace, 173, 195; of institutions, 295

Administrations of gifts, 131

Admonition, 18, 173, 213, 256, 272

Affirmation: of believers, 43, 121, 195-96, 301; of God's voice, 177, 277, 279

Agape, 14

Agencies of the church, 143, 176, 179, 201, 229, 241, 283

Akoloutheō, 219

Alienation, 169

'am, 17

'am Elohim, 16

American Standard Bible (ASV), 160

Amplified Bible, The, 160

Anabaptism, 211

Apollo, revelation of, 113

Apostasy of Israel, 15, 17

Apostle(s), 114, 118, 132, 179, 212, 272

Apostolic calling, 277

Assurance, 58, 271

Atonement of sins, 33, 189

Authenticity of the local church, 210, 211

Authority: chain of command, 104, 282; divine, 54, 92, 174, 175, 219; human/secular, 13, 171, 174, 220, 297, 298, 300; in ministry, 258; of church leaders, 152, 274, 281, 295, 298, 300; of the Bible, 255; self-authenticating, 298, 300

Baker's Dictionary of Theology (Harrison, ed.), 161

Baptism, 93, 118, 120, 219; of Jesus Christ (*see* Jesus Christ, baptism of); with Holy Spirit, 92, 93, 114, 285

Basic Christianity (Stott), 290

'bd, 74, 81

Beatitudes, 55

Belief in Christ, 59, 269

Believer-priests, 12-13, 40, 42-43, 46, 104, 173, 180, 222, 225, 248, 249, 284, 287, 295

Bible Alive, The, 206

Bible college, 242

Bible Men of Faith, 215

Bible study (studies), 68, 157-58, 161, 198, 199, 214-16, 290, 291; evangelistic, 179; for children, 205; groups, 216; guides, 155, 158, 159, 161

Bible Study Fellowship, 154

Bible versions and translations, 160, 232

Billy Graham (Pollock), 128

Blessing(s): Abraham, source of, 28; for believers, 51, 80, 136, 146, 167, 261, 271, 272; of abundant life, 133; of Israel, 16

Blood: of Jesus Christ, 35; sacrificial, 12, 34

Board: church, 40, 47, 96, 179, 245, 275, 280, 282, 301; meetings, 197, 198, 199; of deacons, 134, 280

"Body gifts," 122, 123, 148, 150, 173, 194, 301. *See also* Specific gifts

Body-life, 231

Body Life (Stedman), 48, 128

Boldness in ministry, 61, 246, 247

Born-again experience, 186

B'rith, 15, 28

Building up of body, 116-18, 120, 121-22, 148, 157, 194, 212

Call(ing): of people of God, 74, 147; of the church, 145, 208, 258, 283; to carry out Christ's incarnation, 41; to commitment, 222; to discipleship, 223, 224; to faith, 265; to full-time Christian service, 18, 282; to minister, 12-14, 18, 31, 117, 149, 151, 152, 176-81, 190, 202-3, 206, 223, 241, 245, 249, 250, 252, 266, 267, 271, 274, 276-78 *passim*, 281-82, 287, 295, 301; to obedience, 219

Index of Subjects

Index of Subjects

Index of Subjects

134; of gifts, 125-26, 128; of God's will/voice, 103, 267; of needs, 250, 252, 255; spiritual, 98

Disciple-making, 223, 228, 229-30, 233

Disciples:

—of Jesus Christ, 101, 175, 219, 226-28, 233; building of, 42, 151; Christ's incarnation in (see Incarnation of Jesus Christ); goal of, 231; love among, 191, 269; relationship with Christ, 222; to disciple the nations, 13

—of Jesus Christ (the Twelve): Christ's continued incarnation through (see Incarnation of Jesus Christ); foot-washing of, 79; selecting, 127, 221; teaching of, 31, 57, 92, 93, 97, 143, 219, 230, 255; to disciple, 223, 230, 269

—of John the Baptist, 54, 220

Discipleship, 117, 151, 154, 157, 211, 213, 219-37, 250, 258, 259, 301; cost of, 269; goal of, 224, 229, 231; groups, 154, 202, 206, 226, 228, 230; rabbinical, 221-22; training, 206, 219, 221-22, 224, 229, 230, 233

Discipline, 42, 69, 75, 215, 225, 232, 234, 236, 249, 250, 273, 300

Discipling process. See Discipleship

Distinguish between spirits, ability to, 114

Distribution of gifts, 131

Diversity in body, 119-20, 211

Divorce, 233-34, 244

Doulos, 81, 83

Drug(s), 66, 67, 69, 242-44, 252; addict, 63, 179, 244; clinic, 244; research teams, 247; seminars, 247

Dualism, Thomistic, 254-55

Dynamic Church Ministries, 206

Ecology of the church, 211

Ecclesiastical systems, perpetuating, 224

Ecstatic experiences in Greek culture, 113, 115, 116

Edge of Adventure, The (Miller and Larson), 288

Edifying one another, 115. See also Building up of body

Eighth Day of Creation (O'Connor), 126, 128

Elder(s), 42, 65, 80, 96, 127, 131, 132, 134, 136, 155, 179, 225, 231, 242, 258, 261, 281, 282, 289, 302; counsel of, 274, 276-77, 279-80. See also Leaders, church

Empowered: by God, 11, 31, 147; for ministry, 99, 165, 209

Encourage(ment), 11, 42, 63, 115, 122, 168, 192, 197, 200-5 passim, 220, 230, 249, 253, 257, 258, 261, 266, 285, 287; gift of, 104-6, 119, 124, 259; of Scripture, 251

Endurance, 221, 230, 251, 270

Energemata, 129

Ephesus, church at (Ephesians), 64, 96, 118, 172

Epistles, New Testament, 266; "body" in, 117; "deacon" in, 83; discipleship in, 221; Holy Spirit in, 90, 95, 101, 148; Paul's teaching in, 73; "servant"/"slave" in, 83. See also Scripture Index

Epistle to the Romans, The (Stifler), 161

Equality of believers, 18

Equipping of believers for personal ministries, 95, 121, 122, 148, 152, 212, 241-61, 287

Eternal life, 73, 189, 265, 270

Ethiopian eunuch, 96

Ethnoi, 17, 29, 52, 144

Ethnos, 14, 15

Evaluation: of one's calling/vision, 274, 276; of practices in the church, 143-44

Evangelical(s), 166; witness, 178

Evangelism, 122, 150, 165, 189, 191, 208-14, 247, 287; gift of, 213, 259. See also Sharing one's faith

Evangelism in Depth, 208

Evangelist, 122, 126, 132, 203

Evangelistic: Bible studies, 179; campaigns, 206-7; fruitfulness, 211; leadership, 212; lifestyle in church, 207-8, 213-14; ministry, 191; team, 191

Everyone a Minister, 48

Evil, 95, 100, 126, 166, 171, 174, 190, 192, 193, 194, 211, 273

Example, 41; of believer-priests, 42-43; of Jesus Christ, 74, 79-80, 83, 171, 221, 222; of leaders, 174,

Index of Subjects

creation, 213; of gifts, 111; of godlike motives, 101; of testaments, 147; with God's will, 11, 145, 165; with Scripture, 94, 98, 144, 149, 279, 301

Head of the church. *See* Jesus Christ, Head of the body

Healing, 127; by Christ's disciples, 60, 61, 62; by Jesus, 54, 56, 63, 90-91; by the Holy Spirit, 91, 257; divine, 256; gift of, 111, 113, 129, 132

Healing Gifts of the Spirit, The (Sanford), 128

Health, of body of Christ, 170

Heaven, 36, 78, 213, 219; kingdom of *(see* Kingdom of heaven)

Hebrews. *See* Israelites; Jews

Hellenists. *See* Greeks/Hellenists

Helps, 81; gift of, 132, 258

"Here's Life, America," 207-8

Hierarchical structure(s), 296, 297; church as, 13, 280; of ministries, 281-83, 299; under the old covenant, 40

Hierarchies, status, within church, 275

History: God entered, 189; linked to future, 56; source of church practices, 143, 183; versus tradition, 183

Holiness, 82; God of, 17; of believers, 16-17, 33, 35, 36, 40, 57, 73, 118, 167, 175, 213; of God, 35, 36, 147; of Jesus Christ, 12, 90; revealed in covenants, 35, 37, 40; teaching, 39, 73

Holy Spirit: Companion in world, 94 95, 101; contemporary voice, 95; Counselor, 94-95, 101; creativity of, 248; director of church, 96-97, 148; empowering, 101, 104, 209; filling of, 61, 101, 125; fruit of *(see* Fruit of the Holy Spirit); given to believers, 89, 95, 149, 191, 241, 267, 269, 284; given to Old Testament people, 93; Giver of gifts, 111-37, 148, 149, 150; Guide, 94-95, 96, 99, 100, 101; Interpreter of the Word, 93, 98, 101; in Jesus Christ, 76, 77, 89-93, 96; link of the body, 17; living link between God and believers, 93-94, 101, 147; ministry

of, 35, 93, 96, 98, 104; mouthpiece of God, 60, 93, 96 *(see also* God, voice of); operation on human beings, 90; power of *(see* Power of the Holy Spirit; revealer, 97, 98, 101; role in church, 89, 95-102, 111-37, 147-48; role in creation, 89-90, 92, 93; Teacher, 93-101 *passim;* voice of, 97, 98, 100, 147, 149, 151, 152

Hope, 18, 36, 62, 115, 118, 170, 175, 189, 193, 194, 251, 270; of glory, 17

Hospitality, 42, 64, 119, 175, 194-95, 257, 258, 259

House, spiritual, 295

House church, 20, 21

Household, God's, 272

House of prayer experience (H.O.P.E.), 286

Humanity: of Jesus Christ, 92 *(see also* Incarnation of Jesus Christ; restored, 166, 175

Humility, 47, 78-79, 117, 167, 222

Identity: new covenant, 38, 40, 146; of believers, 14, 18, 31, 38, 40-42, 51, 57, 74, 121, 145-46, 196; of God, 27; of Jesus as God, 80; of people of God, 11, 147, 149, 241, 245, 266, 275, 287; of people of Israel, 15-17, 29-30, 144, 145

—of church, 117, 121, 145, 149, 295; functional, 295; relational, 295; spiritual, 295

Idolatry, 16, 113, 175, 192

Idols, 16

Image of Jesus Christ. *See* Christlikeness

Immortality, 13, 16, 175, 192

Incarnation of Jesus Christ, 14, 34, 59, 74, 78, 80, 83, 91, 92; continuing in lives of believers, 37, 40, 41, 55, 59, 82, 100, 101, 145-46, 148, 150-51, 195, 245

Indigenousness, 226, 229, 277

Individualism, 97, 209

Inductive Bible study, 158

Informality: of discipling, 221; of interaction within body, 199-200

Injustice, 13, 16, 167, 168, 171

Inner city ministry, 183-84

Inspiration: character of, 129; divine, 113; of the Holy Spirit, 90

Index of Subjects

Institution: church as a, 66, 201, 245; human/secular, 295-96; maintenance of, 179

Institutional: ministries (see Ministry, institutional); roles, 202, 229; structure(s), of the local church, 14, 42, 143, 178, 230; transaction, 203-4, 214

Institutionalization, of clergy-laity distinction, 103; of injustice, 171; of ministry, 152, 176, 201, 248, 283; of the priesthood, 39

Institutionalized Christianity, 227

Integrity, 248, 249

Interaction: lack of, 198
—types, 197-200; Type I, 197-98, 199; Type II, 198, 199; Type III, 199, 200, 206

Intercession. See Prayer, intercessory

Interpersonal/transactional church climate, 198, 202, 203, 204

Interpretation: of Scripture, 99, 161, 165, 267, 273; of tongues, gift of, 114, 115, 116

Introduction to the New Testament (Thiessen), 161

Israel: disobedience of, 15, 17, 58, 190, 266; God's kingdom in, 56; identity of, 15-16, 145; in need of renewal, 90; lost sheep of, 62; moral code of, 32 (see also Covenant, Mosaic; Law, Mosaic); new covenant with, 29, 31 (see also Covenant, new); relationship with God, 15-17, 27-30, 63, 74-75, 144-45, 147; religious leaders of, 55, 60, 125; servant of God, 147. See also Israelites; Jews

Israelites, 37, 39 (see also Jews); commitment to God, 16, 74; God's commands to, 265; God's promises to, 16, 27

Jerusalem, 75, 96, 210, 268

Jesus Christ: anointing of, 90, 92; Apostle, 33; ascension of, 89, 92-93, 101; baptism of, 53, 93; birth of, 53, 93; chief cornerstone, 272; conception of, 90; consecration of, 90; crucifixion of, 14, 31, 55; death of, 31, 33, 35, 37-38, 77-78, 99, 143, 145, 147, 209, 213, 214; example of (see Exam-

ple, of Jesus Christ); fullness of, 213-14; Good Shepherd, 135, 265; Head of the body/church, 12-13, 96-97, 119, 135, 148, 208, 281, 295-300; Head over every power, 213; High Priest, 12, 33-36, 38, 40, 145; humanity of, 32-33; incarnation of (see Incarnation of Jesus Christ); Judge, 172; King, 29, 53-57, 60, 62-63, 65, 76, 94, 146-47; lordship of (see Lordship of Jesus Christ); Master, 229; Messiah (see Messiah); mind of, 102, 266, 273; preaching of, 54, 64; Prophet, 55; resurrection of, 55, 92, 143, 147, 170, 209, 213, 219, 270; reign of 213, 214; return of, 146; sacrifice of, 12, 31, 34-36, 39-40, 77, 118, 145, 189, 194; Servant (see Servanthood of Jesus); Son of God, 32, 55; suffering of (see Suffering, of Jesus Christ); Teacher, 80 (see also Teaching of Jesus); temptation of, 53, 91; will of, 13, 95, 298 (see also God, will of); work of, in world, 11, 93, 212

Jew(s): believers in Christ, 17, 144; need for redemption, 73. See also Israelites

Journal, 124, 125, 127, 130, 133, 225, 228, 231, 273

Joy: evidence of Christ's reality, 170, 226; fruit of the Spirit, 100; in hope, 194; in maturing, 181; in what God is doing in the church, 42; of creating, 129; of salvation, 90; serving with, 126, 133; sharing, 119, 157, 190, 211; within the believer, 216, 251

Judah, 16, 30, 75, 96, 165, 168

Judaism: postexilic, 219; rabbinic, 220

Judea, 96

Judge (v.): a brother, 99, 172, 274; Lord will judge, 52-54, 74, 171, 193; others, 172, 175, 195, 204, 271

Judges of Israel, 16

Judgment, 95, 273; Jesus' pronouncement of, 63; man's, 98, 266, 273, 277; of the Word of God, 143, 144, 149, 266; on disputable matters, 172; to come, 189, 196

Index of Subjects

Justice: believers' concern for, 167, 175; deprived of, 61, 168, 190; fruit of the kingdom, 65, 89, 147; lifestyle of, 75; neglected, 63, 75; of God, 209; of Jesus Christ, 52-53, 56, 62, 76, 89, 101

Kaphar, 35
Kindness, 100, 118, 167, 174, 194, 202, 256
Kingdom: doctrine of, 51ff., 150; ethic, 64; fruit of (see Fruit of the kingdom); of God/heaven, 51, 53, 56, 62, 68, 146-47, 150-51, 169, 209, 275, 284, 296, 300; of the enemy, 166, 172; of the Son, 51-52, 57, 61, 89, 94, 95, 146, 147, 213; people, 51, 57, 63, 146, 147; power, 59; priestly, 13; proclamation, 91; teaching, 229
King James Version, 160
Kings of Israel, 16
Knowing God (Packer), 155
Knowledge: complete, 173; gift of, 101, 113, 132; in Christ, 17; of Christ, 51-52, 212; of God, 40, 225, 228; of the truth, 174; renewed, 100
Koinonia, 212

Laity, 11, 13, 18-19, 41-42, 122, 143, 245, 275, 283, 295. See also Clergy/laity distinctions
Land covenant. See Covenant, land
Laos: definition of, 11-12, 14-15, 17, 28, 144; identity as, 11-12, 15, 18, 30, 38, 74, 78, 144, 147, 149, 245, 249, 253, 273, 287
Last Supper, 79, 92
Law (Mosaic), 39, 41, 63, 97; as covenant, 28, 29-31, 32, 271 (see also Covenant, Mosaic/law); condemns, 37; fulfillment of, 191, 193; God's guidance into life of love, 190; obedience to, 75, 98, 102; statement of righteousness, 35, 36, 37, 54, 98; teaching of, 220-21, 270; versus grace, 73; written on hearts and minds of believers, 100, 102
Laying on of hands, 111
Laymen, 12, 18, 20, 24. See also Laity
Leader(ship):
—church: gift of, 119; pastoral (see

Pastor); practices, 143; responsibility of, 298; role of, 22, 24, 45, 47, 97, 134, 152, 176-81, 197-200, 202-3, 224, 225, 226, 241, 242, 245, 252, 253, 266, 276, 280, 282, 285, 295, 296, 298, 300; servanthood of, 80-81, 83, 122, 135, 174, 175, 222, 245, 296-301; spiritual, 152, 178-79, 202, 245, 267, 276, 282, 283, 296; team, 205-6; training of, 224
—gifts, 212, 259, 282, 295. See also Administration
—of ministries, 156, 157, 266
—secular, 80, 174, 296-98
Leading: of God, 42, 247, 248, 268, 274, 280, 282, 283, 295; of the Holy Spirit, 96, 97, 284
Leitourgia, 212
Levitical priest(hood). See Priesthood, Mosaic
Lifestyle, 273, 295; based on Christ, 66, 93; evangelistic, 207-8, 213-14; kingdom, 61; missionaries, 258; new, 33; of believers, 35, 149, 211; of congregations, 45, 266; of love, 75; prescribed by Law, 75; servant, 77
Lights in the world, believers as, 174-75
Living Bible, The, 160
Lordship of Jesus Christ, 57, 69, 80, 99, 101, 148, 149, 170, 214, 222, 227, 266, 280, 281, 285, 286
Love, 47, 74, 103, 125, 146, 184, 221, 257, 269; characteristic of the kingdom, 64, 101; community of (see Community, Christian); example of, 178, 269; expression of, 21, 67, 68, 83, 191, 196; for anyone in need, 169; for enemies, 55, 175, 192, 204; for God, 94, 98, 167, 168, 221, 231, 270, 272, 284; for nonbelievers, 175, 191, 193, 195, 204; fruit of the Spirit, 100, 114-15; gift of, 135; God's, 36, 75, 94, 95, 100, 175, 186, 189-90, 192, 193, 195-96, 204, 213, 221, 269-71, 275; Jesus' self-sacrificial, 38, 82, 100-1, 117, 169-70, 175, 191, 194, 203-4, 245, 253, 255, 301; life(style) of, 75, 118, 126, 175, 190; -motivated obedience, 94, 147;

Index of Subjects

Index of Subjects

Index of Subjects

24, 96, 143, 152, 176-78, 201, 202, 203, 229, 230, 248, 275, 280; discipleship, 259; ministry, 229, 277. *See also* Agencies; Structures, church

Promised Land, 15, 27, 29, 58

Promises: covenant, 15-16, 28-30, 33, 36-38, 271; of God, 27-29, 93, 145, 189

Prophecy: gift of, 101, 103, 113-14, 115, 119, 129, 132, 269; messianic, 54; Old Testament, 34, 53-54, 63, 92-93, 116

Prophet(s), 75-77, 90, 92-93, 97, 114, 126, 132, 145, 146, 190, 212, 268, 272; Jesus Christ as, 55

Prostitutes, ministry to, 63, 179, 184-85, 192, 243, 246

Protestantism, 103

Psychoanalysis and Psychotherapy, 36 Systems, 251

Psychology, science of, 251

Purity, example of, 178, 221, 269

Purpose(s): common, in community, 211; for ministry, 165, 221; God seeks through church, 150, 165, 169, 175, 176. *See also* Vision

Rabbi, 220-22

Rabbi-disciple pattern of education, 220

Rabbinic Judaism, 220

Rabbinical discipleship, 221-22, 225

Reason, Holy Spirit as source of man's, 90

Recognition of gifts. *See* Gifts, spiritual, recognition of

Reconciliation of God and man, 12, 38, 172, 209-10, 213

Recreation in the body, 43

Redeem mistakes, 284

Redemption, 35, 39, 73, 76, 147, 213, 265, 269, 275

Reformation, 254-55

Reformers, 12-13, 38, 227, 254-55

Regale sacerdotium, 13

Rejoice: in suffering, 175, 270; with those who rejoice, 194

Relationships: among believers, 42-43, 79-80, 83, 114, 117, 119, 121-22, 150, 157, 170, 189-92, 194-97, 203, 210, 213, 214, 223-25, 234, 247, 250, 252, 274, 278, 297, 300-1; between believ-

ers and nonbelievers, 66, 105-6, 151, 177, 185, 193, 196, 203-4, 210, 214, 243, 246; between counselor/counselee, 257; between God and His people, 18, 28-30, 36, 78, 81-82, 94, 144-45, 170, 180, 190, 196-97, 210, 215, 265, 267, 268, 273; between God and Israel *(see* Israel, relationship with God); between God and man, 11, 32, 189, 190; between Holy Spirit and believers, 93, 94, 101, 173, 266; between Holy Spirit and the twelve disciples, 92, 101; between Jesus and believers, 17, 94, 106, 114, 195, 219, 221, 224, 266, 286, 296; covenant, 16-17, 28, 52, 75, 78, 82, 145; of Jesus Christ to the Father, 94; of Jesus Christ to the Holy Spirit, 90-91, 95 *(see also* Holy Spirit in Jesus Christ); of world, shattered, 170; transformation of, 189, 190

Renewal: movements, 211, 286; of creation, 101; of Israel, 90; of the church, 13, 143, 181; of the covenant relationship, 17; of the mind, 149; within believer, 38, 143, 166, 194, 286. *See also* Transformation

Renewal and Refreshment (R & R) ministry (Trinity Church, Seattle), 154-57

Renewed mankind, 167

Repentance, 53, 174

Resources: of the church body, 167, 168, 205; sharing, 190; spiritual, 172; stewardship of, 42, 211

Respect, 171, 251; for authority, 297

Responding: to needs *(see* Needs, responding to); to one another in ministry, 247, 252, 300; to the voice of God. *See* God, voice of; Obedience

Responsibility of believers: entrusted to laity, 13, 46, 135, 143, 295; for discipleship, 223; for ministries, 152, 154, 156, 205, 258, 277, 280-82, 284, 295, 299; in servanthood, 81; shared, 205, 249, 252; to be guided by the Holy Spirit, 257; to listen and respond to God's voice, 98, 152, 180, 248, 266, 267, 280, 284; to live in

Index of Subjects

power of the Spirit, 102; to live in presence of God, 40, 180; within body of Christ, 135, 146, 147, 149, 280, 298, 301

Responsive obedience to God. *See* Obedience

Responsiveness: to one another, 256; to the Holy Spirit, 100

Restoration: of humanity, 166, 175; of image of God in the believer, 213; to fellowship, 32, 172

Resurrection of believers, 189

Resurrection of Jesus Christ. *See* Jesus Christ, resurrection of

Retreat(s), 203, 287, 290; center, 286

Revelation: character of, 129; God's in the Bible, 94, 98, 116, 143, 144, 147, 150, 165, 250, 251, 267; interpretation by the Holy Spirit, 98, 101

Revised Standard Version (RSV), 160

Revival: continued, 272; meetings, 203

Righteous behavior, 54, 196

Righteousness, 75, 95, 174, 175; from the Holy Spirit, 90-91; Jesus' acts of, 56, 63, 101; law, a statement of, 35; life of, 82, 118, 167; new-covenant approach to, 35; of God, 36, 52, 58, 62, 82, 169; of the kingdom, 54n, 61, 64, 89, 91, 147; slave to, 73

Robert's *Rules of Order*, 134

Roles of church leaders. *See* Leaders, church, role of

Roman Catholic Church, 38. *See also* Catholic churches

Romans (McGee), 161

Romans (Neighborhood Bible Studies), 161

Romans: The Freedom Letter (Johnson), 161

Romans Verse by Verse (Newell), 161

Rome, church at (Romans), 121, 126, 173, 251

Ruling, gift of, 132

Sabbath, 54

Sabbath-rest, 58

Sacrifices: animal, 36; for sins, 32-36, 39-40, 63, 175; of Christ (*see* Jesus Christ, sacrifice of); of prayers and praise, 12; personal, 250; self-, 83

Salvation, 33, 36, 38, 77, 92, 131, 158, 196, 208, 209, 257, 272; by faith, 38, 81; by works, 38; joy of, 90

Sanctification, 213; ministry of, 251

Sanctify, 12, 251

Sanhedrin, 60

Satan, 43, 54, 69, 90-91, 172, 269, 270

Satanic forces, 171

Security, 134, 247

Self-control, fruit of the Spirit, 100

Self-controlled life, 167, 202

Self-discipline, 215

Selfishness, 127, 169

Seminary, 242

Sensitivity: of leaders, 287; to congregation, 276; to God's voice, 178, 268, 272; to needs of others, 241, 244, 252

Septuagint, 14, 51

Sermon on the Mount, 54

Servant: -citizens, 89; Greek definition, 73; Hebrew definition, 74-76; Jesus Christ as, 74, 76-83, 94, 147, 297; -leader, 80, 122, 174, 175, 296-98, 300 (*see also* Leaders as servants); lifestyle, 77; ministry, 78, 81, 94; of the Lord, 13, 74-83, 90, 92, 95, 97, 122, 147, 171, 174, 250, 258, 269; people, 76, 83, 147, 149, 247, 253. *See also* Servanthood; Service; Slave(ry)

Servanthood: biblical, 73-74, 78, 82, 149, 151, 258, 297; of Jesus, 60-61, 83, 89, 253; teaching, 229. *See also* Service; Slave(ry)

Servant Songs, 76-77, 83

Service, 228, 241, 245, 259, 270, 276, 278, 287; full-time Christian, 18, 143, 201, 242; in church programs, 143, 176 (*see also* Programs, church); institutionalizing, 150; kinds of, 113-14; ministry of, 276; Old Testament idea of, 74; to others, 14, 18, 73, 82, 83, 112, 125, 126, 147, 149, 151, 177, 195, 212, 223, 229, 232, 298; to the Lord, 16, 18, 21, 82, 85, 101, 112, 121, 125, 126, 148, 174, 177, 190, 212, 223, 241, 257, 272; training for, 226; within the body, 42, 118, 131,

Index of Subjects

Surveys, Bible, 161
Swedish marking system, 158
Synagogues, 53

Tabernacle, 32, 34-35, 39
Talents: from God, 112, 117, 121, 126, 148, 149, 178, 204, 272; natural, 129
Talmidim, 220
Teacher, Sunday school, 111, 176, 177, 198, 224, 275
Teaching: gift of, 114, 119, 129, 132, 212, 258, 274, 301; ministry of, 42, 150, 174, 202, 259, 301; of Christ, 53, 59, 74, 91, 92, 93, 95, 147, 219, 272; of Scripture, 102; of the Law, 220-21; within the church, 41, 42, 123, 173, 178, 201, 204, 213, 254, 258, 272, 275, 282, 300, 301. *See also* Training
Team: ministry, 114, 122, 156, 191, 192, 204-6, 225, 236, 244, 247, 249, 252, 253, 258, 259, 261, 279, 284, 301; missionary, 221, 258
Temptation(s), 33, 169; of Jesus, 53, 91; overcoming, 43, 298
Ten Commandments, 32. *See also* Law; Covenant, Mosaic
Test: God's will, 144; ministries, 282-83
Testify: believers must, 95; Holy Spirit will, 95, 101; of God's presence and power, 75
Testimony: of faith in Christ, 126; unified, of will of God, 249
Testing of Jesus in desert, 91
Thanksgiving to God, 51, 170, 271
Theology, 143-44, 149, 227, 233-34, 250-51; core (*see* Core theology); definition of, 11
Theology of Christian Education, A (Richards), 301
Theology of Church Leadership, A (Richards), 281, 285
Thessalonians, 191-92
Thomistic dualism/theology, 254-55
Through Gates of Splendor (Elliot), 84
Timing of ministries, 279
Tongues: gift of, 111, 113-18 *passim*, 122, 129, 194, 269; interpretation of, 114, 115

Torah, 220, 222
Tradition, 103, 178, 180-81, 183; challenging, 143; church, 103, 144
Traditionalism, 133
Training: believers to respond to God's voice, 267, 272-73; discipleship (*see* Discipleship); in ministry, 151-52, 157, 201, 205, 241, 242, 249, 250, 252, 253, 255, 258, 301
Transformation: agent of (Holy Spirit), 148; of believers, 35-36, 40, 41, 99-102, 119, 143, 144, 146, 149, 151, 159, 166, 172, 196, 233-34, 269, 270, 298; of relationships, 189, 190; of society, 56, 63, 167; power for, 31
Trinity, Godhead, 59, 89, 91, 94, 130
Trinity Church (Seattle, Washington), 42, 65, 67, 104, 123-25, 149, 154, 156, 202, 225, 233, 235, 236, 237, 242-46, 249, 252, 254, 258-61, 268, 271
Trust, 115, 194; church leaders, 134; in the Lord, 78, 145, 270, 271, 284; one another, 247
Truth, 95, 115, 152, 157, 159, 174, 197, 257; about God's love, 195; application of, 113, 198; expressions of, 227; God's 144, 209, 251, 269; knowledge of, 174; of the gospel, 189, 196, 210; Spirit of, 94; spiritual, 98, 199; Word of, 269

Understanding, 252, 256
Unger's Bible Handbook, 161
Unity: in honor and function, 115-16; in love, 114-15, 117; in the faith, 212; in the Holy Spirit, 113, 118; in worship, 116; within the body, 43, 48, 114, 117-23, 134, 175, 212, 215, 230, 249
Upper Room, 31, 99, 170
Upper Room Discourse, 93

Values of the church, 143-44, 169, 298
Vision: common, 287; communicating, 176-79, 180; confirmation of, 279; congregational, 179, 181; ministering, 244; of God, 165-81, 183; of prophets, 92, 93, 103; per-

322

Index of Scripture References

Index of Scripture References

Index of Scripture References

Index of Scripture References